Spiritual Traditions and the Virtues

Spiritual Traditions and the Virtues

Living Between Heaven and Earth

MARK R. WYNN

OXFORD
UNIVERSITY PRESS

OXFORD
UNIVERSITY PRESS

Great Clarendon Street, Oxford, OX2 6DP,
United Kingdom

Oxford University Press is a department of the University of Oxford.
It furthers the University's objective of excellence in research, scholarship,
and education by publishing worldwide. Oxford is a registered trade mark of
Oxford University Press in the UK and in certain other countries

First Edition published in 2020

Impression: 1

Published in the United States of America by Oxford University Press
198 Madison Avenue, New York, NY 10016, United States of America

British Library Cataloguing in Publication Data

Data available

Library of Congress Control Number: 2019957827

ISBN 978-0-19-886294-9

Printed and bound by
CPI Group (UK) Ltd, Croydon, CR0 4YY

For my parents, Robert and Alison

my first teachers in the ways of spiritual traditions

Acknowledgements

I would like to express my deep gratitude to the many scholars who have helped to extend and clarify my thinking on the themes of this book. While it is my name that appears on the cover, I am very much aware that this work is in fact the product of an intellectual community, of which I am just one small part. The text has its origins in the Wilde Lectures, which I gave at the University of Oxford in Hilary Term of 2015, under the title 'spiritual traditions and human possibilities'. I am grateful to the Board of Electors for the invitation to give those lectures, and especially to Brian Leftow who hosted the series, and offered detailed and highly constructive comments after each lecture. Chapters 1–7 of the book follow closely the text I produced for the first seven lectures in the series of eight, and I have tried throughout to retain the direct and, I hope, accessible style of the original draft. I am grateful to the audience for their helpful questions and observations, and especially to John Cottingham, Brian Leftow, Paul Lodge, and Richard Swinburne for their many, always insightful observations.

I am also fortunate to have been able to rehearse the concerns of the book at various workshops and seminars. I list them here in broadly chronological order, from 2014: the Royal Institute of Philosophy conference on Supererogation, University College Dublin; the Welsh Philosophical Society annual conference, Gregynog; the National Humanities Center workshop on Religion and Emotion, North Carolina; the Logos workshop on Religious Experience, University of Notre Dame; various events in Oxford, including a conference on The Philosophy of Richard Swinburne, a workshop on Faith and Reason, and the 2017 British Society for Philosophy of Religion biennial conference; symposia on Faithful Attitudes, University of Manchester, and Religion and Aesthetics, University of Nottingham; presentations at the Institute for Theology, Imagination and the Arts, University of St Andrews, the Philosophy Group, The Open University, and at the Theology and Ethics

Seminar and the Centre for Catholic Studies, Durham University; conferences on Cross-Disciplinary Perspectives on Well-Being and Measurement, at the Center for Health and Happiness, Harvard University, and on Happiness and Well-Being: Integrating Research Across the Disciplines, St Louis University; and workshops on Concepts of the Divine at the University of Innsbruck and on God and Morality at the University of Southampton. I am grateful to those who organized and contributed to these occasions, each of which I found highly productive in deepening my understanding of the issues I discuss here.

I also appreciate my very great good fortune in being able to participate in recent years in a dynamic philosophy of religion group in the north of England, pioneered by the late David Efird. David was a great builder of intellectual communities, and associated friendships, and this text would not have been possible but for the inter-personal and intellectual milieu that he created in bringing together colleagues in philosophy of religion from York, Durham, Leeds and Sheffield. The core motifs of this volume were first presented on these occasions. I think of David as the founder of the movement of thought he called 'analytic spirituality', an approach that has very evidently shaped the central concerns of this discussion. He is sorely missed by me and his many friends in the field.

I would also like to convey my warm thanks to my friend and for many years my colleague Robin Le Poidevin, who very generously read and incisively commented upon several draft chapters. And I am grateful for the many kindnesses of all my colleagues in the Centre for Philosophy of Religion at the University of Leeds, including, to name only the staff associated with the Centre, Jamie Boulding, Mikel Burley, Simon Hewitt, Chris Kenny, Rachel Muers, Tasia Scrutton, Scott Shalkowski, Gabrielle White, Roger White, and Adam Willows. I am also indebted to other friends and colleagues who have been very actively engaged in developing Philosophy of Religion in the North, notably T. Ryan Byerly, Joshua Cockayne, Christopher Insole and David Worsley.

Taking a longer view, I would like to acknowledge how my sense of the philosophy of religion and how it might proceed has been very much influenced by my first teachers in the field, my DPhil supervisors, Brian Davies and Richard Swinburne, who have continued most generously to take an interest in my work, and by a number of generative conversations, some of them rather brief conversations, over the years with, among others, David Brown, Clare Carlisle, Sophie Grace Chappell, Sarah Coakley, David Cooper, Christopher Cowley, Fiona Ellis, Siobhán Garrigan, Tim Gorringe, Christopher Hamilton, Victoria Harrison, Douglas Hedley, Mike Higton, Ian Kidd, Dave Leal, Tim Mawson, Michael McGhee, David McPherson, Andrew Moore, Yujin Nagasawa, Andrew Pinsent, Michael Rea, John Schellenberg, Christopher Southgate, Christina Van Dyke, Hami Verbin, Judith Wolfe, and Bill Wood.

I owe a special debt of thanks to John Cottingham, whose advocacy in recent years of a 'humane' approach to the philosophy of religion has been profoundly formative for my thinking about the matters I address in this book, and also to Eleonore Stump, for her always wise counsel, unflagging encouragement, and exemplification of what it is to think about the spiritual life with depth. I would also like to offer warm thanks to two reviewers for the Press, for their perceptive comments on the manuscript, and to Tom Perridge and the dedicated team at OUP for their judicious guidance and support. There are many others who have also played a significant role in deepening my appreciation of the themes of this text, whose names I have not recorded here, and I thank them too, and apologize in advance for the more egregious omissions from this list. Needless to say, the many errors in the discussion which remain are to be attributed to me alone!

Finally, and most importantly, I want to acknowledge my family, in all its branches, around the globe, especially Kate and Rowan, without whose support this venture would never so much as have begun. I would also like to recall here the foresight of my mother's grandfather, Walter Broxap, whose generosity in funding her education is, I believe, one more enabling condition, without which this book would not have come to be.

Copyright Acknowledgements

Chapter 4 uses material from Mark Wynn, 'Aesthetic Experience and Spiritual Well-Being: Locating the Role of Theological Commitments', *International Journal of Philosophy and Theology*, 79:4 (2018), 397–409, DOI: 10.1080/21692327.2018.1475250, reprinted by permission of the publisher (Taylor & Francis Ltd, http://www.tandfonline.com).

Chapter 5 uses material from 'Tradition', in F. Aquino and W. Abraham (eds), *Oxford Handbook of the Epistemology of Theology* (Oxford: Oxford University Press, 2016), pp. 126–40, reprinted by permission of the publisher.

Chapter 6 uses material from 'Aesthetic Goods and the Nature of Religious Understanding', in F. Ellis (ed.), *New Models of Religious Understanding* (Oxford: Oxford University Press, 2017), pp. 116–33, reprinted by permission of the publisher.

Contents

Introduction

Setting the Scene

The primary focus of this volume is the nature of spiritual traditions. Among other matters, I shall consider the distinctive character of the goods to which spiritual traditions are directed; the structure of such traditions, including the connection between their practical and creedal commitments; the relationship between the various vocabularies that are used to describe, from the insider's perspective, progress in the spiritual life; the significance of tradition as an epistemic category; and the question of what it takes for a tradition to be handed on from one person to another. So while this discussion will, I hope, make some contribution to the discipline that we standardly call the philosophy of religion, it will have a rather different focus from some familiar ventures in the field, in so far as it is not concerned in the first instance with questions about, say, the metaphysics of the divine nature or sacred reality otherwise conceived, or with the epistemology of religious belief, but with the nature of spiritual goods, and of traditions that seek to cultivate such goods. Some of these more familiar questions will be addressed in time in this text, but only relatively late, and then only through the lens that is provided by the earlier account of the nature of spiritual well-being.

So the enquiry constitutes in this way a methodological proposal: rather than approaching the nature of spiritual or religious truth by beginning with metaphysics, or epistemology, we are to begin with the spiritual life, and with the detail of particular spiritual traditions. In the course of our enquiry, I hope to show the fruitfulness of a study of this kind, but provisionally, at this early stage of the discussion, I suggest that there are three general merits that we should associate with such an

Spiritual Traditions and the Virtues: Living Between Heaven and Earth. Mark R. Wynn, Oxford University Press (2020).
© Mark R. Wynn.
DOI: 10.1093/oso/9780198862949.001.0001

approach. First of all, this conception of our task recognizes that practitioners of the religious and spiritual life are motivated most fundamentally, at least in many cases, by the prospect of securing an important practical good: their relationship to the central claims of their tradition is not one of simple intellectual assent, but grounded in their pursuit of a life that bears a certain kind of significance. The account which follows will provide a much fuller specification of this understanding of spiritual traditions, but if this is in general terms the way in which we are to understand spiritual and religious forms of life, then it makes some sense for philosophers of religion to take as their starting point a consideration of the nature of spiritual goods, and the claim they make upon us. It is the commitment to these goods, so I shall argue, that holds the more theoretical elements of a religious or spiritual conception of the world in place.

Secondly, the approach we shall follow recognizes that, while the philosophical imagination can contribute a certain amount to our appreciation of the nature of spiritual goods, nonetheless, if we wish to understand such matters in any depth, then we should also turn to lived traditions of religious practice, which constitute in effect extended experiments in human possibilities—and a long, perhaps centuries-long, sifting and trial of certain spiritual ideas for creatures of our particular physical and mental constitution. Spiritual traditions are instructive, then, both because they set before us a wide range of conceptions of the nature of spiritual goods, a wider range than we could hope to concoct from the vantage point of the arm chair, and because they allow us to reach a judgement not only on the theoretical fruitfulness of those conceptions, but on their capacity to order a human life in practice, given the constraints of human nature. So in this way, the approach invites philosophers of religion to engage more fully than they have sometimes done with the data of religious life, and this too will be a productive turn, I think.

While this proposal aims to take seriously the data provided by particular spiritual traditions, its concerns are not simply descriptive: I hope to develop an analytical framework that will allow us to understand the nature of spiritual goods, as they have been conceived in particular traditions, and at the same time to identify some of the considerations that are relevant for the critical assessment of varying conceptions of the spiritual life. In this way, a third benefit of this kind of enquiry is, I hope, that its findings will be of rather direct interest to practitioners of the spiritual and religious life, since it will propose both a framework for understanding their practice, and a way of conceiving of the spiritual productiveness of that practice.[1]

Some Key Themes

For the reader who would like to proceed directly to those parts of the discussion that are most germane to their own interests, and also for the reader who would find it helpful to have, at the outset, a plan within which they can locate the main phases of the enquiry, I shall close these introductory remarks with a brief, chapter by chapter summary of some of our main concerns. Others may prefer to read the text as it stands, without these prefatory comments, and they will enjoy, I hope, the rather different experience, the experience of those who attended the lectures, of encountering various themes somewhat unannounced.

In Chapter 1, I introduce some of the guiding questions of the investigation, here drawing on Pierre Hadot's text *Philosophy as a Way of Life*. These questions include: how should we understand the nature of spiritual goods? What is the relationship between a tradition's world view and its conception of the well-lived human life? How should we conceive of the connection between the different vocabularies that can be used to describe progress in the spiritual life, for instance, those involving metaphysical and experiential categories? What epistemic conditions, if any, does a world view need to meet if it is to be capable of informing a spiritual ideal of life? And what is the contribution of

---

[1] There will be differences of view on this matter, but it might be argued that in some central respects, the philosophy of religion literature of recent years has done relatively little to inform the practice and self-understanding of 'ordinary believers', and indeed relatively little to engage the attention of theologians and other-than-philosophical theoreticians of the relevant traditions. Of course, being of interest to religious and spiritual practitioners is not the sole measure of adequacy for a philosophical treatment of religion, and depending on our concerns, it may well be that it is not even a very important measure, but having this property is, I take it, a merit, other things being equal.

tradition in shaping our understanding of the spiritual life? The key concept that runs through this volume is Thomas Aquinas's notion of infused moral virtue, and in this chapter, I also introduce this notion and consider its fruitfulness for addressing the second of these questions, concerning the relationship between world view and ideal of life. I contrast Aquinas's account of these matters, according to which some spiritual goods—the goods that are the object of the infused moral virtues—cannot be identified independently of reference to our theological or metaphysical context, and Hadot's account, according to which ethical or spiritual ideals come first, and provide the basis for metaphysical commitments. I note some reasons for thinking that this distinction between the two authors should not be too sharply drawn.

Having sketched the idea of goods that are relative to our theological or metaphysical context, I consider next, in Chapter 2, some varieties of such goods, taking as my focus two instances of infused moral virtue: abstinence and neighbour love. I note a distinction between these two: in the case of abstinence, the introduction of a theological frame has the effect of lifting an action that would otherwise be morally permissible but under-motivated into the realm of the obligatory, whereas in the case of neighbour love, the introduction of such a frame constitutes as obligatory an action that would otherwise be supererogatory. I consider how we can understand this difference by distinguishing between the kinds of good that can be produced by the infused moral virtues, and noting that one of these kinds of good, what I call an extended good of reason, is present only in the case of neighbour love. I then explore the relevance of extended goods of reason for a consideration of the practical rationality of religious commitment, noting how this kind of good allows the religious way of life to appear as worthwhile from a secular vantage point.

In the next two chapters, I further develop the notion of infused moral virtue, by considering how the target goods of these virtues can be realized in domains additional to those that Aquinas discusses. In Chapter 3, I examine in particular how our world-directed experience can be deemed more or less appropriate relative to a theological narrative, and how it is capable therefore of realizing the kind of good that is the object of the infused moral virtues. I call these goods 'hybrid goods' to mark the fact that they share their subject matter with the acquired moral virtues (since they are concerned with our relations to the created order) and their teleology with the theological virtues (because here the measure of success for our relationship to creatures is provided by reference to relationship to God). In this chapter, I also consider how a story of progress in the spiritual life that is rehearsed in an experiential idiom may be related to one that is cast instead in metaphysical terms. To develop the account, I examine in particular the relationship between Aquinas's understanding of spiritual growth, expressed in terms of the acquired and infused moral virtues, and John of the Cross's narrative of the various phases of the spiritual life. On this basis, I consider how experiential and metaphysical perspectives on spiritual development are mutually informing, while at the same time they also exhibit, relative to one another, a significant degree of independence.

In Chapter 4, I discuss another domain within which hybrid goods may be realized, again seeking to extend the range of such goods beyond what is envisaged in Aquinas's account. This time, I examine the contribution of bodily demeanour to the spiritual life, distinguishing the phenomenon that is of interest for us from behaviour that is theologically appropriate because morally efficacious. I also explore the idea that the hybrid goods that arise in this context have an aesthetic character. I consider the novelty of this proposal by introducing two other accounts of the aesthetic significance of the body for the spiritual life, here drawing on the work of Jeremy Begbie and George Pattison. I suggest that the approach developed in this volume occupies a middle ground, by affirming that there are distinctively theological aesthetic goods, while at the same time retaining, and extending, conventional measures of aesthetic excellence.

In Chapter 5, I discuss the contribution of tradition to the spiritual life. I begin by reviewing the implications of the work of Anselm and Aquinas for our understanding of these matters, before proposing that the notion of hybrid goods offers a further way of thinking about the role of tradition. Notably, traditioned patterns of thought may be important if a community is to be able to test hypotheses about the nature and extent of the relations of congruence that may hold between various theological narratives and our world-directed thought, experience and behaviour. I contrast this vision of the role of tradition with the much thinner role that is implied in Hadot's account of the spiritual life, noting how a difference of view about the nature of spiritual goods can drive a difference of view about the place of traditioned forms of enquiry in the spiritual life.

In Chapter 6, I turn to the question of what kind of assent a person needs to give to a theological narrative if it is to support their pursuit of hybrid goods whose realization is tied to the truth of the narrative. Here I expound Aquinas's account of faith as in the relevant senses cognitive, action-guiding, voluntary, confident, and certain, and note how the idea of hybrid goods allows us to understand the spiritual life in comparable terms. On this basis, I propose that faith is best conceived not as first of all a commitment to a world view, from which we are then to read off a set of practical implications, nor as first of all a commitment to a way of life, which then calls for the introduction of a supporting world view, but instead as a commitment to a way of life and world view taken in combination. In this way, the notion of hybrid goods allows us to develop an account of the practical reasonableness of particular forms of the spiritual life, where it is axiological questions at least as much as evidential or epistemic questions that determine the shape of that life.

In the concluding chapter of the book, I consider how this conception of spiritual goods provides a framework for the assessment of theological narratives. In brief, a narrative will make more of a demand on our adherence, in spiritual terms, to the extent that its truth would enable the realization of hybrid goods that run broad and deep. I call this the principle of spiritual good, and compare it with other ways of trying to map the basic structure of religious thought, notably the 'great-making principle' that has been propounded in perfect being theology. This second principle offers a divine-nature-focused route into the question of what we are to think in religious terms, whereas the proposal I am developing begins rather with the nature of spiritual goods, and is to that extent more human-nature-focused. I consider how the principle of spiritual good may enable us to integrate otherwise apparently quite disparate fields of enquiry, and how it may throw light on the entrenched character of some disagreements in philosophical theology. I also compare this principle to a related principle that William James presents in his essay 'The Will to Believe'. James is also interested in the idea that prospective spiritual 'benefits' may provide a measure for the adequacy of religious thought, but the benefits with which he is concerned are, characteristically, psychological in nature, unlike hybrid goods, which have inherently a theological structure. There follows a short conclusion to the book—short enough to require no summary here!

Overall then, this discussion aims to develop a philosophical appreciation of the spiritual life. Specifically, it seeks to show how a certain notion of spiritual good, one that is rooted in Thomas Aquinas's account of infused moral virtue, can generate a distinctive vision of human life, and the possibilities for spiritual fulfilment. For reasons that will become apparent, we could say that this is a vision of how it is possible to live between heaven and earth. Since the key phases of the discussion are bound together by a single core concept, namely, Aquinas's notion of infused moral virtue, I propose to begin by introducing this concept, and exploring some of its implications for an understanding of the structure of the spiritual life. This will be the task of Chapter 1.

1

Philosophy as a Way of Life

Introduction

In this chapter, I shall provide an initial sketch of the subject matter of our investigation, by saying a little about the structure of spiritual traditions, understood as I shall understand them here. I shall approach these matters by drawing a distinction between Thomas Aquinas's treatment of the spiritual life and that of Pierre Hadot, who has famously proposed that the philosophies of the Hellenistic world were most fundamentally bodies of spiritual practice, or what he calls 'ways of life'. Once we have addressed these questions concerning the constitution of spiritual traditions, we will then be in a position to consider, in later chapters, a range of additional questions concerning, among other things, the nature of spiritual goods, and the role of spiritual traditions in enabling human beings to order their lives to such goods.

Let us begin, then, by examining Hadot's account of the structure of spiritual traditions, before considering how Thomas Aquinas's notion of infused moral virtue can be brought to bear on these same issues.

Pierre Hadot on the Spiritual Life

I have taken the heading for this chapter from the title of Pierre Hadot's celebrated study of philosophy in the ancient world. (In English translation, that text also bears the title *Philosophy as a Way of Life*.[1]) If we begin with a very generic conception of a spiritual tradition, as one that

---

[1] See *Philosophy as a Way of Life: Spiritual Exercises from Socrates to Foucault*, tr. M. Chase (Oxford: Blackwell, 1995). Parts of this work were first published as *Exercices Spirituels et Philosophie Antique* (Paris: Etudes Augustiniennes, 2nd edn, 1987).

Spiritual Traditions and the Virtues: Living Between Heaven and Earth. Mark R. Wynn, Oxford University Press (2020).
© Mark R. Wynn.
DOI: 10.1093/oso/9780198862949.001.0001

is concerned with the proper ordering of a human life in practical, emotional, and experiential terms, where that ordering is in some way relative to a picture of the fundamental nature of things, or perhaps grounded in a sense of the constraints on human beings' capacity to know the nature of things, then ancient philosophical traditions, as Hadot represents them, will also count as spiritual traditions. In this book, I shall also be concerned with spiritual traditions in broadly this sense, that is, as bodies of practice and theory, elaborated over time, together with correlative forms of feeling and experience. So here is an initial reason for taking Hadot's approach, and his account of philosophy in the Greco-Roman world, as a starting point for our discussion of the nature of spiritual traditions.

In this chapter, I shall use Hadot's work to introduce a number of questions that will be integral to our enquiry. I shall concentrate on one of these issues in particular, namely, the question of how to represent the relationship between two key components of at least many spiritual traditions: on the one hand, a certain way of life and, on the other, a conception of the fundamental nature of things.

We can put the following general question to any account of the structure of the spiritual life: once we have distinguished between the various elements of that life, should we assign one of these elements priority, by beginning with an understanding of that element, and then reading off the character of other elements? As we shall see shortly, Hadot seems to favour an approach of this kind: his account treats one component of the spiritual life as primary, and then introduces other features according to their role in supporting this first component. In the course of this book, I shall argue, on the contrary, that the central elements of the spiritual life should be considered in the first instance in combination, with none being assigned the sort of unilateral priority that seems to characterize Hadot's position. I shall make a start on presenting this case in this chapter by comparing Hadot's treatment of these questions with Thomas Aquinas's handling of some related matters in his discussion of neighbour love.

Let us begin by considering Hadot's conception of the philosophical schools of the Greco-Roman world as a way of broaching the wider theme of the structure of spiritual traditions. As you would expect from its title, Hadot's book is a defence of the claim that ancient philosophies were, at root, ways of life. Here is his own account of how we are to understand this proposal:

> In order better to understand in what way ancient philosophy could be a way of life, it is perhaps necessary to have recourse to the distinction proposed by the Stoics, between *discourse about* philosophy and *philosophy itself*. For the Stoics the parts of philosophy – physics, ethics and logic – were not, in fact, parts of philosophy itself, but rather parts of philosophical *discourse*. By this they meant that when it comes to teaching philosophy, it is necessary to set forth a theory of logic, a theory of physics, and a theory of ethics....But philosophy itself – that is, the philosophical way of life – is no longer a theory divided into parts, but a unitary act, which consists in *living* logic, physics and ethics.[2]

On this account, 'philosophy' is most fundamentally a 'way of life', and the role of 'philosophical discourse' is to serve as an aid to the process of personal formation that is required for the leading of a given way of life. To see more exactly how this connection between the discourse and the way of life is supposed to work, let us take one of Hadot's examples. Hadot writes that Epicureanism is:

> a philosophy which seeks, above all, to procure peace of mind. Its goal is consequently to liberate mankind from everything that is a cause of anguish for the soul: the belief that the gods are concerned with mankind; the fear of post-mortem punishment; the worries and pain brought about by unsatisfied desires...[3]

Here Hadot sets out the 'philosophy' or way of life that defines Epicureanism. The philosophy is, in brief, one involving 'peace of mind', and the Epicurean sets himself to realize this way of life, and the associated freedom from mental disturbance, by removing various possible sources of anxiety. As Hadot notes, for the Epicurean, one such source is

---

[2] Ibid., pp. 266–7, source's emphasis.   [3] Ibid., p. 222.

the 'fear of post-mortem punishment'. And the Epicurean commitment to atomism addresses precisely this anxiety, by providing a picture of the fundamental nature of things that will render such fears groundless. How? Because from the truth of atomism, it will follow that at death a person will simply decompose into their constituent atoms, so that there is no enduring subject who could be the object of post-mortem punishment—or, for that matter, reward. So here is one simple picture of how a certain philosophical discourse—in this case, atomism—can be in the service of a way of life. According to Hadot, then, in Epicurean thought, atomism is, at root, not a theoretical or speculative commitment concerning the fundamental nature of things, but an idea whose point is to enable a certain way of life.

On Hadot's account, if atomism is to play this life-regulating role for the Epicurean, then it is not enough that the adept should simply assent to its truth. Indeed, on this account, it is not immediately clear that assent to the truth of atomism is required at all. What is clearly required is that the Epicurean should acquire the habit of thinking of themselves in the light of this atomic conception of the nature of things—whether or not this entertaining of the view also involves assenting to it. Hence Hadot remarks of 'philosophical theories' that:

> in the Hellenistic and Roman periods, they were reduced to a theoretical, systematic, largely concentrated nucleus capable of exercising a strong psychological effect, and easy enough to handle so that it might always be kept close at hand (*procheiron*). Philosophical discourse was not systematic because it wanted to provide a total, systematic explanation of the whole of reality. Rather, it was systematic in order that it might provide the mind with a small number of principles, tightly linked together, which derived greater persuasive force and mnemonic effectiveness precisely from such systematization. Short sayings summed up, sometimes in striking form, the essential dogmas, so that the student might easily relocate himself within the fundamental disposition in which he was to live.[4]

---

[4] Ibid., p. 267.

If we follow this account, then we should say that the role of a 'philosophical discourse'—such as Epicurean atomism—is not, in the first instance, to provide an 'explanation' for the nature of things. The discourse is introduced, then, not so much to satisfy various epistemic desiderata, but—to put the point in Hadot's terms—for the sake of 'exercising a strong psychological effect' and for its 'persuasive force'. So the discourse provides the aspiring philosopher with a picture of the nature of things which they are to bear actively in mind—not necessarily, it would seem, to assert. By the practice of the requisite spiritual discipline, the philosopher aims, then, to become habituated to thinking of themselves in the terms provided by this depiction of the world, so securing their release from the anxieties to which they might otherwise fall prey.

Hadot argues that other ancient philosophies also exhibit this same sort of connection between a body of discourse and a certain quality of life. Stoicism, for example, represents resignation to events in the outer world as an ideal of life, where this ideal is supported by Stoic pantheistic discourse, according to which all events are ordered by a cosmic reason, so that everything works for the best. By acquiring the habit of thinking of events in these terms, Hadot proposes, the sage ceases to be troubled by worldly change, and thereby achieves the Stoic ideal of resignation. Here again, on Hadot's account of the matter, the reason for adopting the discourse is fundamentally 'psychological' rather than epistemic: the discourse is worthy of adherence because of its therapeutic effects, and not because of, say, its explanatory power, considered as a theory of the nature of things.

Hadot elaborates on this account of ancient philosophical traditions in various ways, but in summary form, the structure of his view seems to be as follows. The 'philosopher' begins with a conception of the good human life, as involving for instance (if we are Epicureans) freedom from anxiety, or (if we are Stoics) resignation to events in the outer world. Granted some such conception, the sage then seeks to adopt the requisite means for realizing the good life so understood, and to this end engages in various spiritual disciplines, which are designed to help them internalize the world view specified in the relevant philosophical discourse. If these exercises are efficacious, then the adept will become habituated to thinking of themselves in the terms of that world view, and will thereby achieve a way of life in which their favoured psychological and moral condition can be enduringly realized.

There is a further feature of Hadot's account of ancient philosophical traditions that it is worth noting here, since it raises a question that will be of some importance for our discussion in later chapters. Hadot writes:

> If one admits, as I do, that the various philosophical schools of antiquity were characterized above all by their choice of a form of life, which is then justified *after the fact* by a given systematic construction (for instance, Stoicism is the choice of an attitude of coherence with oneself, which is later justified by a general theory of the coherence of the universe with itself) – then it is easy to understand how one can remain faithful to one's choice of a form of life without being obliged to adhere to the systematic construction which claims to found it.[5]

In these remarks, we see, once again, Hadot's commitment to the priority of the way of life over the world view or 'systematic construction'. But this text also reveals that, for Hadot, this stance carries the implication that Stoicism, Epicureanism and the other ancient philosophical schools are not of merely antiquarian interest. These schools might have been of merely antiquarian interest *if* they had been grounded in a 'general theory' of some sort, such as Epicurean atomism or Stoic pantheism.[6] Why? Because such theories can become—and indeed these theories in particular evidently have become—in certain respects, outmoded. And if the rationale for Stoicism, for example, is simply to live according to the vision of the world given in such a theory, then the obsolescence of the theory will entail the obsolescence of the way of life. But if, on the

---

[5] Ibid., p. 282. This passage is in the Postscript to the text, and Michael Chase, the translator, explains: 'In April-May 1992, M. Hadot was kind enough to respond to some questions I had asked him during the course of our preparation of this translation. What follows is a translation of our exchange. All notes are my own': p. 285. I take it, then, that the emphasis in this passage derives from Hadot.

[6] See too Hadot's suggestion that to ensure their enduring importance, we are to 'reduce these philosophies to their spirit and essence, detaching them from their outmoded cosmological or mythical elements': ibid., p. 273. I discuss this passage shortly.

contrary, Stoicism is most fundamentally a set of practical and emotional commitments, of the kind that Hadot describes, and if Stoic 'discourse', that is, Stoic metaphysics, is just a rhetorical device which is helpful for sustaining those commitments, then we can be Stoics today, providing simply that we share the relevant commitments, and regardless of whether we subscribe to the conception of ultimate reality that was typical of Stoicism in the ancient world. Like the ancient Stoics, Hadot thinks, the modern Stoic will need a 'philosophical discourse' of some sort, if these practical and emotional commitments are to be motivationally accessible. But there is no requirement on modern Stoics to use the very discourse that was preferred by their ancient counterparts; instead, they are free to adopt a discourse that is better suited to contemporary habits of thought.

It is also worth noting Hadot's comment in this text that a 'systematic construction' may 'claim' to ground a way of life—which indicates his willingness to concede that some ancient philosophers took their discourse to provide the basis for their way of life. Allowing for the possibility that some philosophers in the ancient world read their practice in these terms, Hadot is clearly of the view that this interpretation is, in fact, mistaken. From his perspective, it is his own account that discloses the real import of ancient philosophical practice, and the real basis for thinking in terms of the relevant world view. Although he does not say so here, Hadot presumably thinks that any attempt to start from a 'systematic construction', and to 'found' a way of life on this basis, would, in fact, be indefensible, whatever the proponent of such an approach in the ancient world may have thought, since no world view can have the epistemic status that would be required for it to play this grounding role. On this reading of his position, Hadot's view is that we must represent the real drift ancient philosophies as he does, on pain of thinking of them as simply irrelevant for modern questions about how we are to live.

Hadot's account raises a question about what it would be for a philosophical discourse to become outmoded. After all, given what he says about the 'psychological' and 'persuasive' rather than epistemic grounds for adopting a given philosophical discourse, it would seem that, in his view, I do not need to suppose that a world view is true for it to play a spiritually efficacious role in my life. So we might ask: allowing that a given philosophical discourse has ceased to seem a plausible candidate for truth, and has in that sense become outmoded, why suppose that it will thereby lose its capacity to ground a spiritual practice? Why think, then, that modern Stoicism, for example, needs a modernized form of philosophical discourse—why can it not make do with the ancient version, even if that version seems most likely to be false, from our perspective?

Although Hadot does not address the question, we could respond on his behalf by supposing that while a given philosophical discourse can play a spiritually efficacious role in my life even if I do not take it to be true, I must still allow that its picture of the world has some reasonable prospect of providing at least a guide to the nature of things. If I come to suppose, on the contrary, that Stoic discourse, for example, has no claim to provide even an approximation to the truth, then it is hard to see how attending to this particular account of the nature of things could rationally motivate the practice of coming to respond to the world in the ways that are commended in Stoic ethics. By contrast, even if I suppose that the Stoic world view, considered in all its detail, is most likely false, I can still find its picture of the world to be properly action-guiding and emotion-regulating, providing that I suppose that there is some prospect that the world is, in respects relevant to the Stoic ideal of life, at least something like that. For if the world is something like that, then the Stoic picture can still serve, even if only approximately, as a guide to the nature of things, and therefore as a guide to right action, so far as right action is action that is properly responsive to the nature of things.

On this reading of Hadot, in affirming the Stoic world view for the purpose of engaging in a spiritual practice, I am not committed to the thought that the world view is true, but I am committed to the idea that it is a serious contender for truth, considered as a general guide to the nature of things. I take it that on Hadot's perspective, we can't say more than that on behalf of any world view. After all, if a world view were able to make a stronger claim to truth, then it could after all function as a 'systematic explanation' of the nature of things, and we would then have good reason to begin our reflections on how to live with 'philosophical discourse', before reading off the implications of such discourse for our way of life—and Hadot's position is evidently defined by its opposition to that picture. Rather, it seems that, for Hadot, there are various world views that are at least contenders for truth, and we can therefore exercise a measure of choice between them—and on his approach, we should of course choose the one that best supports our favoured way of life.

On this reading of Hadot, a given world view does not exert a merely mesmeric kind of power, through sheer force of repetition. Instead, its capacity to motivate the person to lead a certain way of life is mediated at least in part by the thought that this picture has some sort of claim to track fundamental features of reality, even if it is allowed that the same can be said for other world views. Granted this reading, we can see how the Stoic world view could indeed come to be outmoded for the purpose of sustaining a way of life—not by virtue simply of coming to seem false, considered in all its detail, but by ceasing to appear as a candidate even for the title of rough or approximate guide to the nature of things. So this account allows us to suppose both that epistemic considerations are, as Hadot supposes, of secondary importance—since the epistemic requirements that a world view must satisfy are on this approach relatively undemanding, and do not fix our choice between competing philosophical discourses—and that a world view's spiritual significance is not altogether detached from its claim to represent the nature of things.[7]

Whatever the stance we take on these issues, it is clear that for Hadot, ancient spiritual traditions are not only live practical possibilities for us today, but also repositories of a kind of wisdom, from which we may hope to learn as we consider how to order our lives here and now. In support of this theme, he remarks:

we shall find in the ancient traditions of the various philosophical schools – Socratism, Platonism, Aristotelianism, Epicureanism, Stoicism,

---

[7] Compare Hadot's comment that: 'What's interesting about the idea of spiritual exercises is precisely that it is not a matter of a purely rational consideration, but the putting in action of all kinds of means, intended to act upon one's self. Imagination and affectivity play a capital role here: we must represent to ourselves in vivid colors the dangers of such-and-such a passion, and use striking formulations of ideas in order to exhort ourselves': ibid., p. 284. The suggestion that spiritual exercises do not rest on a 'purely' rational basis perhaps invites the kind of reading we have just offered, which gives such considerations a role, of a subordinate kind.

Cynicism, Skepticism – models of life, fundamental forms in accordance with which reason may be applied to human existence, and archetypes of the quest for wisdom. It is precisely this plurality of ancient schools that is precious. It allows us to compare the consequences of all the various possible fundamental attitudes of reason, and offers a privileged field for experimentation. This, of course, presupposes that we reduce these philosophies to their spirit and essence, detaching them from their outmoded cosmological or mythical elements, and disengaging from them the fundamental propositions that they themselves consider essential.[8]

Here again, now more explicitly, Hadot acknowledges that his reading of the import of ancient philosophical traditions diverges at least in part from the reading that would have been offered by some practitioners of those traditions. But bracketing that point, Hadot's suggestion is that the ancient philosophical schools can teach us, in the present, something of fundamental importance—something we could not know a priori or by reference to social scientific sources. In brief, these traditions teach us what follows in practice from the attempt to live according to a certain 'attitude of reason'—such as the Stoic attitude of resignation to outer events, or the Epicurean attitude of freedom from anxiety. They teach us, then, the extent to which various ways of life, and associated ideals, are in fact practicable, given the constraints of our human nature.

As we have seen, Hadot allows for the possibility of a modern Stoicism or a modern Epicureanism that has abandoned the discourse of ancient Stoicism and Epicureanism. This view might suggest that it is simply the way of life of these ancient philosophies that is of enduring interest, and not the 'philosophical discourse' that was part of their mental discipline. But this does not follow, I think. Granted Hadot's view, we should allow that ancient philosophies can be instructive for us today both because they can teach us about the kind of world view that is best suited for the inculcation of a given way of life, and by virtue of disclosing the kind of spiritual exercise that is likely to be effective in instilling a given world view. In other words, ancient philosophies can teach us not merely that

[8] Ibid., p. 273.

certain ways of life are realizable, but also the conditions under which they can be realized, including here the kinds of discourse that are apt to promote a given mode of engagement with the world, and the kinds of spiritual practice that are apt to promote the motivationally effective internalization of that discourse.

I have spent some time expounding Hadot's views in part because I find some of these views at least initially attractive, as an account of the nature of the spiritual life, but more fundamentally because his discussion enables us to distinguish a number of questions that can be used to structure an enquiry into the nature of spiritual traditions of the kind that we are about to conduct. Some of the more obvious questions that emerge in the course of Hadot's account of the ancient philosophical schools are these.

How should we conceive of the relationship between world view and practice? There is an obvious sense in which Hadot prioritizes practice over world view—after all, on his view, we are to start from the recognition that a certain way of life is worth following, and move from there to consider which world view will make the way of life motivationally accessible. In another, more practical sense, Hadot prioritizes the world view, since we are to entertain the relevant world view first of all, with a view to shaping our emotions in the ways required for the realization of the favoured way of life. So Hadot's discussion invites us, first of all, to consider the structure of the spiritual life: which of world view and way of life comes first, if either, and in what sense? This is a question to which I shall return shortly.

Hadot's remarks also invite us to consider the nature of the motivational power of a world view. On his approach, we have seen, there is no need to assert the truth of the world view in all its detail, although it may be an implication of his position that the view should be taken to have a reasonable prospect of being at least an approximate guide to the nature of things. So his discussion also directs us to the question of what sort of epistemic status we should assign to a world view, if any, if it is to support the leading of a spiritual life.

Hadot's discussion also raises very clearly the question of what we might hope to learn from spiritual traditions, when we consider how we are to order our own lives in spiritual terms here and now. As we have seen, he has an account of these matters, proposing that there are certain deep-seated truths about human possibilities that are disclosed in, and only in, spiritual traditions, in so far as these traditions involve a kind of centuries-long testing of the practicability of various ideals of life for creatures such as ourselves. And finally, Hadot's approach also invites us to consider the relationship between the vocabularies that are used to describe the spiritual life, in so far as we require one idiom for what he calls 'philosophical discourse' and another, more experiential idiom for talking, however inchoately, about the quality of mind, and associated mode of life, that this discourse is supposed to enable.[9]

Each of these questions has an important part to play, I think, in ordering an enquiry into the nature of spiritual traditions, and their significance, if any, for us today. And I hope to address all of them in the course of this investigation. As it happens, I also think that Hadot's approach to each of these issues is at best radically incomplete, and this volume could be read as an extended examination of why his account needs elaboration in all of these respects. In the present chapter, I shall concentrate on Hadot's description of the structure of the spiritual life. Later chapters will consider the other questions that emerge in the course of Hadot's discussion, including these matters: the epistemic status required by a world view if it is to play an action-guiding role in the spiritual life; the relationship between the various vocabularies that can

---

[9] Hadot is explicit on this point. See for example his remark that in the ancient world: 'Scientific knowledge was objective and mathematical, whereas cosmic consciousness was the result of a spiritual exercise, which consisted in becoming aware of the place of one's individual existence within the great current of the cosmos and the perspective of the whole, *toti se inserens in mundo*, in the words of Seneca. This exercise was situated not in the absolute space of exact science, but in the lived experience of the concrete, living, and perceiving subject': ibid., p. 273. Here it is implied that while a world view can be communicated 'objectively', the quality of 'lived experience' that defines a particular philosophical way of life cannot be so described. See too his comment that: 'Everything which is "technical" in the broad sense of the term...is perfectly able to be communicated by teaching or conversation. But everything that touches the domain of the existential...for instance, our feeling of existence, our impressions when faced by death, our perception of nature, our sensations, and a fortiori the mystical experience, is not directly communicable. The phrases we use to describe them are conventional and banal; we realize this when we try to console someone over the loss of a loved one. That's why it often happens that a poem or a biography are more philosophical than a philosophical treatise, simply because they allow us to glimpse this unsayable in an indirect way': ibid., p. 285. This account suggests that spiritual exercises will need to deploy other kinds of verbal expression, in addition to the theoretical idiom of 'philosophical discourse', if they wish to communicate, in verbal terms, the state of mind that is the goal of the exercise.

be used to chart spiritual development; and the significance of tradition for our understanding of spiritual goods. But let us begin with the question of the structure of the spiritual life.

Having introduced Hadot's perspective on this question, I am going to consider a rather different approach, which I have taken from Thomas Aquinas. Aquinas makes a good interlocutor for our purposes both because he writes clearly and systematically, and because his views have a certain spiritual, and not only philosophical and theological, authority within one central strand of the Christian tradition, namely, Roman Catholicism. So by anchoring our account of the spiritual life in his perspective, we can be confident that our discussion will be, to that extent, attuned to the concerns of at least one living and widely influential spiritual tradition.

As I noted in the Introduction to this volume, the various phases of this enquiry will be bound together by a single concept, namely, Thomas Aquinas's notion of infused moral virtue. The remainder of this chapter will offer a first intimation of the fruitfulness of this notion for an assessment of the questions that we have derived from Hadot.

Thomas Aquinas on the Christian Life

At the core of any Christian account of the nature of the good or worthwhile human life will stand a conception of neighbour love. And if we wish to consider Aquinas's view of the Christian life, it is natural, then, to turn first of all to his treatment of neighbour love. Of course, Christians have thought of neighbour love as good, and indeed, for themselves, as obligatory for a variety of reasons. Most simply, they are bound to think of this way of life as required, for them, because it is after all mandated by Jesus himself.[10] While he accepts, naturally, that neighbour love is binding upon Christians for this reason, Aquinas offers another rationale for its status—as obligatory—in the Christian conception of the good life when providing an account of neighbour love as a theological virtue.

[10] See for example Mark 12:30–1.

When developing this account, Aquinas does not take the appropriateness of neighbour love to be evident simply from a consideration of human nature, in the way that the appropriateness of the precepts of the natural law, and the actions they enjoin, is in principle evident simply from a consideration of human nature.[11] Instead, the appropriateness of neighbour love turns out to depend, in his view, on a certain conception of our metaphysical context, as disclosed in revelation. Let us see how he develops this idea.

In *Summa Theologiae* 2a2ae Question 25, Aquinas puts to himself a question about the scope of neighbour love, by asking whether it extends to our enemies, ourselves, to our bodies, to the angels, and so on. In general terms, his answer is that I am to treat as my neighbour any creature who will share in the beatific vision. Here, for example, is his answer to the question of whether the angels are properly the objects of neighbour love. While this particular question may seem to be of no very pressing importance from the perspective of our own time, Aquinas's answer is representative of what he says when determining the bounds of neighbour love in other cases too, so is worth considering at least for that reason:

> the friendship of charity is founded upon the fellowship of everlasting happiness, in which men share in common with the angels. For it is written (Mt. 22:30) that 'in the resurrection…men shall be as the angels of God in heaven.' It is therefore evident that the friendship of charity extends also to the angels.
>
> (ST 2a2ae. 25. 10, ellipsis in the original)[12]

We are all familiar with the idea that truths about the past can shape the character of our moral relations with others in the present. To take a very simple example, if I have wronged someone, say by breaking a promise I made to them, then, prima facie, I have a reason to make good that wrong in the present, if there is opportunity to do so, at least by

---

[11] For a fuller treatment of these matters, see the discussion of 'acquired' temperance in Chapter 2.

[12] Here as elsewhere, unless otherwise indicated, I am using the translation of the Fathers of the English Dominican Province (New York: Benziger Brothers, 1947).

offering an apology, and perhaps by other means. In this passage, Aquinas seems to envisage another, less familiar kind of connection: perhaps truths about the future can also shape the character of our moral relations with others in the present? To take the particular case that he cites here, perhaps the truth that the angels will, in the eschatological future, share with us in a 'fellowship of everlasting happiness' establishes the appropriateness of a certain attitude towards them here and now?

There are obvious practical reasons why future-referenced truths do not in fact play much of a role in shaping our assessment of our moral relations to others, since the future is of course, from our human vantage point, very often uncertain. But the considerations that make it appropriate for me to apologize in the present for a past wrong would presumably make it appropriate for me to apologize in the present for a future wrong, were I to know of that wrong in the present. For instance, were I to know here and now that I will, culpably, harm another person, then it looks like I have prima facie a reason to apologize to them here and now, if there is opportunity to do so.

The case that concerns Aquinas is not quite so straightforward as that of harm, but it is not too difficult to think of parallels between the example that he gives and morally significant truths about the past. If I once had a close friendship with someone, one that involved sharing in fundamental goods, then there is ready moral sense in the idea that I can be called upon to act in certain ways in the present, as a condition of honouring the history of the friendship. And we might suppose that this is so even if the friendship has now lapsed. Analogously, Aquinas seems to be supposing that a truth concerning my friendship with someone in the eschatological future, where that friendship involves sharing in a uniquely profound good, namely the vision of God, or participation in the divine life, can also call for practical acknowledgement in my relations with the person in the present.

The relationship between truths concerning my friendship with another person, whether in the past or the future, and the kind of conduct that I am thereby called to exhibit in my relations with them in the present seems to be broadly one of existential congruence. If I know that a person has been or will be my friend, then my conduct towards them in the present is in principle open to assessment as being more or less adequate, more or less fitting—more or less congruent—relative to those truths about our friendship. These considerations need not be overriding: the fact that a particular action or thought would dishonour the friendship need not show conclusively that I should not act or think so. That judgement will depend upon the overall balance of reasons. But truths concerning the history of a relationship, or its putative future, do seem to be properly part of the mix of reasons to which I can held accountable in my relations to another person in the present.

The appeal to theological context makes it relatively easy for Aquinas to introduce truths about the future, as he does here when speaking of the beatific vision. He is writing, evidently, as a Christian theologian, and can therefore presuppose certain fundamental Christian claims about the course of human lives. However, even from this theological vantage point, there may be some uncertainty about which human beings in particular will participate in the beatific vision. A universalist about salvation, or someone who thinks that there is a simple empirical marker of whether or not someone is saved, will not take themselves to be subject to such uncertainty. But Aquinas's position is not to be identified with either of these perspectives. And we might ask then: if there is indeed a degree of uncertainty about whether a given individual will share in the beatific vision, should there not also be, for Aquinas, a matching uncertainty about whether that individual is to be shown neighbour love? After all, it is, he has told us, a person's sharing in the beatific vision that grounds the appropriateness of showing them neighbour love. And consistently with this general approach, Aquinas is explicit that the demons, whom we know to be damned rather than saved, are not to be shown neighbour love, for the reason that we will not share with them in the beatific vision.[13]

There is perhaps a tension here between Aquinas's account and standard Christian teaching. Aquinas is suggesting that the appropriateness of neighbour love is grounded in a future truth concerning the beatific vision, and if it is uncertain whether a particular individual will share in that vision, then should it not be in the same measure uncertain whether

[13] See ST 2a2ae. 25. 11. ad 2. I comment on this text in footnote 14.

that individual is properly the recipient of neighbour love? But presumably, for the Christian, there can be no uncertainty about whether we are to treat other human beings as our neighbour. Or to raise a related difficulty, if as many Christians have supposed, not all human beings share in the beatific vision, then how can it be appropriate to regard all human beings as properly the objects of neighbour love? And yet it is surely a mark of neighbour love that it does rightly extend to every human being; famously, it is supposed to extend even to one's enemies.

I take it that Aquinas's answer to these concerns would be to appeal to the possibility, relative to our present epistemic vantage point, that any given human being will share in the beatific vision. Relative to that vantage point, it is appropriate for me to treat any given human being as my neighbour, even if it should turn out that some of those to whom I extend neighbour love will not in fact share in the beatific vision. We could put the point by saying that in these matters we are to adhere to a kind of precautionary principle: if it is possible, from my epistemic vantage point, that an individual has a relatively elevated moral or onto-logical status, then I am to treat them as having that status, even if it is also possible, from that same vantage point, that they have another, lower status. In other words, I am to make it my priority to treat all those who will share in the beatific vision with appropriate regard, even if this policy means running the risk of treating some who will not share in the beatific vision with a regard to which they are not entitled. More ambi-tiously, we might suppose that it is not only true relative to my epistemic vantage point that it is possible for a given human being to attain the beatific vision: perhaps this is, in addition, a metaphysical possibility for all human beings, ante mortem, given the nature of human freedom. Aquinas also seems to allow for this case.[14] And for present purposes, I shall proceed on the assumption that sharing in the beatific vision is in fact an ante mortem possibility for each human being.

---

[14] See Aquinas's comment that: 'In this life, men who are in sin retain the possibility of obtaining everlasting happiness: not so those who are lost in hell, who, in this respect, are in the same case as the demons.' ST 2a2ae. 25. 11 ad 2. By possibility here, Aquinas seems to mean metaphysical possibility.

Comparing Aquinas and Hadot

In structural terms, this account of the spiritual life might sound rather like Hadot's perspective. In Aquinas as in Hadot, we find both a vision of the good life and a conception of our metaphysical context, where the second appears to ground the first: where Hadot appeals to Stoic pantheism and Epicurean atomism to motivate the Stoic and Epicurean ideals of life, Aquinas appeals to the narrative of the beatific vision as the basis for the Christian ideal of neighbour love. And we might add that in the work of both authors, the relevant world view does not need to be taken in all its detail as evidently true, if it is to motivate the practice: it is enough that it should be a contender for being at least an approximation to the truth (if we follow my reading of Hadot on this point) or enough that it should represent an epistemic possibility (if we follow my reading of Aquinas's account of the preconditions of neighbour love).

On closer reading, however, it turns out that there are some significant differences between Hadot's picture of the spiritual life and Aquinas's. As we have seen, Hadot represents the approach of the ancient philosophical schools (whether or not they realized as much themselves) in the following terms:

> the various philosophical schools of antiquity were characterized above all by their choice of a form of life, which is then justified *after the fact* by a given systematic construction (for instance, Stoicism is the choice of an attitude of coherence with oneself, which is later justified by a general theory of the coherence of the universe with itself).[15]

The emphasis here—'justified *after the fact*'—is Hadot's, and indicates categorically that for him, the judgement about the appropriateness or fittingness of a given way of a life comes first, and that we are to introduce a world view only as a second step, as a means of inculcating the state of mind that is required for the leading of that way of life.

---

[15] *Philosophy as a Way of Life*, p. 282.

By contrast, for Aquinas, it seems clear that a judgement about the appropriateness or fittingness of neighbour love is to be grounded in the relevant world view: here, the view given in the narrative of the beatific vision. This is evident from the case of the demons, which Aquinas distinguishes from that of the angels in these terms:

> The possession of everlasting happiness is not impossible for the angelic mind as it is for the mind of a demon; consequently the friendship of charity which is based on the fellowship of everlasting life, rather than on the fellowship of nature, is possible towards the angels, but not towards the demons.   (ST 2a2ae. 25. 11 ad 1)

From this passage, it is clear that 'charity'—that is, neighbour love—is not to be extended to the demons, for the reason that they can have no part in the beatific vision. So here the judgement about the fittingness of neighbour love, with respect to the demons, depends very directly on a judgement about the nature of our metaphysical context. In this passage, possibility and impossibility seem to signify metaphysical possibility and impossibility: the impossibility of the demons' sharing in the beatific vision is, presumably, a function of the radical corruption of their nature. And it is this impossibility that places the demon beyond the scope of neighbour love.

As I have noted, it may be that Aquinas is also committed to the thought that a given individual is properly the object of neighbour love, for me, if it is epistemically possible, for me, that they will share in the beatific vision, even if in fact they will not do so—and, we might surmise, even if it is metaphysically impossible for them to do so. There is no inconsistency here, between Aquinas's handling of the case of the demons and what seems to be his stance towards human beings who will not attain the beatific vision. Where human beings are concerned, we have to be guided by judgements of epistemic possibility, when determining whether an individual is properly the object of neighbour love: for all I know, any given human being will attain the beatific vision. (This will be my epistemic position whether or not I know if it is metaphysically possible for this individual to attain the beatific vision.) By contrast, in the case of the demons, we are able to make reliable judgements of metaphysical impossibility: here, we can judge that an individual's nature is such that they will not participate in the beatific vision.

So the case of the demons shows that, for Aquinas, the question of whether a certain way of life is an ideal for me—here the way of life defined by the practice of neighbour love—is connected to the question of metaphysical context. If I were to know that my fellow rational creatures are in all cases demons, and that my relationship to them is, therefore, not one of prospective fellowship in the beatific vision, then neighbour love would cease to be an ideal of life for me, or at least cease to be obligatory for me. (For ease of exposition, I shall drop the qualification about obligatoriness in what follows. In each case, the point is that the normative status of the way of life is a function of metaphysical context.) Accordingly, when considering whether we are to treat other human beings, and the angels, as our neighbours, Aquinas does not appeal to the self-evident goodness of the practice of neighbour love, but to a theological datum, concerning our future life with God.

In sum, Hadot and Aquinas seem to differ on this point: Hadot takes the appropriateness of a way of life to be evident independently of metaphysical context, so that a person's commitment to a given way of life can serve as the ground for their commitment to a philosophical discourse or world view; by contrast, Aquinas's account suggests that the fittingness of a way of life, or at least of certain ways of life that he deems spiritually important, is tied to a judgement about metaphysical context. On Thomas's view, if we were come to know that the relevant context does not obtain, then the way of life would cease to be an ideal for us. To put the distinction between the two in another way, the goodness of ways of life appears to be intrinsic for Hadot, or at least independent of metaphysical context, whereas for Aquinas their goodness is a function of their relationship to our metaphysical context.

On Aquinas's account, then, it would make no sense to take neighbour love to be an ideal for human beings independently of any reference to metaphysical context, and then—as a second, discrete step—to ask about what world picture or, to use Hadot's expression, what 'philosophical discourse' might be helpful in inculcating that way of life. Why would this make no sense? Because on his account, the goodness of the way of life is a consequence of its congruence with our metaphysical context; and to determine that the way of life is good, we need therefore to identify, first of all, the relevant metaphysical context.[16] To take the case of neighbour love again, the goodness of this practice, so far as it is directed at our fellow human beings and the angels, follows from its congruence with an eschatological truth concerning our relations with our fellow rational creatures; and an assessment of the goodness of the practice cannot proceed independently, therefore, of reference to this metaphysical context.

Of course, for Hadot, as we have been reading him, motivating a given way of life depends upon appeal to a world view. But there remains this difference: when he considers metaphysical context, Aquinas is concerned with the question of whether a given way of life (such as neighbour love) is to be counted as good, whereas when Hadot considers metaphysical context, he is concerned with the question of whether a given way of life, which can be judged good independently of reference to any such context, can be motivated effectively, by reference to a world view that has some prospect of being at least an approximation to the nature of things. To put the point concretely, on Hadot's account of the matter, if the Epicurean should learn that atomism is, for certain, not an approximation to the truth, then he should not surrender the thought that tranquillity of life is an ideal. Instead, he should simply recognize that this ideal cannot be supported by reference to atomism, and that he should therefore search for another world view, one that has some prospect of being true, considered as a general guide to the nature of things, and whose truth would provide a basis for his practice.

In an attempt to reconcile Hadot and Aquinas, it might be said that Hadot is working with a very thin conception of the spiritual life, and where this conception is concerned, the goods of the spiritual life will turn out to be independent of metaphysical context. And we might add that we can associate a similarly thin account with Aquinas himself. For instance, we could say that the spiritual life is grounded most fundamentally in a commitment to the principle that good is to be done and

---

[16] In Chapter 2, I shall complicate this picture a little, when distinguishing between the vantage points afforded by a 'rule of reason' and a 'divine rule'. But we can come to those matters in due course.

evil avoided. (This is the first principle of the natural law for Aquinas.)[17] And if the spiritual life is conceived in these terms, then the fittingness of that life will not, after all, vary with metaphysical context. (This first principle of the natural law is, I take it, a conceptually necessary truth for Aquinas, so valid regardless of context.) The case of neighbour love is different on this point, it might said, only because it involves a thicker description of the nature of the spiritual life. So perhaps Aquinas's position and Hadot's are not at odds with each other, but are just different specifications of the spiritual life, one relatively thick and one relatively thin, with the result that one is sensitive to metaphysical context while the other is not?

However, while it may be true that Aquinas's conception of the spiritual life can in part be cast in these terms, it is clear that on his view, we need a relatively thick conception of the spiritual life, of the kind provided in his discussion of neighbour love, if we are to say much of action-guiding import about the nature of a good human life, whereas for Hadot, I take it, this is not the case. There is, after all, nothing in Hadot's account to suggest that the introduction of a world view or metaphysical context expands our conception of the nature of the good life—on the contrary, the world view serves simply to motivate a way of life whose character, and goodness, has already been established, independently of reference to metaphysical context. If that is so, then the difference between Hadot and Aquinas on this point is not a function simply of their particular angle of view on the spiritual life, but reflects a substantive difference about how we are to characterize that life if our object is to indicate how we are in fact to live.

From the picture I have presented so far, we might conclude that while Hadot advocates beginning with the way of life, and then moving to the metaphysics, Aquinas favours a shift in the opposite direction, from metaphysics to ethics. Again, Hadot's position is clear enough. See for example his remark that:

> As a matter of fact ethics – that is to say, choosing the good – is not the consequence of metaphysics, but metaphysics is the consequence of ethics.[18]

---

[17] ST 1a2ae. 94. 2.   [18] *Philosophy as a Way of Life*, p. 283.

But it would be a mistake, I think, to see Aquinas as proposing simply that we invert this arrangement and move in the other direction, from a set of metaphysical to a set of ethical commitments. This is a matter we will examine more carefully in the discussion of religious faith in Chapter 6. But very briefly, we can note here that for Aquinas, the believer's assent to the Christian narrative, concerning the beatific vision and other such matters, is not epistemically required, but on the contrary voluntary. And what engages the believer's assent to that narrative, I shall argue, here following at least the spirit of Aquinas's text, is the goodness or attractiveness of the picture of reality that it extends—where that picture includes not only various proposals concerning the nature of ultimate reality, such as the idea that there is a God, but also an indication of what goods will be realizable in a human life should those proposals be true.

To see more exactly how this account runs, let us take again the case of the beatific vision. If it is true that we will one day share with other human beings in the vision of God, then our lives can bear an additional significance here and now, in the ways we have discussed, when they stand in a relationship of congruence to that truth. And when the believer assents voluntarily to the idea of the beatific vision, and commits herself to a correlative form of life, she is moved at least in part, on this view, by the prospect of realizing this additional significance in her own life. It is, then, the attractiveness of the way of life, relative to the metaphysical picture, that engages the believer's will, and elicits her assent to the picture.

Of course, this account raises a great many questions—including questions about whether religious faith is to be considered, therefore, as merely a kind of wish-fulfilment, where the person subscribes to certain claims for the reason simply that she would like them to be true, because of the good that will then attach to a human life. But these are matters we can defer to later discussion. For present purposes, I note simply that Aquinas's position is not simply that we are to determine the nature of the metaphysical facts, independently of any reference to the way of life that those facts would enable, and only then ask about how we are to live.

The Distinctive Character of Aquinas's
Account of the Spiritual Life

Let us suppose for now that this is the right way of reading Aquinas. If that is so, then we can distinguish his position from two others. Firstly, as we have seen, Aquinas's account of the Christian life differs from Hadot's representation of the life of the philosophical sage, because for Aquinas, we are not to begin with a commitment to the way of life— where the goodness of that life is judged independently of metaphysical context—and only then to introduce a world view. Secondly, Thomas's account is also different from that of those philosophers of religion who aim to establish the truth of various metaphysical claims on the basis of evidence, or perhaps by reference to religious experience, considered as distinct from 'evidence', before moving to a judgement about what way of life would be good granted that metaphysical vision.[19] Aquinas's position seems to differ from this approach because it takes the assent to a given metaphysical picture to be voluntary, rather than as grounded simply in epistemic considerations. Let us think a little further about these distinctions. Once again, we can take the beatific vision as representative of a wider class of cases.

I have been suggesting that, for Aquinas, in assenting to the truth of the beatific vision, the Christian assents not just to a world view, but to a world view understood in conjunction with a correlative way of life. On this account, the attractiveness of the doctrine of the beatific vision consists in part in the fact that it enables human lives to exhibit a distinctive kind of goodness here and now, in so far as we relate to other human beings as our neighbours here and now; and it is at least in part this truth about the doctrine that draws the believer to assent to it. If all of this is so, then we should take Aquinas to be committed to the view that in assenting to at least some fundamental propositions of faith, we

---

[19] The concern of a broad swathe of the literature in the philosophy of religion to 'prove' or 'disprove' the existence of God is, arguably, rooted in this sort of orientation—where it is assumed that the question of whether or not we should engage in religious practice is to be addressed by, first of all, resolving the question of whether or not the relevant metaphysical claims are true.

assent, in the first instance, neither to a metaphysical vision in isolation from any practical commitment nor—as in Hadot—to a practical commitment considered independently of any metaphysical vision, but to a metaphysical vision that has embedded within it a certain conception of the good human life. In these cases, it is this package, comprising the way-of-life-and-metaphysical-vision-in-combination, that elicits the assent of faith.

In sum, Hadot and Aquinas agree that we are free to choose between different forms of spiritual life. But they hold differing views of what the spiritual life is, and they disagree, therefore, about the objects of that choice: for Hadot, the choice is between different ways of life understood independently of metaphysical context, whereas for Aquinas, as I have read him, the objects of choice are ways-of-life-with-an-associated-metaphysics, so that the way of life and world view are taken in conjunction. For some philosophers of religion, we should follow another approach again, and begin with a metaphysical vision understood independently of any reference to human lives, where this vision is affirmed on epistemic or other grounds, and only then are we to move to an account of the nature of the well-lived human life.[20]

Each of these approaches takes a view about how we ought to represent spiritual traditions when we compare them with one another for

---

[20] For an example of this final approach, consider Richard Swinburne's comment: 'If there is no God, humans have no obligations to give their lives to prayer or philosophical reflection or artistic creativity or helping to enrich the spiritual, intellectual, and physical lives of others, good though it is that these things be done. But if all talents depend totally on God, and if doing these things is the way to form our characters and those of others over a few years of earthly life to fit us for the life of heaven, then to use our lives in some such way passes into the realm of the obligatory': 'The Christian Scheme of Salvation', in Michael Rea (ed.), *Oxford Readings in Philosophical Theology*, vol. 1: *Trinity, Incarnation and Atonement* (Oxford: Oxford University Press, 2009), p. 305. If we grant Swinburne's claim that God's existence can be shown to be 'more probable than not', it seems to follow that we can ground these aspects of religious practice in a (probabilistic) proof of the existence of God. (On the question of the probability of divine existence, see Swinburne, *The Existence of God* (Oxford: Oxford University Press, 2nd edn 2004), p. 342.) It is important to add that Swinburne's treatment of these questions is not restricted to what he says regarding the existence of God, where the truth of a religious belief can be established first, and then various practices inferred from the belief. For a fuller account of his approach, see his text *Faith and Reason* (Oxford: Oxford University Press, 2nd edn, 2005). For further discussion of the three approaches I distinguish here, see my chapter, 'Renewing our Understanding of Religion: Philosophy of Religion and the Goals of the Spiritual Life', in P. Draper and J. L. Schellenberg (eds), *Renewing Philosophy of Religion: Exploratory Essays* (Oxford: Oxford University Press, 2017), ch. 5.

the purpose of determining which, if any, to adopt. So the difference between these accounts is of some importance, if we wish to reach a judgement about which form of the spiritual life, if any, we should follow. We could answer the question of which of these accounts is to be preferred by considering whether human beings, in varying cultures, have in fact begun, and perhaps still begin, with an ideal of life, and then moved to a supporting metaphysical story, as Hadot proposes, or whether they have proceeded the other way about, by moving from the metaphysical story to a vision of an ideal of life, or whether, finally, they have taken themselves to be choosing between ways of life and metaphysical schemes considered in combination. In the next chapter, I want to address not this sociological issue, but rather the question of which of these approaches makes best sense, in philosophical terms, regardless of which has typically been implied in actual human choices.

To conclude, I hope that in this chapter we have succeeded in distinguishing between several approaches to the structure of the spiritual life, where that structure can be understood in very general terms by reference to Hadot's distinction between a way of life and a 'philosophical discourse'. And I hope we have identified some initial ways in which these matters can be illuminated by reference to Aquinas's conception of infused moral virtue, and specifically his account of neighbour love considered as such a virtue.

2

Religious and Secular Conceptions of the Human Good

Introduction

Chapter 1 had two primary objectives: to introduce some of the key questions that will guide this enquiry into the nature of spiritual traditions, drawing on the work of Pierre Hadot for this purpose; and to examine how Thomas Aquinas's concept of infused moral virtue can be used to address one such question, concerning the structure of spiritual traditions, and the relationship between the way of life of a tradition and its 'philosophical discourse'. In the present chapter, I am proposing to extend this discussion by thinking further about the concept of infused moral virtue, and its importance for the following questions, which have their roots, once again, in Hadot's work: how should we conceive of the relationship between spiritual goods and their metaphysical context? How should we think of the relationship between religious or spiritual and what we might call secular conceptions of the human good? And how should we understand the practical reasonableness of participation in religious traditions? As we shall see, these questions turn out to be connected in various ways. To address them effectively, we need, first of all, to develop our understanding of the nature of infused moral virtue, and to that end, I shall begin by considering the relationship between the infused moral virtues and their acquired counterparts, before exploring a significant distinction between two examples of infused moral virtue, namely, neighbour love and infused temperance.

Spiritual Traditions and the Virtues: Living Between Heaven and Earth. Mark R. Wynn, Oxford University Press (2020).
© Mark R. Wynn.
DOI: 10.1093/oso/9780198862949.001.0001

Thomas Aquinas on Infused Temperance

It is well known that Aquinas distinguishes between acquired and infused forms of the moral virtues.[1] The acquired moral virtues derive of course from a process of habituation, of the kind that Aristotle described. For instance, a person can acquire the virtue of justice by repeatedly performing just acts, with the result that the performance of such acts becomes habitual, or second nature, for them, so that they then perform those acts as a just person.[2] Aquinas reasons that the infused moral virtues must be different in this respect. Since these virtues are concerned with a goal that is not given with human nature, namely the goal of flourishing in relation to God, where that flourishing is understood in specifically Christian terms, they cannot be instilled, he thinks, by way of some process of habituation, or acquired simply by human effort: they must instead be conferred upon the person directly by God, which is to say that they must be 'infused.'[3] Similarly, the goal at which these virtues are targeted cannot be apprehended, he thinks, simply by reasoned consideration of what will be conducive to the flourishing of creatures of our kind, but must instead be revealed by God.

We can bring these matters into sharper focus by turning to Aquinas's handling of a particular case. In the following passage, he is explaining the distinction between acquired and infused temperance:

It is evident the measure of desires appointed by a rule of human reason is different from that appointed by a divine rule. For instance in eating, the measure fixed by human reason is that food should not harm the health of the body, nor hinder the use of reason; whereas

---

[1] For present purposes, I simply bracket the question of the intellectual virtues.

[2] For this account, see Aristotle's *Nicomachean Ethics*, Book II.

[3] Aquinas writes: 'human virtue directed to the good which is defined according to the rule of human reason can be caused by human acts: inasmuch as such acts proceed from reason, by whose power and rule the aforesaid good is established. On the other hand, virtue which directs man to good as defined by the Divine Law, and not by human reason, cannot be caused by human acts, the principle of which is reason, but is produced in us by the Divine operation alone. Hence Augustine in giving the definition of the latter virtue inserts the words, "which God works in us without us" (Super Ps. 118, Serm. xxvi)': ST 1a2ae. 63. 2.

[the] divine rule requires that a man should *chastise his body and bring it into subjection* [1 Cor 9:27], by abstinence in food, drink and the like.   (ST 1a2ae. 63. 4)[4]

Acquired temperance is governed, of course, by a 'rule of human reason'. The example that Aquinas gives here is the rule that eating 'should not harm the health of the body': this is a rule 'of reason' because it serves a goal whose nature can be fixed independently of revelation. (We do not need to defer to Scripture to determine that bodily health is good, or that certain dietary practices are beneficial, or detrimental, to bodily health.) By adhering consistently to this rule, that is, by repeatedly eating in ways that do not harm the body, a person can become habituated to so eating; and thereby they can acquire through their own efforts, with respect to this particular domain of activity, the virtue of temperance. Here Aquinas conscripts Aristotle's story of the acquisition of the moral virtues into his own conception of the moral and spiritual life.

However, for Aquinas, there is of course a further goal that can be served in our practices of eating and drinking: not only the goal of health of the body, and the goal of ensuring that reason's operation is unimpaired by any bodily disturbance, but also the end of being properly related to God. (As we shall see, these goals are not simply discrete.) This further end is served by a different pattern of activity, one which is identified here in Aquinas's phrase 'chastising the body'. When this phrase is located in its original literary setting, in Paul's first letter to the Corinthian church, it becomes clear that this practice is directed to the end of relationship to God in the afterlife. Paul's text reads:

> Everyone who competes in the games exercises self-control in all things. They then do it to receive a perishable wreath, but we an imperishable. Therefore I run in such a way, as not without aim; I box in such a way, as not beating the air; but I discipline my body and make it my slave, so that, after I have preached to others, I myself will not be disqualified.   (1 Cor 9:25–7, New American Standard Bible)

---

[4] Translation from the Blackfriars edition of the *Summa Theologiae*, ed. T. Gilby (London: Eyre & Spottiswoode, 1964–74).

So adherence to the divine rule that is appropriate to eating has as its goal an 'imperishable wreath', which is to say, the goal of relationship to God in eternity. (It is notable that, as in his discussion of neighbour love, Aquinas here anchors the fittingness of an infused virtue in the beatific vision.) This goal was not known to Aristotle, who for Aquinas stands as the supreme exemplar of what can be known by natural reason. And for Aquinas, this is, indeed, a goal which cannot be grasped by unaided reason, and which is to be accepted, therefore, as a datum of Scripture and affirmed in faith.

The picture of the moral and spiritual life that Aquinas provides in this sketch of acquired temperance and its infused counterpart points to a two-tier account of the significance of human activities: there are activities whose sense is evident from a consideration of human nature and the conditions of our flourishing as human, and there are activities whose sense is relative to an end that is not given simply with human nature, but apprehended only in revelation. So these two kinds of significance have different kinds of ground: one is grounded in human nature, the other (to take the case that Aquinas gives here) in the beatific vision, that is, in a pattern of life that is beyond nature. And the two kinds of significance are also subject, therefore, to different epistemologies: the first is defined by a goal that is knowable in principle from an examination of human nature, while the second concerns a goal that can be identified only through revelation. And from this it follows, Aquinas thinks, that they will also have different aetiologies: by their own efforts human beings can relate themselves appropriately to goals such as the health of the body, but they cannot by their own efforts bring themselves into an appropriate practical and emotional relation to the Christian God, not even if they should have, from revelation, some conception of how that relationship is to be conceived in Christian terms.[5]

While they differ in these respects, there is for Aquinas no inconsistency between the practice of the acquired and infused forms of a given virtue. To take this same example, it seems clear that the pattern of life that is appropriate to infused temperance, that is, abstinence, should not

---

[5] For Aquinas's reasoning on this point, see ST 1a2ae. 63. 2, cited in footnote 3.

harm the body. Hence, the rule that is the measure of the acquired form of the virtue is presupposed in the rule that governs the infused form.[6] And consistently with this position, Aquinas notes with approval the custom of exempting children from the full rigours of practices of abstinence, on the grounds that such practices pose a risk to their bodily health:

> In children there is a most evident reason for not fasting, both on account of their natural weakness, owing to which they need to take food frequently, and not much at a time, and because they need much nourishment owing to the demands of growth, which results from the residuum of nourishment. Wherefore as long as the stage of growth lasts, which as a rule lasts until they have completed the third period of seven years, they are not bound to keep the Church fasts: and yet it is fitting that even during that time they should exercise themselves in fasting, more or less, in accordance with their age.

Aquinas goes on to note that even so, there are certain occasions when children are required to fast according to the standards of grown men and women—but this is not the normal case, and is permitted only for the sake of averting some catastrophe. And in so far as it serves to ward off catastrophe, this practice also serves, at least indirectly, we might suppose, the health of the body. Aquinas comments:

> Nevertheless when some great calamity threatens, even children are commanded to fast, in sign of more severe penance, according to Jonas 3:7, 'Let neither men nor beasts ... taste anything ... nor drink water'.
>
> (ST 2a2ae. 147. 4 ad 2, tr. Fathers of the
> English Dominican Province)

---

[6] In general, Aquinas thinks of the acquired form of a given virtue as preparing the way for the receipt of the infused, which builds upon and extends, and does not displace, the acquired form of the virtue. Hence he writes: 'Acts produced by an infused habit, do not cause a habit, but strengthen the already existing habit; just as the remedies of medicine given to a man who is naturally healthy, do not cause a kind of health, but give new strength to the health he had before' (ST 1a2ae. 51. 4).

It is worth distinguishing this sort of case from the abstinence that is proper to infused temperance: when speaking of the abstinence appropriate to temperance, Aquinas has in mind, I take it, not only the requirement to fast in preparation for religious festivals, or in the face of potential 'calamity', but a general habit that will govern the person's practice throughout the year. In the case both of special fasting and of generalized abstinence, the ultimate goal of the practice is, of course, relationship to God. But there is a further difference between the two cases in so far as special fasting aims to effect some change in our present circumstances, whereas abstinence, we have seen, is directed in the first instance to the person's relationship to God in the beatific vision. To put the point in Scriptural terms, we might understand the significance of abstinence by saying that it is the 'pure in heart' who will 'see God' (Matthew 5:8), and that the role of abstinence is, then, to instil such purity.

So granted Aquinas's treatment of the idea of abstinence, and granted the conception of the limits of proper abstinence that is evident in Christian practices of fasting, it is clear that in this domain, of dietary practice, adherence to the 'divine rule' presupposes, in the normal case, adherence to the relevant rule of reason. So there is no conflict between the two rules. The divine rule is, however, more stringent, since it requires not only that a person should not harm their body, but also that they should aim at a further goal, which will entail restricting their consumption of food beyond what would be necessary simply for the sake of preserving bodily health. Hence all of those habits of eating that are consistent with the divine rule will also be consistent with the rule of reason; but some of those habits of eating that are consistent with the rule of reason will not be consistent with the divine rule, because by the standard of the divine rule, they will involve eating to excess.

These reflections allow us to frame a question: what should the person who does not assent to the doctrine of the beatific vision make of the practice of abstinence? Well, we have seen that abstinence is consistent with the rule of reason that operates in this context. So the person who acknowledges this rule (understood as Aquinas understands it) but not the divine rule that is relative to the goal of the beatific vision should not think of the practice of abstinence as wrong. But abstinence does involve a stringent set of demands—in fact, significantly more stringent demands than those required simply for the sake of ensuring health of the body and the unimpeded operation of reason. So from the vantage point of the person who subscribes to the rule of reason but not the divine rule, it looks as though abstinence, while not wrong, is under-motivated. Of course, such a person can at the same time recognize that from the perspective of the person of faith, the practice of abstinence is adequately motivated, because ordered to an end—the end of relation-ship to God in the beatific vision—that the person of faith acknow-ledges. But someone who does not share this perspective has no motive to engage in abstinence, it seems; and if such a person is certain that there is no beatific vision, then from this vantage point, they should take the practice of abstinence to involve a kind of misdirection of human effort and concern, and to that extent a kind of failing, even if not strictly a moral failing.

When we examine the virtue of neighbour love, we shall see that a question of this same kind is to be answered rather differently. But before turning to that discussion, let us try and clarify two further mat-ters. First of all, how should we understand the idea that abstinence is ordered to relationship to God in the beatific vision? Or in general terms, how are we to think of the relationship between a practice and the spiritual goal to which it is directed? And secondly, how might we relate this discussion of the two varieties of good that attach to human acts—one relative to human nature, one relative to our 'supernatural' calling—to the account of the goods of the spiritual life that we devel-oped in Chapter 1? Here we can consider in particular the question of whether this distinction may help us to accommodate, in some measure, Hadot's understanding of the goods of the spiritual life.

The text from 1 Corinthians that Aquinas cites in his discussion of infused temperance may suggest that the relationship between the prac-tice of abstinence and participation in the beatific vision is broadly speaking causal. After all, in that text, Paul is citing the case of the ath-lete, who disciplines their body in order to prepare themselves for 'the games'; and the point of such discipline is, of course, to make it more likely that the athlete will prevail in an athletics contest, and win the prize of a 'perishable wreath'. And by extension, we might suppose that the object of the kind of bodily discipline that Paul is describing is to improve the person's chances of attaining the beatific vision, so they can win an 'imperishable wreath'. And perhaps, similarly, Aquinas is thinking of abstinence as in some way causally efficacious, that is, as capable of improving the abstinent person's chances of attaining the beatific vision? In this spirit, we might suppose that abstinence is spiritually fitting because of its role in removing impurities of character, so making it more likely that the person will attain the beatific vision.

But alongside this story, we can set another. In so far as it involves purity of heart, or absence of craving, abstinence can also be seen as appropriate to, or to use the phrasing we adopted in Chapter 1, congruent with, the beatific vision; and in that case, it can count as an attempt to live out here and now a life that is patterned on the life that one is called to live with God. This reading of the rationale for abstinence resembles the account of neighbour love that we developed in Chapter 1, where the appropriateness of neighbour love was understood not in terms of its making participation in the beatific vision more likely, but by reference to the thought that this form of life gives due acknowledgement to a prospective relationship of friendship, which will be realized in the beatific vision. Similarly, it would be possible to think of the practice of abstinence as a matter of giving due acknowledgement, here and now, to the truth that we will one day share in the life of God in the beatific vision, rather than as an attempt to help bring about that state of affairs. Here the congruence, or fittingness, of one's present mode of life relative to one's final end is to be understood, we might say, in existential rather than causal terms.

While it is worth distinguishing between these two accounts, there is no need, for our present purposes, to decide between them. Indeed, on some points, it is possible to combine them. For instance, it may be that abstinence enables a person's participation in the beatific vision precisely because it involves a mode of life, here and now, that is appropriate to the enjoyment of that vision. And on any account, abstinence is presumably congruent with the beatific vision, and this provides a reason for engaging in the practice here and now, whether or not it is thought to be an effective means of improving a person's chances of participating in the beatific vision. It is also worth noting that accounts of these two types do not exhaust the possibilities. For instance, as we saw in Chapter 1, we also find in Aquinas the view that the fittingness of neighbour love can be grounded not only in the already established truth that we will one day share with others in the beatific vision, but also in the mere possibility (read epistemically or metaphysically) that we will do so. And we could reason similarly in the case of abstinence.

In Chapter 1, we considered whether we could assess the goodness of a way of life independently of reference to its metaphysical context. The goodness of dietary practices that are attuned to the health of the body might suggest that we can indeed judge a way of life, or a practice that forms an integral part of a way of life, as good, independently of reference to metaphysical context. (In general terms, this is, of course, Hadot's position.) It is only when we consider the goods relative to a divine rule, it might be said, that we need to refer to metaphysical context. Why? Because it is only here that the good of the practice flows from, or perhaps simply consists in, its bearing an appropriate relation, what I have called a relation of congruence, to its metaphysical context.

However, even in the case of the goods that are the object of a rule of reason, there may be an implicit reference to metaphysical context. After all, if our context is one in which harm of the body can serve as a route to metaphysical good, then it would not be so clear that a practice that avoids harm of the body is to that extent overall good. And of course, it is not hard to find religious and spiritual traditions which have thought of harm of the body in precisely these terms, and have encouraged various practices of 'self-mortification' for that reason. So we may be able to say that a particular dietary practice is good in so far as it does not harm the body. Lack of harm, or more positively, promotion of bodily health, must, after all, count as good considered in themselves, given what we mean by 'harm' and by 'health'. But whether a practice that has this property is for that reason worthy of our adherence will depend at least implicitly on assumptions about metaphysical context. If harm of the body, of relevant kinds, is a route to purification of the soul, or serves to prepare a person for a further life, in which their true fulfilment consists, then it may be doubted whether the practice of eating so as to preserve the health of the body is overall good, even if it is good in part, in so far as bodily health considered in itself is a good.

To take stock, drawing on Aquinas's discussion of acquired and infused temperance, we have seen how we can draw a distinction between two respects in which a practice may prove to be good: first, its goodness may be relative to human nature, in so far as the practice is ordered to the well-being of the person in bodily and other terms; and secondly, its goodness may be relative to metaphysical context, in so far as the practice is congruent with that context, existentially and perhaps causally. As we have seen, it seems that we also need to refer to metaphysical context if we are to judge that a practice is overall good, and not good simply in so far as it respects the relevant rule of reason.

Having discussed infused temperance, let us return to Aquinas's treatment of neighbour love. Since we examined neighbour love in Chapter 1, we can be briefer here. Consideration of neighbour love reveals, I am going to suggest, a further respect, in addition to the two just noted, in which a spiritual practice can be deemed good. Before proceeding to this discussion, it is worth mentioning briefly the grounds for treating neighbour love as an infused moral virtue. Aquinas himself regards such love as a theological virtue, and I take it that in so doing his concern is at least in part to indicate the integral connection between love of God and love of neighbour: as he says, 'it is specifically the same act whereby we love God, and whereby we love our neighbour.'[7] However, if we consider neighbour love in distinction from love of God (allowing that in practice the first form of love is rooted in the second, for conceptual reasons), we can see that it exhibits the same structure as infused temperance and the other infused moral virtues: it is directed to our relations with creatures (specifically, our relations with rational creatures), where the measure of success in our relations to these creatures is provided by reference to our relationship to God. So for our purposes, I will continue to count neighbour love as an example of an infused moral virtue, understanding by an infused moral virtue one that has this dual

---

[7] The full text reads: 'Now the aspect under which our neighbour is to be loved, is God, since what we ought to love in our neighbour is that he may be in God. Hence it is clear that it is specifically the same act whereby we love God, and whereby we love our neighbour. Consequently the habit of charity extends not only to the love of God, but also to the love of our neighbour.' ST 2a2ae. 25. 1.

focus, of being world-directed and at the same time ordered to relationship to God.[8]

Aquinas on Neighbour Love

In the case of acquired and infused temperance, it is relatively easy to chart the difference that is made to our assessment of the nature of the good human life by the introduction of a theological or metaphysical context. Here, we can see directly how appeal to the beatific vision, as a frame for understanding the significance of human choices, results in a more stringent practical ideal, one that serves not simply the goal of health of the body and the unimpeded exercise of reason, but also the goal of congruence with this truth concerning our future life with God. As we saw in Chapter 1, the appropriateness of neighbour love, as a practical and attitudinal ideal, is also dependent upon metaphysical context, in so far as such love is attuned to a future truth concerning our relations with human beings and other rational creatures in the beatific vision. But while it is easy to identify an acquired correlate for infused temperance, it is harder to see what the acquired correlate of neighbour love might be. So here it is not quite so straightforward to track the difference that is made by the introduction of a theological context simply by laying alongside one another the rule that serves as the measure of the acquired form of the virtue (the putative case of 'acquired charity') and the rule that serves as the measure of the infused form of the virtue. So let us begin by thinking a little further about this question, of the difference that is made in this domain by the introduction of a 'divine rule'.

It is clear that Aquinas regards neighbour love as a more demanding practical ideal than any that could be grounded in a consideration of the ends that are proper to human beings simply in virtue of their humanity. This is pragmatically implied in his general approach. If neighbour love added nothing to the requirements of the natural law, then there would

---

[8] Aquinas distinguishes such world-directed virtues from the 'theological' virtues, which aim directly at God. See ST 1a2ae. 63. 3 ad 2.

be no need to supplement the discussion of the natural law that Aquinas gives in the first part of the second part of the *Summa Theologiae* with the discussion of neighbour love that he presents in the second part of the second part. I take it that the point of the further discussion is certainly not to remove the requirements that we can see to obtain on the basis of natural law considerations alone; nor is Aquinas's purpose simply to reaffirm those requirements: instead he intends to show how they are to be extended.

This difference between the rule appropriate to neighbour love and the correlative rule of reason is also implied in the thought that neighbour love is not acquired but infused, so cannot be produced by any amount of human effort. Here again, it seems to follow that the requirements of neighbour love are relatively demanding, so demanding indeed that human beings cannot fulfil them simply by their own efforts.[9] The relatively stringent character of the requirements of neighbour love is also suggested by Jesus's reply to the lawyer's question 'who is my neighbour?' (Luke 10:29). Famously, Jesus responds by rehearsing the story of the good Samaritan. Here again, it is contextually implied that the ideal of neighbour love is relatively demanding. If it were not, then the example of the Samaritan would fail to be morally instructive.

Moreover, Christians have commonly thought of the moral code of the New Testament as a radicalization of the ethic that is given in the Hebrew Bible. To take just one example of how this thought may be grounded in scriptural sources, Jesus is reported as saying: 'You have heard that it was said to the people long ago, "You shall not murder, and anyone who murders will be subject to judgment". But I tell you that anyone who is angry with a brother or sister will be subject to judgment' (Matthew 5:21–2 New International Version). Here there is an implied contrast between the requirements of the New Law and those of the Old Law, on the grounds that the first are relatively demanding. And if neighbour love, construed as Jesus construes it, is at the core of this New Law, then it seems to follow that the requirements of neighbour love

---

[9] We should recall here that in Aquinas's view, in the normal case, the infused form of a given virtue builds on and extends the acquired form. See again ST 1a2ae. 51. 4, cited in footnote 6.

must count as relatively demanding, when compared with those of the Old Law and, we might surmise, those that can be established simply by reference to human nature.[10]

So there is a broad swathe of contextual evidence that supports the idea that neighbour love involves a relatively stringent practical ideal. We can further substantiate this claim by considering some of the dimensions of such love. Let us take first the scope of neighbour love. As we have seen, Aquinas takes neighbour love to be universal in scope: it extends to all human beings. (It also extends to some, but not all, non-human rational creatures.) Suppose we turn to contemporary moral philosophy for a view of the nature of the 'rule of reason' that operates in this domain. A number of familiar philosophical treatments of the nature of our obligations, or responsibilities, to other human beings suggest that those obligations are conditional upon the individual having an attribute that some but not all human beings possess—say, the capacity for autonomous choice, however exactly 'autonomy' is conceived, or the capacity to feel pleasure and pain, or to flourish in certain respects, where the presence or absence of these capacities is in principle open to empirical verification. So far as a moral scheme has this character, then it will be less demanding than the ideal of neighbour love with respect to scope, because the moral regard that it enjoins will extend to some but not all human beings.

When laid alongside at least some contemporary philosophical visions of the moral life, neighbour love also seems to be relatively demanding in attitudinal terms. For instance, if the moral life is thought to be fundamentally a matter of acting beneficently, or bringing about good outcomes, then by comparison, neighbour love will count as attitudinally demanding. For neighbour love, understood as Aquinas understands it, requires not simply that I should benefit other human beings, but also that I should think of my relationship to them under the category of 'friendship'. When Aquinas considers the question 'whether charity is friendship?' (ST 2a2ae. 23. 1), he replies emphatically that it is. And he notes that wishing good to the other, while necessary for such friendship, is not sufficient. As he says, in addition:

---

[10] For Aquinas's account of the relation between the Old and New Laws, see ST 1a2ae. 107. 1.

a certain mutual love is requisite, since friendship is between friend
and friend: and this well-wishing [in the case of friendship] is founded
on some kind of communication.   (ST 2a2ae. 23. 1)

As we would expect, Aquinas also supposes that in this life, such friendship will remain imperfect, since the 'communication' or 'conversation'
(23. 1 ad 1) that we will enjoy with our neighbour in the beatific vision
remains, in this life, relatively undeveloped.[11] Even so, on his view, it is
clear that if we are committed to living according to the ideals of neighbour love, then our relationship to others can be assessed, here and now,
not only in terms of beneficence, but also attitudinally, in so far as our
attitudes to other human beings here and now should be congruent with
the truth that we will one day enjoy a perfected relationship of friendship with them. Accordingly, Aquinas thinks, our relationship to others
here and now should already be answerable in some measure to the
standards that are appropriate to friendship, and for this reason that
relationship should itself be a kind of friendship, even if one that remains
in some respects inchoate. So here again, compared with at least some
familiar moral schemes, neighbour love appears to be relatively
demanding.

Lastly, neighbour love may also appear to be relatively demanding in
terms of what it requires of us in practical terms in our dealings with
those human beings who do fall within its scope. Moral philosophers
disagree of course about the nature of our responsibilities to other
human beings. Some philosophers have thought that morality requires
us not to harm others, but imposes no requirement to benefit them,
except in cases where they are in dire need, and we can relieve that need
at minimal cost to ourselves.[12] If the moral life has this form, then I will

---

[11] He writes: 'Man's life is twofold. There is his outward life in respect of his sensitive and
corporeal nature: and with regard to this life there is no communication or fellowship between
us and God or the angels. The other is man's spiritual life in respect of his mind, and with
regard to this life there is fellowship between us and both God and the angels, imperfectly
indeed in this present state of life, wherefore it is written (Phil. 3:20): "Our conversation is in
heaven." But this "conversation" will be perfected in heaven, when "His servants shall serve
Him, and they shall see His face" (Apoc. 22:3, 4). Therefore charity is imperfect here, but will
be perfected in heaven': ST 2a2ae. 23. 1 ad 1.

[12] See for instance John Arthur's defence of this principle: 'we should require people to help
strangers when there is no substantial cost to themselves, that is, when what they are sacrificing

be morally required to pull a drowning child from a pool of water, if I can do so at no great cost to myself; but I will not be morally required, not even as a matter of imperfect duty, to relieve poverty that is consistent with the needy person's basic nutritional needs being met, or to relieve poverty that is life-threatening if in doing so I would have to significantly impoverish myself. Relative to such a conception of the moral life, neighbour love looks to be relatively demanding in practical terms. The good Samaritan seems, after all, to do rather more than would be required of him granted this conception of the moral life: notably, by entrusting the injured man to the innkeeper, in the manner that he does, the Samaritan not only relieves his dire need, but helps to ensure his full recovery.

Of course, moral philosophies can be more or less exacting in their conception of our duties to other human beings. For example, on a maximizing version of consequentialism I could be obliged to significantly impoverish myself in order to raise the material well-being of others to a point well above the level at which basic nutritional needs have been met.[13] However, famously, these approaches do not appear to fit our ordinary moral intuitions: they seem to be revisionary with respect to conventional moral thought. So, as far as our ordinary conception of our responsibilities to others is concerned, there is some reason to say that the standards of neighbour love are relatively demanding, in terms of what they require of us practically in our dealings with those who fall within their scope.

We are now in a position to put to the virtue of neighbour love the kind of question we earlier put to the virtue of infused temperance. Neighbour love, we have seen, aims at congruence with a future truth concerning our relations with others in the beatific vision. But what should a person who does not subscribe to that vision make of the practice? For present purposes, let us suppose that we can agree on the

would not mean significant reduction in their own or their family's welfare': 'Famine Relief and the Ideal Moral Code', in H. LaFollette (ed.), *Ethics in Practice: An Anthology* (Oxford: Blackwell, 2nd edn, 2002), p. 590.

[13] Peter Singer is the best-known advocate of such an approach, and Arthur's discussion, cited in footnote 12, is a response to the case that Singer develops in his article 'Famine, Affluence, and Morality', *Philosophy and Public Affairs*, 1:3 (1972), 229–43.

content of the relevant rule of reason that operates in this domain, and agree that compared with the requirements of this rule, neighbour involves a relatively stringent ideal not only attitudinally, but also in terms of its scope and its injunctions regarding our conduct towards those individuals who fall within its scope. From the vantage point of such a person, who does not subscribe to the idea of the beatific vision, neighbour love is presumably morally permissible: it affords others the kind of regard to which they are entitled under the relevant rule of reason, while also doing more besides. Let us take those respects in which neighbour love asks more of us, with respect to attitude, scope and seriousness of practical concern, than is asked of us by the relevant rule of reason. Should the person who does not affirm the beatific vision say that in these respects the practice of neighbour love is permissible but under-motivated?

From this vantage point, neighbour love will appear under-motivated to the extent that it goes beyond what duty requires, but it is not clear that it is under-motivated in the sense that we can find no good moral reason for the practice in these respects. On the contrary, from the vantage point of the relevant rule of reason, it looks as though the practice of neighbour love, when it goes beyond what is required by that rule, is morally commendable. Take again the example of the good Samaritan. From the vantage point of the rule of reason, he does more than is required; but it does not follow that his action in this regard is, from a moral point of view, lacking in merit. What he does is, on the contrary, from that point of view good and indeed praiseworthy.

There is one complication it is worth noting here. Let us think of duties of 'imperfect' obligation as duties to benefit others which, by contrast with duties of 'perfect' obligation, cannot be claimed from us as a matter of right by any one individual. Suppose for instance that I am relatively affluent, and that I am morally obliged, therefore, to make some reasonably significant contribution to the support of charitable causes. If we take this obligation to be an 'imperfect' duty, then while I will be required to benefit people who are less well off than myself, I will not be morally obliged to make any particular individual the object of my charitable giving. (Let us allow, plausibly, that the stock of needy individuals is reasonably extended, so that there are various ways in which I might reasonably fulfil the requirement to donate, say, a certain proportion of my income to people whose material circumstances are less favourable than my own.)

If we return to the case of the good Samaritan, we might now raise this possibility: perhaps the Samaritan's actions exceed his duties of perfect obligation (he does more than he is required to do to benefit this particular individual), but not (when we take account of his wider practice of charitable giving) his duties of imperfect obligation. If we are to sustain the idea that neighbour love involves a relatively stringent ideal, then it will be necessary to suppose, on the contrary, that the Samaritan does more than he is required to do by any obligation that can be grounded in a 'rule of reason', whether that obligation be one of perfect or imperfect duty. So for our purposes, we need to rule out the possibility that the Samaritan goes beyond what duty demands only with respect to perfect duties.

I take it that the example is indeed to be understood in this spirit: it would require a rather contrived reading to suppose that the Samaritan is actually thinking that because he has not benefited anyone in the recent past (or is unlikely to do so in the near future), he'd better be especially generous to this individual, in order to meet his duties of imperfect obligation. The import of the example is, rather, that the Samaritan recognizes that, whatever may be true of his wider giving, he has a duty to this very individual, because this very individual is, in theological terms, his neighbour. So the Samaritan's actions in this case are not going to be explicable by supposing that he is after all adhering to a rule of reason, where that rule encompasses duties of imperfect as well as duties of perfect obligation. So from here on, when I talk of going beyond duty, of the kind that can be grounded in a rule of reason, I shall understand this expression in the way just indicated—that is, as a matter of going beyond what duties of perfect and imperfect duties of obligation together demand.

With that clarification in place, we can return to the question of how the requirements of infused temperance and neighbour love compare with the requirements of their respective rules of reason. From the vantage point of the relevant rule of reason, the practice of abstinence, we have seen, seems pointless: it does no more to realize the good that is the end of that rule than do other, less demanding dietary practices. Let us consider now why matters should be different in the case of neighbour love. The rule of reason that is the counterpart for the divine rule that is the measure of neighbour love presumably aims at human well-being or flourishing in some respect. This rule requires us to take some heed of the well-being of others, while setting a fairly tight cap on the extent to which such considerations constrain our choices. From the vantage point of this rule, the good Samaritan fulfils his obligations to heed human well-being, and does more than he is required to do in respect of this same good, of human well-being. To this extent, then, his behaviour is morally intelligible from the vantage point of the relevant rule of reason: from this perspective, he goes beyond what duty requires, not arbitrarily, but in such a way as to bring about more of the very good that is the end of the rule of reason, so far as that rule has as its goal human well-being.

We could summarize this difference between infused temperance and neighbour love by saying that in the case of neighbour love, but not of infused temperance, the introduction of the relevant divine rule lifts certain actions that would otherwise have been supererogatory (that is, beyond duty and praiseworthy) into the realm of the obligatory.[14] By contrast, the divine rule that is the measure of infused temperance lifts certain actions that would be, from the point of view of the relevant rule of reason, permissible but without point into the realm of the obligatory.

In turn, we can understand this difference by supposing that while infused temperance realizes simply two kinds of good, neighbour love realizes in addition a further good. Infused temperance realizes those goods that are mandated by the relevant rule of reason: for instance, the good of bodily health. It also realizes a further good that is relative not simply to our human nature, but to our sharing in the life of God in the beatific vision. This further good will obtain in so far as our habits of eating are congruent with this 'supernatural' end. Neighbour love also realizes goods of these kinds: it realizes those goods that are mandated by the relevant rule of reason (for instance, the good of the alleviation of

[14] For a fuller, and careful and subtle, account of the nature of supererogation, see David Heyd, *Supererogation* (Cambridge: Cambridge University Press, 1982), ch. 6.

dire human need, under the requisite conditions) and the good of comportment towards others that is congruent with the beatific vision. But in addition, as we have seen, neighbour love realizes a further kind of good, one that is not mandated by the relevant rule of reason, but which is even so intelligible from the vantage point of that rule, in so far as the bringing about of this good will count from that vantage point as commendable because supererogatory. There is no counterpart for this kind of good in the case of infused temperance. There would be such a counterpart if infused temperance did more to promote the health of the body than is mandated by the relevant rule of reason, but if we follow Aquinas's account of abstinence, there is no reason to think of infused temperance as motivated by this consideration, or as promoting this outcome.

For ease of reference, let us call these three kinds of good 'goods of reason' (for example, the good of bodily health in the case of infused temperance), 'theological goods' (for example, the good that is realized when my habits of eating are congruent with the beatific vision), and 'extended goods of reason' (for instance, the good that obtains in so far as the good Samaritan's action not only satisfies the relevant rule of reason, but does more besides to promote the human good as measured by that standard). In general, we may say, spiritual practices are aimed at (at least) these three kinds of good: goods of reason, extended goods of reason, and theological goods.

We can use this distinction to address a question I posed earlier: to what extent are the goods that are the objects of spiritual practices visible from the vantage point of the person who does not share the metaphysical assumptions of the practice? Goods of reason are, of course, immediately evident from this perspective: to see these goods, there is no need to have adopted the metaphysical assumptions of the spiritual practice. (However, even here, I have suggested, certain metaphysical assumptions may need to be in play if the relevant outcome is to be considered not simply good in itself, but good all things considered.) By contrast, theological goods are not evident independently of metaphysical context. Of course, a person who does not share these metaphysical assumptions can still grasp what the person of faith is aiming at when they adhere to the relevant divine rule. But theological goods are realized only in so far as human activity is in fact congruent with its metaphysical context; so of course, these goods, of congruence with metaphysical context, will not be visible to us unless we grant that the relevant context in fact obtains. Lastly, extended goods of reason are evident from the vantage point of the relevant rule of reason, but from that vantage point they do not appear (as do goods of reason) as morally mandated, but as good while surpassing what morality requires.

In concluding this chapter, I am going to use this distinction between these three kinds of good to consider a question that John Cottingham has posed in his 2009 text *Why Believe?*[15] Here we shall touch on the relationship between religious and secular ethics, and the practical reasonableness of participation in a religious or spiritual tradition.

John Cottingham on the Relationship between Religious and Secular Ethics

In this book, as I understand him, Cottingham sketches a kind of moral argument for religious belief. At the core of this argument is the idea that certain moral commitments will only make complete sense if embedded within a theistic context. So in brief, the case is that if a non-theist finds themselves with such commitments, and wishes to retain them, then they have a moral reason for subscribing to theism. I am not going to examine this argument very closely, or the plausibility of the idea that the particular traits of character that are of interest to Cottingham do indeed fit most readily within a theistic picture of the world. Instead I am going to concentrate on the structure of this account, with a view to addressing some issues that are relevant to our question of the visibility of spiritual goods from a vantage point external to the relevant spiritual practice. We should begin by setting out Cottingham's case in a little more detail.

---

[15] John Cottingham, *Why Believe?* (London: Continuum, 2009).

Cottingham proposes that certain traits of character will only count as virtues when located within the relevant metaphysical context. For example, in a theistic context, humility involves:

> a recognition that... one's gifts, if such they be, are not ultimately of one's own making.... Man is not self-creating. 'It is he who hath made us and not we ourselves.'[16]

On this account, granted a theistic metaphysical context, the patterns of thought and feeling that are typical of humility will be appropriate, for the reason that they give due acknowledgement to the status of our 'achievements'. And in the absence of that context, Cottingham thinks, those same patterns of thought and feeling will cease to be properly motivated. Again, I am not going to consider here the plausibility of the claim that humility, and the other traits that Cottingham examines, do indeed depend for their appropriateness upon a theistic context. The idea that there is some such association between metaphysical context and the claim of certain traits of character to count as virtues is, of course, one that we have explored at some length already. For instance, on Aquinas's account of the matter, the habits of feeling and behaviour that, in part, constitute infused temperance will count as virtuous if we grant the relevant truths concerning our future life with God, but not if we operate simply in terms of a 'rule of reason'. Rather than focusing on the idea that there is such a connection between at least some virtues and their metaphysical context, I want to consider instead the structure of the case for theism that Cottingham builds on the basis of this idea.

Cottingham argues that if the claim of traits such as humility to count as virtues is indeed dependent on metaphysical context, then the secular person who considers humility, or another such trait, to be a virtue faces a dilemma. He puts the point in these terms:

> Secular naturalists have a dilemma here, I think. Either they can go along with Aristotle and simply accept a schema of proper human

---

[16] Ibid., p. 153.

character and conduct that allows no place for humility; or they can acknowledge the moral pull of something like the Christian conception of humility and try to find a secular analogue for it.[17]

Cottingham develops the same sort of case in relation to other traits, such as hope and trust, considered as encompassing attitudes, rather than as directed simply at certain localized states of affairs. And here again, he thinks that the naturalist can from their naturalistic vantage point recognize the goodness of the trait, even if they do not have to hand a ready account why it should count as good:

it is hard to deny that there is something admirable about this [theistic] ethic of hope and trust. And the value is something we seem to recognize not just on a prudential level...Over and above such utilitarian considerations, most of us have a strong intuitive sense of something splendid, something moving, about the human being weighed down with misfortunes and difficulties, who nevertheless manages to keep alive the radiance of hope, as is done in the straining yet resonant self-exhortation at the end of Psalm 43: 'Why art thou cast down, O my soul, and why art thou disquieted within me? Hope in God for I shall yet praise him who is the health of my countenance, and my God.'

---

[17] Ibid., p. 153. We might ask: on Cottingham's view, what is the nature of the connection between metaphysical context and the claim of a trait to count as a virtue? I have tried to spell out this relation in terms of the idea that the trait can be existentially, and perhaps causally, congruent with a given theological context, and deemed good for that reason. Cottingham puts the point in these terms: 'an exhortation to virtue is not just a raw set of prescriptions on how to act, or on what dispositions to cultivate; it necessarily involves a *background of significance*, a wider picture of the goals of human life, or the best way of living. Without such a background picture, any given candidate for a virtue or vice will be isolated from its source of meaning' (p. 154). In the case of humility, Cottingham appeals to the idea that if there is a God, then: 'Man is not self-creating' (p. 153). So here the 'background of significance' involves the idea of creation, and therefore the idea that we cannot claim any deep credit for our achievements, because they are, at root, divinely enabled. This example suggests that relative to the theological truth of creation, certain assessments of human achievements are simply false, and for that reason inappropriate. The account we have presented, following Aquinas, suggests a somewhat different way of developing the notion of a 'background of significance', because here the background is understood in future-referenced terms, and the notion of existential appropriateness is read accordingly. Once again, the focus of our discussion has been upon the realization of hybrid goods, rather than say avoidance of error in one's self-assessment.

Cottingham goes on directly to summarize his perspective in these terms:

> The position so far reached, then, is that these so-called theological virtues [such as humility, hope and trust] are ones which many or most of us, almost irrespective of religious persuasion or its absence, can intuitively recognize as admirable and valuable. And hence, short of biting the bullet and suppressing such intuitions, the naturalist has to construct some secular analogue for these virtues, which will allow them to be preserved as ethically desirable traits of character. But I have suggested that this will not be easy, without a suitable framework in which to locate them...[18]

So Cottingham is proposing a case of this structure: secular people can recognize that humility, trust and hope are genuine virtues; these traits will count as virtues granted a theistic context; given the difficulties of constructing a secular analogue for this theistic context, it is hard to see how they can count as virtues independently of theism; so in the absence of a persuasive secular analogue that can play the role that theistic metaphysics has traditionally played in grounding the fittingness of these traits, we should affirm theism, as a presupposition of our moral commitments.

I am not going to comment on Cottingham's proposal that there is no ready or plausible secular analogue for the theistic metaphysical context that has traditionally grounded the claim of such traits to count as virtues. I am interested instead in another idea that he advances or comes close to advancing here: namely, the idea that the secular person can from their secular vantage point see that traits such as humility and trust are rightly reckoned as virtues. He notes for example that the secular person can 'acknowledge the moral pull of something like the Christian conception of humility', and has some reason, therefore, to try to develop a secular analogue for the 'background of significance' that sustains the claim of humility to count as a virtue in theistic contexts.[19] Or again, he

---

[18] Ibid., pp. 155–6.
[19] This phrase occurs in the passage I cited in footnote 17: ibid., p. 153.

notes that 'it is hard [hard for naturalists and theists equally] to deny that there is something admirable about this ethic of hope and trust'; and he continues: 'many or most of us, almost irrespective of religious persuasion or its absence, can intuitively recognize [traits such as hope and humility] as admirable and valuable'.[20]

On one reading of Cottingham's text, we could take him to be making a case in the style of Hadot, by beginning with the relevant way of life (understood in terms of humility and trust, for example) and moving from there to a claim about metaphysical context, where that context plays the role of fitting and supporting the way of life. But that cannot, in fact, be the structure of his case, I take it, because he is explicitly of the view that humility, for example, will only count as a virtue granted the relevant, that is, theistic, metaphysical context. On this account, it is hard to see how the secular person could have a clear-eyed insight into the status of humility as a virtue, prior to any theistic metaphysical commitment, and then be drawn on that basis to assent to a theistic metaphysics. Why? Because the theistic metaphysics must already be assumed if the trait is to count as a virtue. Cottingham is perhaps acknowledging that any such inference, in the manner of Hadot, would be strained, given his own commitments, when he writes that:

> many or most of us, *almost irrespective of religious persuasion or its absence*, can intuitively recognize [traits such as humility] as admirable and valuable. [my emphasis]

Given his views about the sensitivity to context of a trait's claim to count as a virtue, Cottingham should say, I take it, that we cannot in fact recognize such traits as admirable 'irrespective of religious persuasion'. A secular person may have been raised to think of humility as a virtue, and may in their adult life continue to regard humility as a virtue. But if Cottingham is right, they cannot have a genuine insight into its status as virtue from their secular vantage point. So there is no stable premise here for an argument, addressed to a secular person, which moves from the claim that humility is a virtue to the claim that

---

[20]   As quoted on p. 56: ibid., pp. 155–6.

we ought therefore to adopt a theistic metaphysical framework, as an entailment of that moral commitment.

Of course, there are contexts in which I can move unproblematically from the claim that p to the conclusion that q, on the ground that the truth of p presupposes the truth of q. Why then should I not be able to move similarly from the claim that humility is a virtue to the conclusion that there is a God, if humility's being a virtue presupposes the truth of theism? The difficulty with this inference is that, for these values of p and q, I can have no access to the truth of p independently of reference to the truth of q. If we follow Cottingham in supposing that humility counts as a virtue precisely for the reason that it constitutes a proper response to my status as a creature, made by God, then it is hard to see how I could resolve the question of whether humility is indeed a virtue without first of all taking a view on my metaphysical context. And in that case, there will be no informative argument from the claim that humility is a virtue to the claim that theism is true.

But could there not be ways of recognizing that humility is a virtue without having, first of all, to establish that there is a God, even supposing that Cottingham is right to ground humility's status as a virtue in the truth of theism? For instance, perhaps I can know by testimony that humility is a virtue, supposing that my interlocutor has performed the requisite inference. But this does not seem to be the case that Cottingham has in view. He talks, for example, of a person having a 'strong intuitive sense of something splendid, something moving' in the life of hope, and of 'intuitively recognizing' a trait such as humility as 'admirable and valuable'. Here the person who judges that humility or hope is a virtue is dependent, it seems, not upon testimony but upon some kind of direct, first-hand apprehension of this truth. But it is hard to see, I have been suggesting, how any such apprehension could be well grounded if it does not involve at the same time a recognition of the truth of theism. And in that case, there will be no apologetically useful argument from the idea that humility is a virtue to the truth of theism.

Or again, it might be urged: perhaps it is just a feature of human beings' cognitive architecture that we can have an intuition of the status of humility as a virtue without any (explicit) thought of God?[21] But this proposal also poses difficulties. If theism is true, then we will have, I take it, a reason to trust such an intuition. Why? Because we have some reason to suppose that God, if there is a God, will ensure that our fundamental moral judgements are reliable; and, therefore, we have some reason to suppose that God will confer upon us a faculty that will generate intuitions about the moral status of traits such as humility which are trustworthy. But if a secular person is being asked to address these matters from her secular vantage point, then it is not so clear that she is entitled to trust any such intuition. Given a naturalistic metaphysic, and taking for granted once more Cottingham's claim that the status of humility as a virtue is relative to our metaphysical context, then we should not expect to have any such faculty of intuition. After all, the faculty in question would need to be in some way sensitive, directly or indirectly, to our metaphysical context (since it is metaphysical context that fixes the truth or falsity of claims such as the claim that humility is a virtue). And what reason is there to think that an evolutionary, or other naturalistic, process would, or could, give rise to a faculty of this kind? (Unsurprisingly, there is no empirical evidence of our having such a faculty.) So in this case too, the starting point of the argument—here the assumption that it is appropriate to trust the relevant intuition—seems to presuppose the truth of theism, rather than providing an independent ground for theistic conclusions.

We have been considering the implications of the thought that humility will only count as a good trait of character if theism is true. Specifically, we have been examining the plausibility of this line of reflection: the person who does not already have a theistic perspective cannot, in a clear-eyed way, take themselves to grasp that humility is a virtue; and to urge the secular person to move from the recognition that humility is a virtue to the thought that theism is true is, therefore, to ask them to reason in a circle. In response to this difficulty for the attempt to move from the recognition that a certain trait is good to an affirmation

---

[21] I am grateful to Paul Lodge for raising in discussion the possibility that the intuition may involve some obscure recognition of God's existence.

of theism, we might wonder whether at least some of the goods that are realized in the practice of, for example, humility may be visible from a secular vantage point. Drawing on our earlier discussion, we might suppose that it is in particular the theological goods produced by the practice that will not be visible from a secular vantage point, because this sort of good consists, after all, in the congruence between a certain pattern of life and the beatific vision or some theologically grounded truth. But what if humility also gives rise to 'extended goods of reason'? If it does, then perhaps the secular person who accepts Cottingham's point about the connection between theism and humility's status as a virtue can reason as follows. (For present purposes, let us simply assume that humility does produce extended goods of reason, without pausing to consider their character.)

Humility, of the kind that interests Cottingham, is answerable to a divine rule, and in adhering to this rule, the humble person treats as obligatory what I from my secular vantage point would count as supererogatory. Granted that much, can the secular person not continue as follows, without falling into any confusion: from my point of view, I see, therefore, that humility is an admirable trait, in so far as the standards that are embedded in the practice of humility oblige the humble person to do all that I am required to do by the corresponding rule of reason, and more that is good besides, where this additional good is recognizable as good from my secular vantage point. And granted that much, could not a secular person intelligibly conclude that she does have a pragmatic, moral reason—not necessarily, of course, an overriding reason—for subscribing to theism. Why? Because if she assents to the relevant theistic claims, then she will have a more compelling reason to lead the kind of life that from her current, secular vantage point she deems to be good and indeed praiseworthy. And from that vantage point, would it not be good to have such a reason? From this secular perspective, humility is attractive on account of its role as a source of moral motivation: the person who inhabits the practice, and therefore assents to its theological presuppositions, has more of a reason to do what, from a secular point of view, we already recognize to be good and indeed praiseworthy. Following our discussion of Hadot, we should add that any such case will need to satisfy this epistemic constraint: it will only have application if the person takes relevant portions of the theistic world view to have some prospect of providing at least an approximation to the nature of things. If that condition is not met, then it is hard to see how that world view could have any power to motivate the person.

To see how such considerations might play out in practice, suppose a historian were to claim that in the ancient world some practitioners of the Roman religions converted to Judaism, or became God-fearers, out of respect for its rigorous moral code. We would find this claim intelligible, I take it, and we would not need to think of these converts as in any way deluded. What attracts the convert is, we could say, the prospect of having a more robust reason, perhaps even an obligation, to lead a life that from their current vantage point, external to Judaism, they can see to be good, and indeed praiseworthy. To put the point in the terms that we have been exploring, we could say that these converts are impressed by the capacity of Judaism to give to the convert, once they have assented to its doctrinal claims, an additional reason to realize various extended goods of reason.

I am not going to make a case for the idea that humility does produce extended goods of reason, so that, in this respect, it resembles neighbour love, and not infused temperance. For our purposes, the key consideration is just that a trait which resembles humility, as Cottingham understands it, in so far as its status as a virtue depends on its metaphysical context, can be inserted into an argument of this type if it gives rise to extended goods of reason. And that is to say that appealing to a trait of the kind that is key to Cottingham's case need not, after all, beg the question against the secularist, providing that the trait has this character. Again, the proposal is not that such an argument for theistic commitment should be found compelling, but just that it is not simply self-stultifying. By contrast, an argument which begins not with an appeal to extended goods of reason, but with an appeal simply to the thought that a trait such as humility, understood in Cottingham's terms, is a virtue would appear to be beg the question against the secular point of view.

We shall examine these questions more fully in Chapter 6, where we shall also consider whether some such case might be constructed for theological goods, as well as extended goods of reason, without thereby falling prey to the problem of circularity that seems to arise for arguments that start from a context-independent judgement about the goodness of a certain way of life. In the present chapter, I have sought to draw a distinction between those religiously motivated practices such as abstinence that will seem from a secular point of view as, at best, devoid of point, and those religiously motivated practices, such as neighbour love, that will seem, from a secular vantage point, to be good and even praiseworthy. If we wish to understand the nature of the goods that are produced by spiritual practices, this distinction is of some importance, because it suggests that some of these goods are relatively intelligible from a secular point of view. And in turn this truth opens up a conceptual space, I have argued, for a kind of moral argument for theism. That argument turns on the thought that a secular person, while continuing to occupy her secular vantage point, can think of a theistic ethic as 'admirable' (as Cottingham puts the point) and indeed as preferable to her own. How is that possible? It is possible because she can see that a theistic ethic provides a person with more of a reason than is available from her secular point of view to do those things that she herself recognizes to be good and even praiseworthy.

This case may not be compelling, but it allows us to see how theism and an associated body of spiritual practice can seem attractive, from a secular vantage point.[22] Again, what enables this case are not the goods of reason that are produced by theistic practices (they are equally identifiable and equally realizable from within the framework of a secular ethic), nor theological goods (we have yet to see how they might carry any weight from a secular point of view), but what I have called the extended goods of reason that are produced by theistic practices— namely, those goods that from the vantage point of a secular ethic seem supererogatory, and that a theistic ethic will deem obligatory.

---

[22] We should not expect the case to be compelling—or else the distinction between the obligatory and supererogatory would be hard to sustain.

3

Metaphysics and Experience

Introduction

It is time to take stock. In the opening pages of this volume, we have been considering the nature of the goods that are the object of spiritual practices. In Chapter 1, we compared the perspectives on this question of Pierre Hadot and Thomas Aquinas. In his treatment of neighbour love, Aquinas shows how the goodness of a way of life can be relative to its metaphysical context: on this account, as I have read it, the practice of neighbour love is fitting for us here and now because of its congruence with an eschatological truth concerning our relations with others in the beatific vision. Here, the appropriateness of the way of life consists, at least in part, in its standing in the right relation to our metaphysical context. This connection between the normative status of a way of life and its metaphysical context is equally evident from the case of those who will not share in the beatific vision: indeed, extending neighbour love to the 'demons' is presumably not simply not fitting, for Aquinas, but forbidden. Hadot, I have proposed, takes a different view: on his account, we can, quite intelligibly, identify a way of life as good or worthwhile independently of reference to metaphysical context. Here, the question of context arises only when we consider how to make a favoured way of life motivationally more accessible. So this is the first theme of our discussion so far: at least some spiritually significant goods, I have been suggesting, turn out to be relative to metaphysical context.

In Chapter 2, I sought to extend this theme, by distinguishing some varieties of context-relative spiritual good. I took as my focus two spiritual practices: abstinence and, once again, neighbour love. Here, I argued that some of the goods that are realized in the practice of abstinence are simply those that would be realized by a person who adheres to

Spiritual Traditions and the Virtues: Living Between Heaven and Earth. Mark R. Wynn, Oxford University Press (2020).
© Mark R. Wynn.
DOI: 10.1093/oso/9780198862949.001.0001

the rule of reason that operates in this domain. However, providing that the relevant metaphysical context obtains, the practice of abstinence is also capable of realizing a further good—namely, the good of congruence with a future truth concerning our participation in the beatific vision. Neighbour love, I argued, also realizes these two kinds of good, but differs in making possible a further good, which we need to postulate if we are to understand a disanalogy between neighbour love and abstinence: when viewed from the vantage point of the relevant rule of reason, abstinence appears not as wrong, but as at best under-motivated, whereas from this same vantage point, neighbour love appears as good and even praiseworthy. We can understand this difference by observing that neighbour love, but not abstinence, lifts certain actions that would otherwise have been supererogatory into the realm of the obligatory. Hence from the vantage point of the relevant rule of reason, neighbour love appears not as pointless, but morally commendable. And its goodness in this respect is a matter of its producing, as a matter of obligation, not only goods of reason and theological goods (here like abstinence), but also extended goods of reason—that is, goods that can be seen as good from the vantage point of the relevant rule of reason, but which are not mandated by that rule.

In these first two chapters, then, we have been concerned with the character of context-relative spiritual goods, and the varieties of such goods, drawing on Thomas Aquinas's discussion of two infused moral virtues: neighbour love and infused temperance. In brief, I have been suggesting that an account of context-relative goods should allow both for theological goods and for what I have been calling extended goods of reason. I have also tried to show how this distinction bears on the practical reasonableness of participation in a spiritual tradition.

Clearly, this Thomistic approach understands the spiritual life, most fundamentally, in metaphysical terms: we are to understand the ambitions of that life, and significant transitions within it, by locating the person within their metaphysical context. On this view, spiritual practice is an attempt to live in ways that are properly responsive to that context. In the present chapter, I want to consider how this metaphysical approach can be extended once we understand the spiritual life from the vantage point of experience. Here again, I shall take as my starting point

Thomas Aquinas's discussion of the infused moral virtues. But now we shall be concerned with the question of how the path of spiritual development that Thomas describes might appear to a participant in the spiritual life, that is, to someone who is acquainted first hand with its various phases.

The Vantage Point of Experience

There is a much-discussed thought experiment in philosophy of mind concerning a woman who has perfect knowledge of the science of colour vision—who knows all the relevant facts about the frequency and wavelength of light, the functioning of the optic nerve, and so on—while spending her entire life confined to a room in which there are no coloured, but only black and white, objects.[1] One day, the woman, dubbed Mary in the example, leaves the room, and for the first time she sees coloured things, and sees them as coloured. So she sees, for instance, for the first time, the redness of a rose. It is natural to say that at this point, Mary learns something about the colour red: she learns what red looks like, to a person with normal vision. The philosophical debate around this example concerns whether it counts against a physicalist view of 'the facts': should we conclude that there are non-physical facts, since by assumption, Mary knows all the physical facts about colour before leaving the room, and yet, surely, we might reason, she comes to learn something new about the colour red on seeing a rose for the first time.

This question need not detain us here, but there is a related question that is of some interest for our purposes. Suppose we have produced a comprehensive account of the metaphysical (rather than physical) facts that are relevant to the spiritual life, and the goods that can be realized in that life—by setting out the nature of the beatific vision or whatever if may be. An angel, for example, might be able to produce a complete record of these facts. From this vantage point, we can now describe, in exhaustive detail, the goals of the spiritual life and the theological and

---

[1] Frank Jackson, 'Epiphenomenal Qualia', *The Philosophical Quarterly*, 32:127 (1982), 130.

other goods that can be realized in that life by human beings and other kinds of creature.[2] There remains, though, a question about what it would be like for a human being—for a creature with a specifically human cognitive and sensory apparatus—to lead a life that is congruent with our metaphysical context so understood. It seems reasonable to suppose that an angel, to the extent that its thought is purely intellectual, could not know what it is like for a human being to lead such a life, not even if it knows all the metaphysical facts that are relevant to the spiritual life—any more than it is possible for Mary to know what it is like to see red, even if she knows all the scientific facts that are relevant to colour vision in human beings.

If this is so, then to provide a full record of the spiritual life, as it is conceived by a given spiritual or religious tradition, with particular metaphysical commitments, we will need to supplement a metaphysical description of the structure and goals of that life with a description that picks out informatively what it is like to lead the spiritual life. Similarly, to give a full account of what it is to see red, we will need to add to a purely physical description of the facts (one that speaks in terms of the stimulation of the optic nerve, and so on) a description of what it is like to see red, where the second kind of account cannot be simply deduced, a priori, from the first. To explore these matters further, let us take a particular example of how these two vocabularies, one metaphysical and one experiential, might be related to each other. Here again, I am going to start with the story of the spiritual life that Thomas Aquinas develops by reference to the category of infused moral virtue, but now with a view to re-telling some central episodes from that story in an experiential rather than metaphysical idiom. Once more, Hadot's reflections stand in the background of our discussion at this point, and in particular his suggestion that the subjective feel of a given philosophical 'way of life'—for instance, the felt quality of Epicurean contentment—cannot be captured simply by reference to the 'philosophical discourse' that supports the way of life.

---

[2] In fact, later in this chapter, and again in Chapter 4, I shall question whether we could provide a complete specification of the goals of the spiritual life under these conditions. But for now, for simplicity's sake, let us proceed on the assumption that we could.

Thomas Aquinas on the Spiritual Life

I shall begin by rehearsing once more, this time fairly briefly, Thomas Aquinas's account of the structure of the spiritual life, drawing once again on his understanding of the infused moral virtues.[3] Following Aristotle, Aquinas supposes that our flourishing as human beings consists in part in our having the right dispositions of thought, action, and feeling across various domains—for instance, in relation to food and drink, to take the case we examined in Chapter 2. On this view, our flourishing as human depends, therefore, on our possession of the 'acquired' moral virtues, which can be developed by way of a process of habituation, so that I become just, for example, by means of the repeated performance of just actions. So on this account, we can speak of a specifically human kind of flourishing, one that is relative to the particular constraints and opportunities that are given with our human nature.

Of course, Aquinas supplements this account by supposing that the goodness of a human life can also be assessed by reference to a further, more encompassing goal—namely, the goal of relationship to God. These two ends—of being properly related to our creaturely environment and properly related to God—are not, for Aquinas, simply discrete, since our thriving in relation to our divine context consists in part in our thriving in relation to our material context. Aquinas develops this point by introducing alongside the acquired moral virtues a further set of virtues, the infused moral virtues, which orient us in relation to the world, but in ways that are relevant to our flourishing in relationship to God. These further virtues do not displace but further embed the dispositions that define the acquired moral virtues. Hence Aquinas writes:

> Acts produced by an infused habit, do not cause a habit, but strengthen the already existing habit; just as the remedies of medicine given to a man who is naturally healthy, do not cause a kind of health, but give new strength to the health he had before.   (ST 1a2ae. 51. 4 ad 3)[4]

---

[3] Aquinas allows that there are infused intellectual virtues, as well as infused moral virtues, but for our purposes we can bracket out this strand of his account.

[4] *Summa Theologiae*, tr. Fathers of the English Dominican Province (New York: Benziger Brothers, 1947). Unless otherwise indicated, I shall follow this translation in later quotations. I am grateful to Michael Lamb for some very helpful discussion of this text.

We can see in this passage the basis for a sketch of what it is to grow in the spiritual life. In the normal course of things, a person gains first of all the 'acquired' moral virtues, through the practice of the relevant disciplines of character formation. These are the 'already existing' habits that, in the standard case, are presupposed in the operation of the infused moral virtues. The acquired virtues do not guarantee receipt of the 'infused' virtues—those virtues are a gift from God, and there is no natural regularity, let alone a natural law, linking possession of the acquired to receipt of the infused virtues. Nonetheless we can see the acquired virtues as preparing the way for the receipt of the infused. Minimally, the acquired virtues clear away impurities of character that would make a person less disposed to receive the infused virtues. So while not causing the receipt of the infused virtues, the acquired virtues can create the conditions under which a person is more likely to accept these additional, God-directed virtues, and more likely to act upon them once they have been received.[5]

So in the standard case, we have a narrative of the spiritual life in which the person, first of all, cultivates the acquired virtues, so orienting themselves in relation to created things—including here food and drink and, of course, other human beings. In this way, the person can thrive in their relations to the material world, where the measure of success is provided by their human nature or equally, we could say, by a rule of reason. Thereafter, they can develop further in the spiritual life through receipt of the infused virtues, which in turn take two forms:[6] there are the theological virtues, which relate the person directly to God, and the

[5] For an instructive discussion of these matters, see Rebecca Konyndyk DeYoung, Colleen McCluskey, and Christina Van Dyke, *Aquinas's Ethics: Metaphysical Foundations, Moral Theory, and Theological Context* (Notre Dame, IN: University of Notre Dame Press, 2009), especially pp. 144–7. Aquinas is clear that God does not infuse a virtue 'without our consent'—see ST 1a2ae. 55. 4 ad 6 (cited at *Aquinas's Ethics*, p. 144).

[6] Unsurprisingly, Thomas allows that God is not bound to observe this track of development, since God is free to infuse the habits corresponding to the acquired virtues. Hence he remarks: 'Just as, therefore, sometimes, in order to show His power, He causes health, without its natural cause, but which nature could have caused, so also, at times, for the manifestation of His power, He infuses into man even those habits which can be caused by a natural power. Thus He gave to the apostles the science of the Scriptures and of all tongues, which men can acquire by study or by custom, but not so perfectly.' (ST 1a2ae. 51. 4) In the same way, God is free to infuse the habits corresponding to the acquired moral virtues, without having to wait for the unfolding of the processes of habituation that are normally required for the production of those habits.

infused moral virtues, which relate them to God indirectly, via their relationship to creatures. Aquinas represents the connection between these two kinds of virtue in these terms:

> The theological virtues are enough to shape us to our supernatural end as a start, that is, to God himself immediately and to none other. Yet the soul needs also to be equipped by infused virtues in regard to created things, though as subordinate to God.   (ST 1a2ae. 63. 3. ad 2)[7]

So the infused moral virtues, such as infused temperance and (on the view we have taken) neighbour love, structure the person's relations to created things, so that those relations are now subsumed within a God-directed teleology. This new teleology does not disrupt the earlier teleology that belongs to the acquired moral virtues: for instance, the person's activities of eating and drinking are still ordered to their flourishing as human, but they now serve at the same time the goal of their well-being in relation to God. Hence, to revert to the case of dietary abstinence, the person's habits of eating continue to respect the relevant rule of reason, but are at the same time fitting or congruent relative to the truth that they will one day share in the beatific vision.

From this picture, it follows that the goods of the infused moral virtues have a hybrid character, when compared with those of the acquired moral virtues and the theological virtues. These goods are like the goods of the acquired moral virtues with respect to their subject matter, since both kinds of good concern the person's relationship to the created order. But at the same time, the goods of the infused moral virtues are grounded in a God-directed teleology, and in this respect they resemble the goods of the theological virtues. So in brief the goods of the infused moral virtues are realized in so far as the person succeeds in their relations to the created order (here like the acquired moral virtues), where the measure of success is provided by relationship to God (here like the theological virtues). The notion of infused moral virtue serves then as a conceptual hinge, allowing Aquinas to bring together Aristotle's account

---

[7] Here I am following the Blackfriars translation of the *Summa Theologiae*, ed. Thomas Gilby (London: Eyre & Spottiswoode, 1964–74).

of the well-lived human life, and the account of human flourishing in relation to God that was provided by his theological forebears, and notably Augustine.[8] Here as elsewhere, Aquinas elaborates upon the traditions that he has received so as to provide a picture within which the realms of grace and nature do not just sit alongside one another, but are integrated, by virtue of the fact that grace 'perfects' nature.[9] In this particular case, grace perfects nature in so far as the divine rule that is the measure of the infused moral virtues does not abrogate the rule of reason that is the measure of the acquired moral virtues, but does, in the ways we explored in Chapter 2, present a more radical demand.

To return to the main thread of our discussion, this account suggests a twofold conception of the spiritual life: the spiritual practitioner aims, first of all, to be properly oriented in their relations to creatures across various domains, according to the standards of the relevant rule of reason; and if they are to be properly oriented with respect to their divine environment as well, then the acquired moral virtues need in time to be 'topped up' or extended by their infused counterparts (and also the theological virtues). This picture suggests that in the normal case, the spiritual life moves through two phases: a person builds up the acquired moral virtues, first of all, and those virtues then provide a basis for the receipt of their infused counterparts, which do not displace but strengthen or extend the dispositions that are involved in the acquired virtues.

The central motif of this story of the spiritual life concerns the relationship between divine and human agency, where variations in that relationship define the movement into the condition of spiritual maturity. Such a story can be told in purely metaphysical terms, or told as an

---

[8] Augustine's account of the virtues has at least implicitly the same structure. See his suggestion that created things are simply of objects of 'use', and are to be subordinated to relationship to God, who alone is to be 'enjoyed', which implies that our relationship to created things is to be folded into a divinely directed teleology: *De Doctrina Christiana*, Book I. For fuller discussion of the relationship of Aquinas's thought to Augustinian traditions in moral theology, see John Inglis, 'Aquinas's Replication of the Acquired Moral Virtues', *The Journal of Religious Ethics*, 27 (1999), 3–27.

[9] See Aquinas's comment that 'grace does not destroy nature but perfects it': ST 1a. 1. 8 ad 2. Here he is considering the relation between revelation and 'human reason', but the principle has general application in his thought.

angel would tell it. But it is another matter to say what it would be like from the vantage point of a human being to lead such a life. If we want to capture this further perspective on the spiritual life, we will need another vocabulary. To put the point in the terms we used earlier, just as we cannot record what it is like for Mary to see the colour red by using simply the language of the physical sciences, so we cannot record what it is like for the spiritual person to be drawn into a new relationship to their divine context, through the receipt of the infused virtues, by reference simply to the language of metaphysics. In each case, the language of physics or metaphysics needs to be supplemented through the use of a further, experientially grounded idiom.

John of the Cross on the Condition of Spiritual Maturity

There are various ways in which we might try to develop this experiential counterpart for the story that Aquinas has told. One natural way of proceeding would be by appeal to the work of spiritual writers who have some sympathy for his metaphysical picture of the various phases of the spiritual life. One such author is the sixteenth century Spanish Carmelite, John of the Cross.[10] Although John does not speak explicitly of acquired and infused moral virtues, his understanding of spiritual development does seem to map on to Thomas's story of how the acquired virtues, in the normal case, prepare the way for the infused. Moreover, John was an educated man, who studied theology at the University of Salamanca, and there is no doubt that he was well acquainted with central features of Thomas's thought. And at points indeed, it is clear that he is drawing quite explicitly on Aquinas's metaphysical categories to present his own perspective on the spiritual life.

A nice example of John's experiential extension of Thomas's thought can be found in his account of the condition of the spiritually mature

---

[10] For an instructive account of how Jesuit, rather than Carmelite, traditions may provide an experiential amplification of Aquinas's understanding of the spiritual life, see Nicholas Austin SJ, 'Spirituality and Virtue in Christian Formation: A Conversation between Thomistic and Ignatian Traditions', *New Blackfriars*, 97 (2016), 202–17.

person. We can read this discussion as an affirmation of the distinctiveness of the experiential relative to the metaphysical vantage point upon the spiritual life. In the preamble to the Five Ways, in *Summa Theologiae* 1a. 2. 2, Aquinas famously distinguishes between two kinds of proof—what he calls a 'demonstratio quia' and a 'demonstratio proper quid'.[11] The first concerns an inference to the best explanation, where we postulate a cause to account for the data of observation: here we establish the existence of the cause by reference to its effects. In the case of the second kind of proof, we already know of the existence and nature of a cause, and use that knowledge to read off the likely character of its effects. So here we move in the other direction, and prove the character of the effects from a knowledge of the cause. Of course, for Aquinas, where strictly philosophical enquiry into the existence and nature of God is concerned, we are confined to the route of the demonstration 'quia'— that is, we must start from the observation of various phenomena (such as change, gradation of goodness, and teleological directedness), and move from there to the idea that there is a God who stands as their source.

Now John has inherited this understanding of the constraints on our capacity to know about God philosophically. And in the following passage, taken from his text *The Living Flame of Love*, he is providing, I take it, a kind of experiential amplification of Thomas's remarks. Here, he is talking about the perspective of what he calls the 'awakened' person, that is, the person of spiritual maturity:

> Though it is true that the soul here sees that all these things are distinct from God, in that they have a created existence . . . it knows also that God in His own essence is, in an infinitely preeminent way, all these things, so that it understands them better in Him, their first cause, than in themselves. This is the great joy of this awakening, namely to

---

[11] Thomas writes: 'Demonstration can be made in two ways: One is through the cause, and is called "a priori" [proper quid], and this is to argue from what is prior absolutely. The other is through the effect, and is called a demonstration "a posteriori" [quia]; this is to argue from what is prior relatively only to us.' ST 1a. 2. 2.

know creatures in God, and not God in His creatures: this is to know effects in their cause, and not the cause by its effects.[12]

Two things are worth noting about the relationship between Thomas's account and John's. First, the two positions are consistent. John is suggesting, I take it, that the person of spiritual maturity enjoys a new quality of experience. But this experience does not involve any direct vision of the divine nature. Had John proposed that, then his account could not have been reconciled with Thomas's assessment of the limits of human understanding in this life. But in fact, John's focus in this passage is not upon experience of the divine, but instead upon our experience of the world of everyday sensory things, once those things are seen from the divine vantage point, or apprehended, we might say, according to a divine scale of values.

Speaking of John's text *The Spiritual Canticle*, where a similar vision of human possibilities is set forth, Rowan Williams puts the point in this way:

> The sense of God living constantly in the soul, of God's goodness in all things, of the warmth of reciprocal love – all these things of which the *Canticle* speaks at length are described not at all in terms of revelations granted in ecstasy, but in terms of a general disposition of the soul, a regular daily mode of seeing and understanding, a new light on things.[13]

So, in brief, what John is alluding to is a transformation in the person's experience of the everyday world, by virtue of God's presence in the soul, rather than their apprehension of the divine nature considered as some extramundane object of experience. And in this respect, John does not overstep the bounds for human experience that had been drawn by Aquinas.

---

[12] *The Living Flame of Love by Saint John of the Cross with his Letters, Poems, and Minor Writings*, tr. D. Lewis (London: Thomas Baker, 1919), Commentary on Stanza IV, p. 121.

[13] Rowan Williams, *The Wound of Knowledge: Christian Spirituality from the New Testament to Saint John of the Cross* (Cambridge, MA: Cowley Publications, 1991), pp. 187–8.

Secondly, while John's perspective is consistent with Aquinas's, he is not simply recapitulating the latter's position on the spiritual life, but developing his own distinctive account of human possibilities. John makes this clear when he writes in the passage I have just cited that 'this is to know effects in their cause, and not the cause by its effects'.[14] His intention is not, I take it, to dispute Aquinas's claim, made in *Summa Theologiae* 1a. 2. 2, that when reasoning in natural theological terms, we cannot construct a demonstration 'propter quid', by moving from a knowledge of God's nature to a knowledge of God's effects. But he does appear to be saying that we should distinguish what can be said from the vantage point of natural theology, or metaphysics, and what can be said from the vantage point of experience, and specifically from the vantage point of the world-directed experience of the person of spiritual maturity.

In the realm of experience, even if not in the realm of philosophical argumentation, he is proposing, the perspective of something like the 'proper quid' is possible. For in the realm of experience, it is possible to know 'effects in their cause', rather than knowing 'the cause by its effects'. By tracking Aquinas's form of words in this way, John is, I think, intending to draw our attention to this distinction of perspectives, and to enter a kind of plea for the irreducibility of the experiential perspective to that of metaphysics. In sum, John's experiential account is, I would say, faithful to Thomas's metaphysics, but at the same time, it cannot just be 'read off' from that metaphysics. Given simply a knowledge of Thomas's metaphysics, we would have no reason to anticipate that we can experience things 'in God'. Indeed, given what Aquinas says about the impossibility of the perspective of the propter quid in the domain of philosophical thought about God, we might well conclude that such an experience is, to say no more, not to be expected.

---

[14] In this respect, the awakened person's knowledge resembles angelic 'morning knowledge'. Aquinas distinguishes between the varieties of angelic knowledge in this text: 'Knowledge of the Creator through creatures, therefore, is evening knowledge, just as, conversely, knowledge of creatures through the Creator is morning knowledge': *De Veritate* 8. 16 ad 9, tr. R. W. Mulligan (Chicago: Henry Regnery Company, 1952). My thanks to Nathan Lyons for this reference.

In sum, we have here two vocabularies for talking about the spiritual life: one metaphysical and the other experiential. The first can be used equally by angels and human beings, whereas the second is fitted for the description of the world as it appears to creatures with our specifically human sensory and cognitive apparatus, and what it refers to will to that extent always elude the understanding of a non-embodied creature such as an angel. Accordingly, we should say both that knowing the meta-physical story of the spiritual life in all its detail will not be enough for us to fix what it is like for a human being to live a life so conceived, and that if we are to record what it is like for a human being to live that life, then we will need to have recourse to a rather different, experientially inflected kind of vocabulary.

John of the Cross on the Earlier Phases of the Spiritual Life

I shall return to the question of how we are to understand the experien-tial state to which John alludes here. But first of all, having introduced his account of the condition of spiritual maturity, let us track backwards, by considering what John has to say about the transition from the earlier to the later phases of the spiritual life. John is probably best known for his discussion of the 'dark night of the soul'. Let us begin with a very brief sketch of the structure of the 'night' as he understands it.

The 'night' has, first of all, an 'active' phase, when the person engages in various spiritual exercises in order to purge themselves of disordered desires and attachments. And for a time, John suggests, the spiritual practitioner can find a kind of satisfaction in their growing competence in the performance of these exercises. But these satisfactions will even-tually give out, as the person finds that even their spiritual accomplish-ments cease to serve as a source of consolation. In the 'passive' phase of the 'night', which follows on from the active phase, the person suffers from a generalized break down of thought, desire, and action. John advises that at this juncture, they need simply to accept their incapacity, rather than trying as previously, when in the active phase of the night, to advance their spiritual development by their own efforts.[15] During the passive phase of the night, the person feels alienated from their own agency, and afflicted by a profound sense of their own nothingness. But if they are fortunate, then, in time, a new centre of agency will take root in them, so that they can once again engage with, and find fulfilment in, the everyday world. The person who emerges from the rigours of the passive night will find themselves with a radically re-ordered set of desires: their experience will no longer be shaped and coloured by ego-centric concerns, and the world will therefore assume a new appearance. This is the condition that John is describing, I take it, when in the passage that we have just discussed he speaks of how such a person sees all things 'in God'.

This is the barest outline of what John has to say on these questions, but on this basis, there is reason enough, I suggest, to align his story of progress in the spiritual life, in so far as it turns on the distinction between the active and passive phases of the 'night', with Aquinas's discussion of the acquired and infused virtues.[16] As we have seen, on Aquinas's Aristotelian account, the 'acquired' virtues are produced by a process of habituation. So here the person is actively involved in shaping their habits of thought and action. On the standard narrative, the infused virtues are a later development, and they derive not from the person's agency, but from God's. This movement from activity to passivity, as it emerges in Aquinas's discussion of the spiritual life, is paralleled in John's distinction between the active and passive phases of the night.

So Aquinas and John seem to agree broadly on the structure of the Christian life, in so far as each takes it to consist, in standard cases, of an active followed by a passive phase. But their perspectives on this process of development remain importantly different. If we had Aquinas's account alone, we might have expected the transition from the active to the passive phase to be registered in experience as simply a smooth,

---

[15] A fuller discussion of these matters would need to distinguish between the night of the senses and of the spirit—each of which has an active as well as a passive phase. But this sketch of the general structure of John's account is sufficient for our purposes.

[16] I discuss some of these themes at greater length in my chapter, 'Metaphysics and Emotional Experience: Some Themes Drawn from John of the Cross', in J. Corrigan (ed.), *Feeling Religion* (Durham, NC: Duke University Press, 2017), pp. 53–68.

incremental process, as the infused virtues build on and extend the acquired. But John's account suggests that this movement is experienced as one of rupture: in the passive night, the person's established habits of thought and action break down, and it is only once this point of complete collapse has been reached that a new centre of agency is formed in the person. Hence John can write that:

> God makes [the soul] to die to all that is not naturally God, so that, once it is stripped and denuded of its former skin, He may begin to clothe it anew...[17]

Or again, he comments:

> the Divine fire of contemplative love...before it unites and transforms the soul into itself, first purges it of all contrary accidents.[18]

In each of these passages, John proposes that there is a point of radical discontinuity between the earlier and the later phases of the spiritual life, since God only begins to 'transform the soul' once he has first of all 'stripped' it of 'its former skin' and 'purged it of contrary accidents'. Some commentators have doubted whether John's account is to be read in phenomenological terms;[19] but it seems clear that the passive night is registered as bewildering and even traumatizing, and to this extent his remarks do have, I take it, an experiential reference. And what John says in these terms about the passage from the active to the passive phase of the night suggests a rather different, and more disruptive, process than any that could have been anticipated simply from a reading of Aquinas.

Indeed, Aquinas's account and John's might seem to be contradictory. The first invites the view that the spiritual development of the Christian takes the form of incremental growth, where the habits of thought and

---

[17] *Dark Night of the Soul*, Book II, Ch. XIII, in *The Essential St John of the Cross*, tr. E. Allison Peers (Radford, VA: Wilder Publications, 2008), p. 445.

[18] Ibid., Book II, Ch. X, in *The Essential St John of the Cross*, p. 433.

[19] See for instance Denys Turner's anti-experientialist reading of John along with other authors in *The Darkness of God: Negativity in Christian Mysticism* (Cambridge: Cambridge University Press, 1995).

action that have been established in the process of building up the 'acquired' virtues are not displaced, but extended by the infused virtues. By contrast, John's account seems to postulate a fundamental rupture between the earlier and later phases of spiritual development: from the vantage point of experience, the habits of thought and action that have been acquired in the active phase of the spiritual life are not so much further developed as annihilated; and the person's growth in relation to God seems to involve, then, at least for the duration of the passive night, a radical disengagement from the created order, rather than simply a subsuming of their accustomed relations to creatures within a wider, God-directed teleology.

Reconciling the Two Accounts

This apparent disagreement between the two accounts can be resolved, I think, if we are sensitive to their differences of style and perspective. Thomas is using, I take it, a metaphysical idiom, and recording a shift from the period of the spiritual life when the virtues are simply 'acquired' to the period when they are also 'infused'. Here, the track of spiritual development is understood not in experiential terms, but by reference to variations in the relationship between divine and human agency: first of all, the acquired moral virtues are produced by means of human agency, although God's agency as the first cause is still of course presupposed in this process; and the divine agency is then exercised more directly, as the acquired moral virtues are extended, through the 'infusion' of their God-directed correlates. By contrast, John's account, I am suggesting, is more experiential in character: he is describing what it is like to receive these infused virtues.

To see the compatibility of these two narratives, we might consider a rough analogy. The experience of post-natal depression is connected at least in part, I take it, to the formation in the mother of a new attachment—to her child—where this attachment can appear to demand, and in moral and other terms may really demand, a radical re-ordering of her already established attachments. From the vantage point of the woman's experience, while she remains in the state of depression, this development may be registered in the sense that existing attachments have simply broken down, and in a feeling of deep disillusionment with things and relationships that were formerly sources of fulfilment.[20] On this reading, the depression consists at least in part in the conviction that established attachments have fallen away, and in the lack of any felt recognition of the emergence of new attachments that might provide an alternative source of orientation in the world. John's account of the passive night can sound rather like this, and we might suppose that he too is describing the emergence of a new focus of love—here, a love for God—along with a felt breakdown in established attachments as this new focus of concern begins to take root.

But in post-natal depression, it need not be the case that the mother's established attachments have in fact been annihilated, even if that's how things seem to her during the depression. In time, it may be that her former friendships and other attachments will be restored, and once again registered in feeling, albeit that they will now be newly configured, since they will now fall within a new pattern of attachments, one that accords a central place to her child. In such a case—and no doubt there can be other, rather different cases—it seems reasonable to say that the woman's earlier attachments were not so much eradicated, as simply, for a time, not registered in experience. That they were not eradicated is implied in the fact that when the depression passes, the woman returns with renewed vigour to former friendships and pursuits—which suggests that she retained all along some enduring connection to those very friendships and pursuits.

In sum, if we are to speak from the vantage point of the mother's experience, then we may be inclined to say that for a time, certain attachments seem to have given out; but there is another narrative, consistent with this first narrative, but told in a different idiom, according to which these attachments were not after all excised but were simply, for a time, latent, before becoming evident once again in experience, once the woman has recovered from her depression.

[20] For a reading of postnatal depression in terms of the experience of loss, see Paula Nicolson, *Post-Natal Depression: Psychology, Science and the Transition to Motherhood* (London: Routledge, 1998).

It seems that we can say something similar of the relationship between the accounts of spiritual development given by Thomas Aquinas and John of the Cross: the first is cast in a metaphysical idiom and the second can be read at least in part as a report upon experience, and accordingly while the first yields a story broadly of continuity, and the second a story of disjunction, we need not conclude that they conflict: it may be simply that they are records of one and the same sequence of events, which is being differently described, using different vocabularies, according to whether the vantage point of the author is metaphysical or experiential.

Let us pause briefly to draw together some of the key points from the discussion so far. Using the analogy of Mary stepping out of the monochrome room and into the wider world, we began by suggesting that if we are to understand the spiritual life, we need to do more than simply describe that life as a response to a given metaphysical context, and directed to goods that arise in so far as a person's thoughts and deeds are aligned with that context. We also need to ask what it would be like, experientially, for a human being, for an individual who shares our specifically human intellectual and sensory sensibility, to relate to the world on this basis. The texts of Aquinas and John of the Cross, when read in the way I have proposed, provide a ready illustration of the importance of this distinction of perspectives.

Our two authors share their metaphysical and doctrinal commitments, and agree on the focus of the spiritual life, and they are describing, it would seem, one and the same track of spiritual development. But in reading John's account, we learn something that we could not have known on the basis simply of Aquinas's discussion: we learn that the movement from the active to the passive phase of the spiritual life, or to put the point in Thomas's terms, we learn that the receipt of at least some of the infused virtues, can be, and perhaps is likely to be, registered in experience in terms of disruption and bewilderment, rather than as the progressive refinement of the habits of thought, action, and desire that have been established in the active phase of the spiritual life. The distinction between the metaphysical and experiential vantage points is particularly significant here, because on first inspection, John's account and Aquinas's account appear if anything to contradict each other, and it is only by attending to the difference of idiom that is used, or the difference of perspective that is adopted, that we can see how the two narratives are to be reconciled.

So the case of John and Aquinas suggests that the need for an experiential as well as a metaphysical vocabulary arises not simply because there is a logical gap between the language of metaphysics and of experience—rather as there is a logical gap between the language of physics and of experience, in so far as a description of, say, a given visual experience in terms of wavelength and frequency of light does not fix as a matter of logical entailment what colour is thereby apprehended. We also need an experiential vocabulary because the track taken by spiritual experience can be quite the opposite of what we might have expected given simply a knowledge of the metaphysical facts. (There is no counterpart for this point, I take it, in the example of Mary.) In this way, John's discussion of the spiritual life shows, I suggest, that a set of metaphysical truths concerning the ends of human life need not set any very tight constraints on what it would be like, for a human being, to lead a life that is directed towards those ends. Why? Because in this case, the metaphysical facts, concerning variations in the pattern of divine and human agency, imply, if anything, that the transition from earlier to later phases of the spiritual life will be experienced in terms of incremental growth. But allowing, as John of the Cross would, that Thomas is right about the metaphysical story, it seems that this process of development, while real enough, is experienced not in terms of progression, but of dislocation.

Experience and the Constitution of Spiritual Goods

So far, we have been developing the idea that there is no ready route that will allow us to move from a metaphysical depiction of the spiritual life to a claim about what it is like to participate in the spiritual life so understood, and that we need, therefore, to supplement a metaphysical description of progress in the spiritual life with an experientially inflected account of the facts. I want to suggest now that appeal to these different vocabularies is important not only for an appreciation of what it is like to be engaged in the spiritual life, but also for the characterization of certain spiritual goods. So I want to extend our enquiry by considering the idea that reference to experience is necessary not only to address the question 'what is it like to receive the infused virtues, so that one's life is ordered to spiritual goods?' but also the question 'what do these spiritual goods consist in?' In the ways we have been exploring, the first question can be grounded in the example of Mary, the colour scientist. The second question has no direct parallel in Mary's case, and to see its point, we will need to expand on Aquinas's account of the infused moral virtues.

So let us return briefly to the question of the role of the infused moral virtues in Aquinas's picture of the spiritual life. Aquinas might in principle have partitioned the life of virtue, so that one set of activities would be relevant to our flourishing in relation to creatures, independently of our relation to God, and another set of activities relevant to our relationship to God, independently of our relation to creatures. The category of infused moral virtue prevents this disjunction in the spiritual life. Such virtues are 'moral' (and not simply 'theological') since they are concerned with our relations to creatures: infused temperance, for example, is concerned with the consumption of food and drink, and in general with our relation to the objects of the bodily appetites. But at the same time, infused moral virtues are, indeed, 'infused' and not 'acquired', on account of the fact that their ultimate focus is relationship to God.[21]

So it is an implication of the category of infused moral virtue that our relations to the material order are folded into a larger teleology, since those relations are now relevant not only to our flourishing as human, but also to our flourishing in relation to God. For instance, it is implied in the idea that there is an infused as well as an acquired form of temperance that our relation to food and drink can be caught up into our

---

[21] Aquinas notes that there are two reasons why we need infused virtues, the first of which concerns the pre-conditions of the person's orientation to their divine end: 'The first reason is because there are some habits by which man is disposed to an end which exceeds the proportion of human nature, namely, the ultimate and perfect happiness of man, as stated above (Question [5], Article [5]). And since habits need to be in proportion with that to which man is disposed by them, therefore is it necessary that those habits, which dispose to this end, exceed the proportion of human nature. Wherefore such habits can never be in man except by Divine infusion, as is the case with all gratuitous virtues': ST 1a2ae. 51. 4.

relationship to God. It is for this reason that there is a divine rule, and not only a rule of human reason, in this domain. In brief, then, the role of the infused moral virtues is to draw our relation to created things into our relation to God. The theological virtues also have relationship to God as their end, so are also infused, but they are directed immediately to God, whereas the infused moral virtues relate the person to God mediately, that is, via their relations to creatures, by folding those relations into a God-directed teleology.[22]

From all of this it follows that upon receipt of the infused moral virtues, our relations with the everyday sensory world acquire a new dimension of significance, since those relations are now ordered not only to our flourishing as human, but also to our flourishing relative to our ultimate, divine end. And we might wonder whether our world-directed experience can in some way participate in this change in the import of the sensory world. In other words, can that experience be deemed more or less appropriate relative to our theological context, so that it is capable of realizing the goods that are the object of the infused moral virtues? We can make a start on this question by considering some experiences of spiritual renewal.

It is a commonplace of reports of conversion experience that it is not only the person's thoughts, desires, and behaviour that have changed following conversion, but also their perception of the everyday world. As William James puts the point:

> When we come to study the phenomenon of conversion or religious regeneration, we...see that a not infrequent consequence of the change operated in the subject is a transfiguration of the face of nature in his eyes. A new heaven seems to shine upon a new earth.[23]

---

[22] The point is made concisely and rather beautifully in the passage I cited earlier: 'The theological virtues are enough to shape us to our supernatural end as a start, that is, to God himself immediately and to none other. Yet the soul needs also to be equipped by infused virtues in regard to created things, though as subordinate to God': ST 1a2ae. 63. 3 ad 2, following the translation in T. Gilby, ed. (London: Eyre & Spottiswoode, 1964–74), vol. 23.

[23] William James, *The Varieties of Religious Experience: A Study in Human Nature* (London: Longmans, Green and Co., 1911), p. 151. The theme is familiar from various literary traditions. See for instance the opening lines of William Wordsworth's 'Ode: Intimations of Immortality from Recollections of Early Childhood': 'There was a time when meadow, grove, and stream,/ The earth, and every common sight,/To me did seem/Apparelled in celestial light,/The glory

---

Illustrating this general tendency, one of the converts cited by James remarks:

> Natural objects were glorified, my spiritual vision was so clarified that I saw beauty in every material object in the universe...[24]

And the American divine, Jonathan Edwards, as reported by James, describes his own conversion experience in these terms:

> The appearance of everything was altered; there seemed to be, as it were, a calm, sweet cast, or appearance of divine glory, in almost everything. God's excellency, his wisdom, his purity and love, seemed to appear in everything; in the sun, moon, and stars; in the clouds and blue sky; in the grass, flowers, and trees; in the water and all nature; which used greatly to fix my mind.[25]

While this sort of testimony is in some ways puzzling, its prevalence should lead us to suppose that some such change does indeed occur in many cases of what James calls here 'religious regeneration'. So it is worth the effort to see whether we can identify in general terms what is involved in this sort of transformation in the appearance of the everyday world. Two phenomenological categories seem to be of very direct relevance for this purpose. First of all, it seems that there is a change in the colour or 'hue' of the convert's perceptual field, so that the world now appears brighter or more vivid. And in addition, in some cases, there seems to be a change in the patterns of 'salience' that structure the perceptual field: before conversion, the world appeared relatively 'flat', whereas following conversion, the patterns of salience that inform the perceptual field are more boldly defined, so that objects now stand out more clearly relative to one another.[26]

---

and the freshness of a dream', in Wordsworth, *Poetry & Prose with Essays by Coleridge, Hazlitt and De Quincey* (Oxford: Clarendon Press, 1969; first published 1807), p. 111.

[24] *Varieties*, p. 250.   [25] Ibid., p. 249.

[26] Compare James's description of Tolstoy's experience of a period of existential crisis: 'Life had been enchanting, it was now flat sober, more than sober, dead': ibid., p. 152. See too his

I am going to suggest now that in each of these respects, that is, with regard to salience and hue, the appearance of the world can be assessed, in principle, as more or less adequate relative to our theological context. If so, then these categories will give us one way of developing the idea that our experience of the everyday world is capable of contributing to the realization of the hybrid goods that are the object of the infused moral virtues. In this way, we can also throw some light on the question of why conversion experience takes the form that it does, according to the texts just cited. That is, we can understand why religious renewal should involve not only, say, a new sense of proximity to God in prayer, but a shift in the colouring and contouring of the perceptual field. Let us take first the case of salience.

In our everyday dealings with the world, some objects stand out, as relatively salient, while others are consigned to the margins of our awareness. And implied in a given ordering of the perceptual field of this kind is a judgement about what is properly deserving of attention. For instance, if a large and unfamiliar dog is approaching me, then under normal circumstances, this object will be in the foreground of my awareness, while I remain at most peripherally aware of, say, the colour and shape of the flowers in the garden bed along which the dog is advancing; and in this way, I register in perceptual terms the relative importance of these objects for me. Given this general truth about the way in which the significance of objects can be inscribed in the perceptual field, it follows that we can assess a given pattern of salience in moral and theological terms: a pattern will be morally appropriate in so far as it affords most prominence to those objects that are of most importance in moral terms, and theologically appropriate in so far as the salience of objects is directly proportional to their significance with respect to the relevant theological narrative. In this way, we can understand why conversion experience should involve a change in the patterns of salience that inform the perceptual field. In conversion

---

description of the experience of the man 'sick with an insidious internal disease' whose experiences of laughing and drinking 'turn to a mere flatness' (p. 141). I discuss these examples at greater length in Chapter 7.

experience, we may say, these patterns come to track a divinely ordered hierarchy of values.

To the extent that the world's appearance is so structured, so that an object's prominence in the perceptual field is proportional to its theological significance, then the world, as experienced, will hold up a kind of mirror to the divine mind: the relative importance of objects, as that is recorded in the patterns of salience that inform the perceptual field, will now match the relative importance of these objects from the divine vantage point. This account suggests one way of thinking about the text from Jonathan Edwards that I cited just now. Following his conversion, Edwards takes the divine wisdom to be manifest in the everyday world. As he says: 'God's excellency, his wisdom...seemed to appear in everything.' And perhaps this possibility can be understood, in part, in terms of the idea that the patterns of salience that are inscribed in the perceptual field now reflect the relative importance of things from the divine vantage point—for in that case, the world as it appears will present a kind of image of the divine perspective or divine wisdom.

Some reports of conversion experience suggest that it is not just that some objects are now more salient than previously, while others are less salient, but that the sensory world considered as a whole has taken on a new appearance. We might use the notion of salience to understand this possibility by supposing that the patterns of salience that inform the perceptual field have become in general bolder or more sharply defined. A change of this kind could also count as theologically appropriate. If the perceptual field is relatively flat, then it will fail to register any significant variation in the importance of objects and this, it may be said, must contrast with the divine perspective on the world, which involves, surely, a profound sense of the differentiated import of things. If that is so, then we can understand how a generalized deepening in the patterns of salience that structure the perceptual field may, to that extent, bring the world as it appears into closer alignment with a divine scale of values. This generalized deepening in the patterns of salience that order the perceptual field is consistent, I take it, with a concurrent shift in the relative salience of particular objects, so we are free to combine these accounts when trying to understand how a given change in the world's appearance may be theologically fitting.

The reports I cited just now also speak of the world as taking on a brighter or more vivid appearance following conversion, or as seeming newly 'glorified'. Here, we might suppose that it is the colour or hue of the perceptual field that has changed. While variations in salience may well correlate with changes in hue, the two phenomena seem to be distinguishable. Take for instance the case where I learn that the meat that I am chewing derives from Shuttlecock, the pet rabbit. In that case, we may expect the meat to become newly salient in my experience, relative to other items of experience, but it will also change in its intrinsic phenomenal feel: it will now be experienced as revolting. And this second sort of perceptual change we can regard as a change in hue. An object's degree of brightness in the perceptual field provides one relatively straightforward example of hue, where vision is concerned. Variations in hue also seem to be theologically significant. For if God is the creator, and if the world bears at least in part the vestiges of its divine origins, then, it might be said, it is only appropriate that it should appear to us as bright or vivid, rather than as dull or lacking in lustre. As with the other cases we have been discussing, this appropriateness can be understood in terms of existential congruence, to use the terminology we introduced in Chapter 2.

We have been considering how the notions of salience and hue can provide the basis for an understanding of the ways in which the world's appearance may be assessed for theological appropriateness. Let us think now about how this account may be integrated into our earlier discussion of the goods of the infused moral virtues. In a famous text, Aristotle comments:

> both fear and confidence and appetite and anger and pity and in general pleasure and pain may be felt both too much and too little, and in both cases not well; but to feel them at the right times, with reference to the right objects, towards the right people, with the right motive, and in the right way, is what is both intermediate and best, and this is characteristic of virtue.[27]

---

[27] *Nicomachean Ethics*, Book II, 6, tr. W. D. Ross, revised J. L. Ackrill and J. O. Urmson (Oxford: Oxford University Press, 1980), Book II, 6.

Of course, Aristotle is concerned here with the character of the acquired moral virtues. But we can speak in the same terms of their infused counterparts. For instance, to revert to our earlier example, we should say that in their relations to food and drink, the person of infused temperance will experience pleasure and pain 'at the right times, with reference to the right objects, with the right motive, in the right way', and so on, where once again the measure of rightness here is provided by reference to relationship to God. And as we have seen, in his discussion of infused temperance, Aquinas indicates that a person's habits of food consumption, and associated patterns of thought, can also be assessed as more or less adequate relative to our theological context. Similarly, for Aquinas, neighbour love requires that a person's thoughts and feelings, attitudes and behaviour are rightly ordered in their relations to rational creatures; and we should therefore say that in all of these respects, their mode of engagement with the created order can be deemed more or less fitting, relative to the end of flourishing in relation to God.

So Aquinas's account of the infused moral virtues implies that human beings can realize the hybrid goods that are the object of the infused moral virtues across a wide range of domains—for instance, with respect to food and drink, and in our relations with other human beings—and with regard to a wide range of world-directed kinds of engagement—including our thoughts and feelings, attitudes, and bodily comportment. However, so far as I can see, Aquinas does not touch on the question of whether, and how, our perceptual relations to the everyday sensory world may contribute to the realization of hybrid goods directly, that is, not simply by virtue of their role in guiding, in appropriate ways, our world-directed thoughts and behaviour, but on their own account. But for the reasons we have been considering, it seems that the appearance of the everyday world can be judged more or less appropriate, in its own right, relative to theological context, depending on the patterns of salience that are inscribed in the perceptual field, and the hue of the world as it appears. And if that is so, then we have good reason to extend Aquinas's account of the infused moral virtues, by allowing that there is a further way in which such virtues may be realized, namely in so far as the world's appearance is congruent with our theological context.

In his discussion of the infused moral virtues, Aquinas is concerned with virtues that are 'moral' in the sense of taking as their subject matter our relations to other human beings, including, in the case of temperance, our relations to our own bodies. Interestingly, if we extend this account by allowing for the possibility of hybrid goods that arise in so far as the world's appearance is theologically appropriate, then we seem to have a basis for supposing that the goods of the spiritual life may take an aesthetic as well as moral form. Let us pause briefly to consider how we might develop this theme.

The Contribution of Aesthetic Goods to the Spiritual Life

Reports of conversion experience, including those I cited earlier, commonly have a strongly aesthetic dimension: converts observe that the world appears newly beautified or newly glorified, or as James puts it in his summation of such reports, as 'transfigured' or such that 'a new heaven seems to shine upon a new earth'. It is natural to wonder whether extending the category of infused moral virtue in the way that I have just proposed can help us to understand the aesthetic dimension of conversion experience. After all, this extension is concerned with a transformation in the appearances of things, which suggests in turn that the change is in principle open to appraisal in aesthetic terms. But first of all, let us briefly note another, rather different way of understanding the contribution of aesthetic goods to the spiritual life.

In his discussion of the goals of religious practice, Richard Swinburne has drawn attention to the contribution of aesthetically productive activities to the spiritual life. For instance, speaking of 'beautifying the universe', among other activities or 'tasks', he remarks:

> If there is a God, such tasks will necessarily be vastly more worthwhile than secular tasks – for there will be a depth of contemplation of the richness of life of a person, God, open to us which would not be open if there is no omnipotent and omniscient being.[28]

---

[28] Richard Swinburne, 'The Christian Scheme of Salvation', in Michael Rea (ed.), *Oxford Readings in Philosophical Theology*. vol. 1: *Trinity, Incarnation and Atonement* (Oxford: Oxford University Press, 2009), p. 305.

On this account, if there is a God, then the act of 'beautifying the universe' will come to bear an additional dimension of significance, because it will then prepare the way for, or perhaps in some respects it will just be a form of, the 'contemplation of God'. Similarly, Swinburne notes how 'artistic creativity' will be obligatory if there is a God—because in that case, we will owe God a life that is productive in aesthetic and other terms since, in a particularly profound way, as the source of our being, God is our benefactor. Hence if there is a God, then an aesthetically productive life will satisfy an obligation that would not otherwise obtain; and again, this is a particularly weighty obligation, one that is owed to God as our ultimate benefactor. So for this reason too, an aesthetically productive life will be additionally good, if there is a God.[29] On these grounds, Swinburne maintains that aesthetic goods—such as those involved in 'beautifying the universe' or 'artistic creativity'—will have an additional importance if there is a God. And from this it follows that the truth of theism would give us additional reason to pursue such goods.

In these remarks, Swinburne is concerned with the additional non-aesthetic goodness that will attach to aesthetically significant activities, if there is a God—and not, or at least not explicitly, with the idea that God's existence will enable human lives to bear an additional aesthetic import. For instance, on the second of the accounts I have just mentioned, artistic creativity turns out to be additionally good if there is a God because it will then satisfy a moral obligation, which is to say that it will then be additionally good in moral terms. We might wonder whether the cases of conversion of experience that we have noted are also to be read in these terms, or whether they are, instead, concerned with what we might call distinctively theological aesthetic goods, that is, aesthetic goods which cannot be understood independently of reference to the relevant theological context.

There is some reason to take the second view. The brighter appearance of the world that converts report could be appreciated as beautiful,

---

[29]   Ibid., p. 304. Following Swinburne's usage, we should say that the relevant obligation will certainly be 'objective' if there is a God, and may also be 'subjective'. For this distinction, see ibid., p. 296.

no doubt, from a purely secular point of view.[30] Similarly, we might think of the bolder, more vivid definition of the contents of the perceptual field as beautiful independently of reference to theological considerations. But it is also clear that some converts see the world in its post conversion guise as beautiful, at least in part, on account of its perceived relation to the divine beauty or divine glory. Hence Edwards writes that 'there seemed to be, as it were, a calm, sweet cast, or appearance of divine glory, in almost everything'. And as we have seen, James remarks that in general the experience is one of a new heaven shining upon a new earth. If we take these reports at face value, as a record of the phenomenology of the relevant experiences, then there is some reason to say that the world seems newly beautiful to the convert, at least in part, because the divine beauty now appears to them as manifest in ordinary things. And to the extent that these experiences are to be read in these terms, then we should say that this new-found beauty has inherently a theological structure: the experience of this beauty consists, at least in part, in material objects appearing as translucent to their divine source.

Once again, we can understand this possibility in terms of the categories of salience and hue. For instance, using the notion of salience, we can give some sense to the idea that the world as it appears post conversion holds up a kind of mirror to the divine mind, since it now conforms to a divinely ordered scale of values. We might say, then, that the experience of divine beauty as disclosed in the beauty of ordinary things is a matter of the convert registering the character of the divine mind in visual terms—or following Edwards' formulation, we could say that the material order now appears as diaphanous to the divine 'wisdom' and 'excellence'.

Let us take stock. We have been considering how the appearance of the everyday world can be assessed as more or less adequate relative to theological context, and how it is capable of realizing, therefore, hybrid goods—that is, the kind of good that, for Aquinas, serves as the object of the infused moral virtues. By contrast with the goods that Aquinas discusses in his account of infused temperance and neighbour love, the

---

[30] Aquinas is explicit that 'brightness' (or *claritas*) is a constituent of beauty, along with 'integrity' and 'proportion': see *Summa Theologiae* 1a. 39. 8.

goods that are constituted by the congruence between the world's appearance and our theological context seem to be, at least in part, aesthetic in character. And this is not just a matter of certain aesthetic goods proving to be additionally good in non-aesthetic terms once they are understood from the vantage point of a theological narrative. Instead, the goods that arise in so far as the world's appearance is properly attuned to our theological context are themselves aesthetic in character, since they involve, for example, the everyday world seeming to be transparent to the divine beauty. If all of this is so, then we have the basis for an account of the contribution of aesthetic goods to the spiritual life—where this account is built around Aquinas's category of infused moral virtue, and the associated notion of a hybrid good, and at the same time faithful to the phenomenology of some widely cited examples of conversion experience.

It is worth adding that these theologically grounded aesthetic goods are, potentially, both pervasive and deep—pervasive because they can be realized, in principle, whenever we perceive the world, which is to say in much of our lives; and deep because they concern the appropriateness of our perceptual lives not simply in relation to some finite good, or localized context, but with respect to the divine good and our ultimate context. And if that is so, then there is some reason to suppose that hybrid goods of this kind are of fundamental importance for the spiritual life.

The Pervasiveness of the Change in the Appearance of the World

We have been considering the contribution of experience to the constitution of spiritual goods, and the aesthetic dimension of narratives of conversion, and the role of the notion of infused moral virtue in clarifying each of these themes. Briefly, I am going to propose now that there is a further aspect of conversion experience that can be brought into new focus once we introduce the idea of infused moral virtue.

The conversion experiences that James cites seem commonly to involve a transformation in the appearance of sensory things in general, or at least of large swathes of the natural world, rather than concerning simply certain localized spaces or objects. As James puts the point, these experiences take the form of 'a transfiguration of the face of nature'. Hence, as we have seen, Jonathan Edwards writes of how 'The appearance of everything was altered', and another of James's sources remarks:

I remember this, that everything looked new to me, the people, the fields, the cattle, the trees. I was like a new man in a new world.[31]

Another convert cited by James says:

Natural objects were glorified, my spiritual vision was so clarified that I saw beauty in every material object in the universe...

And another report reads:

how I was changed, and everything became new. My horses and hogs and even everybody seemed changed.[32]

In each of these cases, the accent falls on the pervasiveness of the phenomenological change that arises in conversion experience. In this respect, these accounts tally with John of the Cross's representation of the condition of the 'awakened' person. As we have seen, John describes this condition in terms of knowing 'creatures in God, and not God in His creatures'.[33] And since he talks here simply of knowing 'creatures', without further specification, there is some reason to think that John takes the distinctive knowledge of the person of spiritual maturity to extend to the created order as a whole. And if that is right, then in this respect the 'awakened' person resembles the converts whom James describes: in each case, the movement into spiritual maturity involves a new appreciation of the sensory world in general. While John does not explicitly represent this new knowledge of creatures in terms of a transformation of experience, James's discussion gives us some reason to

---

[31] James, *Varieties*, p. 249. [32] Ibid., both passages, p. 250.
[33] Once again, the text is *The Living Flame of Love*, p. 121.

suppose that such knowledge finds expression in, or perhaps in some measure it takes the form of, a change in the appearance of the everyday world. And if we can read John's text in these terms, then we should think of the 'joy' which he associates with the condition of awakening not as simply a state of bodily feeling, but as radiating out into the world, so that sensory objects are differently experienced.

So taking into account James's examples of conversion experience, and John of the Cross's understanding of spiritual regeneration, we have reason to suppose that, in some central cases, religious renewal will go along with, and partly consist in, a changed perceptual relationship to the everyday world, so that the sensory world in general now appears enlivened or inscribed with new significance. We have already noted some ways in which we might understand such a generalized shift in the world's appearance. For example, we could suppose that this is a way of registering in experiential terms the goodness of the world considered as an object of divine creation. So here is one way in which a metaphysical story—the story of creation—can be matched to the experiential story according to which spiritual growth can involve, in its later phases, a pervasive change in the world's appearance. But we can also understand this experiential change by appealing, once again, to the category of infused moral virtue. Let us consider now how such an account might run.

As we have seen, the notion of infused moral virtue allows us to sub-sume everyday sensory objects—such as other human beings, and food and drink—within a divinely ordered teleology. And as we have also seen, the significance that objects come to bear once they are located within this teleology does not displace the significance they bear when understood from a purely secular vantage point. Why not? Because, to put the point in Aquinas's terms, the divine rule that applies in a given domain will incorporate the rule of reason that operates in that domain, so that when viewed from the vantage point of the divine rule, objects will have all the significance they would anyway have had, when viewed from the vantage point of the relevant rule of reason, and more signifi-cance besides. For instance, to revert to one of our earlier examples, if a person lives by the virtue of infused temperance, then their relations to food and drink will realize both the good of bodily health and at the same time the good of a life that is congruent, in these respects, with our theological context.

If all of this is so, then the Thomistic story of the spiritual life—told in terms of the receipt of the infused moral virtues, where those virtues build on and do not displace the acquired moral virtues—allows us to understand spiritual progress as a matter of everyday objects coming to acquire an additional dimension of significance, once our relation to them has been folded into our relation to God. Moreover, this heightened significance extends potentially not just to this item or that, but to whole domains of experience: in the case of infused temperance, to food and drink and the objects of the appetites in general; in the case of neighbour love, to other people in general; and so on for the other infused moral virtues.

So if we understand spiritual growth by reference to the notion of infused moral virtue, then we should expect spiritual development to involve a heightened sense of the significance of the everyday world: on this account, in the later phases of the spiritual life, sensory objects will retain all the import they anyway have when viewed from the vantage point of a rule of reason, but they will now bear, in addition, a new dimension of significance, when seen from the perspective of the relevant divine rule. In our earlier discussion, we have noted how a generalized shift in the felt significance of the world can be registered in perceptual terms: for instance, through a brightening of the world's appearance, or through a deepening in the patterns of salience that are inscribed in the perceptual field. Putting together these lines of reflection, if the category of infused moral virtue can be used to model progress in the spiritual life, then we have some reason to expect such progress to have a perceptual dimension. And specifically, we have some reason to expect the later phases of the spiritual life to involve, in central cases, a pervasive shift in the appearance of the sensory world, where that shift provides a perceptual counterpart for the spiritual adept's heightened sense of the significance of the everyday world as a whole.

Of course, this expectation seems to be matched pretty precisely by the reports of conversion experience that are cited by William James— and in some measure it also conforms to John of the Cross's account of the possibility of knowing God 'in all things'. And in this way, we might take the data reported by James and by John to amount to a kind of empirical confirmation of the idea that the category of infused moral virtue can serve as a key organizing principle for our understanding of the spiritual life.[34] In contrast with our earlier discussion, here we seem to find that the perspectives of Aquinas and John are broadly consonant, to the extent that Aquinas's concept of infused moral virtue invites something like John's reading of the character of the later phases of the spiritual life. But of course, now we have bracketed all reference to the 'night' as a transitional phase in the spiritual life, and concentrated simply on the end point of that life, so far as it takes the form of an encompassing shift in the felt significance of the everyday world. On this matter at least, it seems that Aquinas's story and John's can be brought into fairly ready alignment.[35]

Concluding Thoughts

In the course of this chapter, we have been considering two broad themes. First of all, we have explored the idea that a metaphysical depiction of the nature of things will fail to set any very tight constraints on the way in which the world so conceived will appear to a practitioner of the spiritual life. I have taken as an illustration of this general truth John of the Cross's account of the various phases of the spiritual life, in so far as it represents spiritual progress in terms of rupture rather than incremental change. While it is consistent with Aquinas's metaphysically informed description of spiritual growth, John's narrative could never have been anticipated given simply a knowledge of Aquinas's discussion. It follows, then, that for a rounded account of the spiritual life, we will

---

[34] James's perspective and that of John of the Cross are, of course, in some respects different from one another. Notably, James is describing a development that can seem to occur simply 'out of the blue', and somewhat instantaneously, whereas John is concerned with an extended process of transformation, which involves, for a period anyway, active participation in spiritual practices.

[35] I present a fuller account of the issues we have discussed here in my chapter, 'Between Heaven and Earth: Sensory Experience and the Goods of the Spiritual Life', in D. McPherson (ed.), *Spirituality and the Good Life* (Cambridge: Cambridge University Press, 2017), ch. 6.

need to pay close heed to experiential reports of spiritual change, rather than assuming that the track of spiritual experience can be anticipated, even in general terms, by reference to the relevant metaphysical facts. We have also considered how any attempt to combine the metaphysical and experiential narratives will need to take careful note of the difference of vantage point that is implied in each.

Secondly, we have been considering the nature of spiritual goods, here building on the account of the constitution of such goods that we developed in earlier chapters. In the present chapter, we have been examining how reference to experience is vital for an understanding of the nature of spiritual goods, because it is not only a person's world-directed behaviour, thoughts, and desires that can be assessed for congruence with metaphysical context, but also their experience of sensory things. If that is so, then an account of the goods of the spiritual life will need to take stock of the ways in which a person's attunement to their theological context may be realized, in part, through their perceptual relationship to the everyday world. So here is a further way of understanding the significance of experience for a depiction of the spiritual life.

This chapter has also contributed to our ongoing enquiry into the fruitfulness of Thomas Aquinas's category of infused moral virtue for an understanding of spiritual growth and the condition of spiritual maturity. We have seen that this category can help us to understand the experiential dimension of the spiritual life in three key respects. First of all, Aquinas's distinction between the acquired and infused moral virtues is consonant with the experience of spiritual development, in so far as that experience involves a felt transition from activity to passivity. Moreover, as just noted, the category of infused moral virtue allows us to understand the role of experience in constituting some spiritual goods—once we recognize that not only thoughts, desires, and behaviour, but also experience of the everyday world can be assessed for congruence with metaphysical context. And lastly, the notion of infused moral virtue enables us to see how there could be a connection between spiritual growth and a heightened sense of the significance of everyday objects and spaces, and thereby a connection between spiritual renewal and a renewal in the appearance of the sensory world.

4

Enacted Example in the Spiritual Life

Introduction

In the course of this volume, we have been considering the nature of the spiritual life and of the goods at which it is aimed. In Chapter 1, we explored the idea that spiritual goods can be grounded in a relationship of congruence between a person's world-directed thoughts, desires, and behaviour, and their metaphysical context. In Chapter 2, we examined how a practice that aims at securing such congruence can be deemed good, and even praiseworthy, from the vantage point of a person who does not share the metaphysical presuppositions of the practice, and how this truth bears on the practical rationality of the spiritual life. And finally, in Chapter 3, we discussed how our perception of the everyday world can be assessed for congruence with metaphysical context, and how a rounded account of a person's spiritual practice needs to take into account, therefore, not only their thoughts, desires, and behaviour, but also their world-directed experience.

In the current chapter, I am proposing to extend this understanding of the nature of spiritual goods by reflecting further on the contribution of bodily practices to the spiritual life. We can take as our starting point a text from Raimond Gaita, in which he speaks of the moral significance of enacted example. In the course of the discussion, I hope to show how the metaphysical and experiential vocabularies that we examined in Chapter 3 can be supplemented by a further way of recording progress in the spiritual life, one which appeals to bodily demeanour. I shall propose that bodily demeanour provides a further source for context-relative or hybrid goods, to be distinguished from the examples of those goods

Spiritual Traditions and the Virtues: Living Between Heaven and Earth. Mark R. Wynn, Oxford University Press (2020).
© Mark R. Wynn.
DOI: 10.1093/oso/9780198862949.001.0001

that we reviewed in earlier chapters. If that is so, then our account of the infused moral virtues will need to be extended in this further respect, so as to accommodate the possibility that not only world-directed experiences but also bodily comportment can be more or less adequate relative to our metaphysical context. In brief, then, this chapter aims to develop an argument that runs parallel to the argument of Chapter 3, but now the focus of our enquiry will be bodily practice, rather than experience of the everyday world. Let us begin by setting out Gaita's example, and considering some respects in which it resembles Thomas Aquinas's account of neighbour love. Granted those parallels, we will then have a basis for building on the example to deepen our understanding of the infused moral virtues, and neighbour love in particular.

Raimond Gaita on the Role of Enacted Example in the Moral and Spiritual Life

In his book *A Common Humanity*, Raimond Gaita recalls his experience as a seventeen-year-old of working as an assistant on a psychiatric ward in a Melbourne hospital. He notes how he was impressed by the 'nobility' of a number of the doctors on the ward, who spoke of the 'inalienable *dignity* of even those patients'.[1] He then recounts an episode which led him to a radically new assessment of his moral relation to the patients. This is how Gaita records the scene, and the emergence of his new insight:

> One day a nun came to the ward. In her middle years, only her vivacity made an impression on me until she talked to the patients. Then everything in her demeanour towards them – the way she spoke to them, her facial expressions, the inflexions of her body – contrasted with and showed up the behaviour of those noble psychiatrists. She showed that they were, despite their best efforts, condescending, as I too had been. She thereby revealed that even such patients were, as the psychiatrists and I had sincerely and generously professed, the equals of those who

---

[1] Raimond Gaita, *A Common Humanity: Thinking About Love & Truth & Justice* (Melbourne: Text Publishing, 1999), p. 18, Gaita's emphasis.

wanted to help them; but she also revealed that in our hearts we did not believe this.[2]

This text, and Gaita's interpretation of it, intersects with a number of the themes that we have been exploring in earlier chapters. Let us draw out some of these connections now.

Gaita goes on to represent the example of the nun as an instance of what he calls 'the impartial love of the saints'.[3] And by this expression, it is clear that he intends to refer to the virtue that is known more conventionally by the name of 'neighbour love'. Hence he writes for example that:

> Because of the place the impartial love of saints has occupied in our culture, there has developed a language of love whose grammar has transformed our understanding of what it is for a human being to be a unique kind of limit to our will.[4]

Here Gaita locates the example of the nun within a wider cultural and linguistic tradition, and that tradition is, I take it, the theological tradition that has spoken of neighbour love as a kind of other regard that is universal in scope, so that it extends to all human beings on the same basis, whether they be afflicted individuals, such as the patients on the psychiatric ward, or possessed of the full range of normal human capacities. By calling the love with which he is concerned 'impartial', Gaita indicates that he is intending to set his account within this larger tradition of thought. Moreover, Gaita's further commentary on this example coheres with several other features of the ideal of neighbour love as we have understood it here, notably the idea that such love is not the product of some process of habituation but, as Aquinas would put the point, 'infused'. For example, Gaita notes that:

It would be no fault in any account of ethics if it failed make fully intelligible what the nun revealed, for she revealed something mysterious.

---

[2] Ibid., pp. 18–19.   [3] For his use of this expression, see, for example, ibid., p. 24.
[4] Ibid., p. 24.

And he continues:

> Seeing her...I felt irresistibly that her behaviour was directly shaped
> by the reality which it revealed. I wondered at her, but not at anything
> about her except that her behaviour should have, so wondrously, this
> power of revelation. She showed up the psychiatrists, but if I were
> asked how, exactly, then I would not elaborate on defects in their char-
> acter, their imagination, or in what would ordinarily be called their
> moral sensibility.[5]

So in Gaita's view, the 'noble psychiatrists', who spoke so eloquently and
sincerely of the patients' dignity, were not lacking in any of the conventional moral virtues. So despite their failings, Gaita is not inclined to
withdraw or qualify his thought that the psychiatrists are 'noble', for they
are in their way the epitome of a certain kind of human goodness. But
even so, the nun's conduct shows that they fall short of another kind of
standard, one that lies beyond the imagining of even a well formed
'moral sensibility'. In the spirit of Aquinas, it is tempting to gloss these
thoughts by saying that the psychiatrists do not lack any of the 'acquired'
moral virtues—any of the virtues that standardly make up a 'moral sensibility' or 'character', and for which we can be held responsible, to the
extent that we are capable of instilling these virtues in ourselves by
our own efforts, via the relevant processes of habituation. But even so,
the psychiatrists' conduct, although not their 'character', proves to be
defective, when laid alongside another measure of excellence, one that
lies outside our conventional moral scheme.

In the first of the passages I have just quoted, Gaita develops a related
line of thought when he notes that we should not expect any system of
ethics to be able to 'make fully intelligible' what the nun revealed,
because what she revealed is 'mysterious'.[6] Again, this thought fits very

---

[5] Ibid., pp. 19–20.
[6] In fact, Gaita later expressed regret at his use of the word 'mystery' in this context, on the
grounds that the term might invite the conclusion that 'there are deep mysteries for deep
people to marvel at': Raimond Gaita, *Good and Evil: An Absolute Conception* (London:
Routledge, 2nd edn, 2004), p. xxxi. Gaita notes in this same passage that his interest is in what
is 'necessarily mysterious', rather than mysterious 'because our epistemic or other cognitive

readily with Aquinas's treatment of the infused moral virtues, and with neighbour love considered as such a virtue. For Aquinas too, no conventional, secular mode of ethical reflection can hope to bring into clear focus the goods at which neighbour love is aimed, and to which it thereby bears witness. Why? Because those goods are only evident, in full, from the vantage point of a revealed or theological conception of human possibilities, and will therefore fail to appear in any purely philosophical account of human beings and the conditions of their flourishing.

Moreover, Gaita writes that in observing the nun's behaviour, his attention was drawn in the first instance not to her, but to what she revealed—and only to her in so far as her behaviour had this revelatory power.[7] Once again, this claim could be made of the infused moral virtues, to the extent that they are not the product of human striving. Just because they cannot be instilled by human effort, any attempt to understand the infused virtues ought to direct our attention away from the human agent in whom they are manifest, and towards the values to which that agent is responsive, whose motivational pull elicits her conduct.

It is natural to suppose that the idea of 'infused' virtue had its origins in certain kinds of experience—perhaps most obviously in experiences of passivity such as those that John of the Cross describes, though not necessarily in experiences of that particular intensity and emotional valence. In such experiences, the person will have a sense of themselves as being moved by an agency that is not their own. And in so far as that agency seems to lead them into newly productive relations with other human beings, and into a newly enlivened perception of the everyday

---

powers are limited'. In this discussion, I have tried to be clear that his concern is indeed with the necessarily mysterious.

[7] See too Gaita's comment that: 'in another person such virtues and the behaviour which expressed them would have been the focus of my admiring attention. I admired the psychiatrists for their many virtues – for their wisdom, their compassion, their courage, their capacity for self-sacrificing hard work and sometimes for more besides. In the nun's case, her behaviour was striking not for the virtues it expressed, or even for the good it achieved, but for its power to reveal the full humanity of those whose affliction had made their humanity invisible': *A Common Humanity*, p. 20. Compare Simone Weil's account of the revelatory power of love for the afflicted person in her text *Waiting on God*, tr. E. Crauford (London: Routledge & Kegan Paul., 1951), pp. 53-4.

world, then it would be natural for the theistically inclined person to suppose that the agency in question is ultimately of divine origin. In the last chapter, we saw how experiential and metaphysical kinds of vocabulary can be integrated within an account of progress in the spiritual life. And speculatively, we might suppose that the relationship between these two vantage points consists, in part, in experiences of passivity helping to generate and then to inform, in this kind of way, the notion of infused virtue.

Gaita's example of the nun, and the interpretive framework within which he situates the example, points to an additional possibility. Perhaps the idea of infused virtue has its origins not only in our experience of our own agency, but also in our experience of the agency of others, when that agency takes broadly the form that Gaita has described in this text. In brief, in so far as the agency of another human being seems to reveal some quality that is not evident from the vantage point of a 'rule of human reason' (to put the point in Aquinas's terms), or to reveal something that is 'mysterious' from the perspective of conventional moral thought (to put the point in Gaita's terms), or in so far as the agency of another human being seems to suggest a deficiency in the conduct of even 'noble' human beings, or of human beings who seem to be in secure possession of the 'acquired' moral virtues, then we might find ourselves moved to suppose that this agency testifies to the possibility of another kind of virtue, one that is answerable to a transcendent order, rather than the immanent order that is tracked epistemically by our 'rules of reason' and motivationally by the habits of thought and feeling that constitute the acquired moral virtues.

This connection between Gaita's account of the nun's conduct and the idea of infused moral virtue is all the more striking in so far as the seventeen-year-old Gaita was, presumably, not familiar with that idea. So if Gaita has succeeded in recording the impressions of his seventeen-year-old self, then we should suppose that his remarks do not derive from any prior acquaintance with the notion of infused moral virtue. Rather, they suggest that, quite independently of any familiarity with that notion, our experience of another person's agency can lead us into a cluster of concepts that are closely connected to the concepts that constitute the idea of infused moral virtue, in the ways we have just noted.

In Chapter 3, we considered the relationship between metaphysical and experiential vantage points on the spiritual life. Gaita's example points to the possibility of another kind of connection—this time, between metaphysical and behavioural vantage points upon the spiritual life. Specifically, we might suppose that there is a connection between the idea of infused moral virtue and our experience of another's agency, where that agency is expressed in a particular kind of bodily demeanour, such as that exhibited by the nun. I have been suggesting that this association may run from the observation of another's agency to the category of infused moral virtue, but more plausibly, we might suppose that the relationship has been, historically, one of mutual influence, like the relationship between metaphysics and experience that we explored in Chapter 3.

So here we have an initial reason for extending the thesis that we developed in Chapter 3: for a rounded conception of the nature of the spiritual life, we need to employ not only metaphysical and experiential vantage points—where the second concerns my experience of my own agency and of the everyday sensory world—but also a behavioural vantage point, where this further perspective concerns my experience of the agency of other human beings. I shall return shortly to this question of why the behavioural vantage point is required for a proper conception of the spiritual life, but first let us think a little further about Gaita's example of the nun.

I have been setting out some of the affinities between Gaita's reading of the conduct of the nun and Aquinas's conception of neighbour love, but these two narratives also seem to differ in some respects. Let us consider these points of apparent difference next.

Gaita on the Priority of Enacted Example
over World View

I have noted how Gaita's account of the 'mysteriousness' of what is revealed in the nun's conduct resembles in certain respects Aquinas's understanding of neighbour love considered as an infused virtue. However, there are other features of Gaita's discussion that cannot be assimilated to Aquinas's scheme quite so readily. Take, for example, the following passage, where Gaita is in effect giving a further gloss on the idea that what the nun revealed was not just contingently—relative to his particular vantage point, say—but essentially 'mysterious'.

> Whatever religious people might say, as someone who was witness to the nun's love and is claimed in fidelity to it, I have no understanding of what it revealed independently of the quality of her love. If I am asked what I mean when I say that even such people as were patients in that ward are fully our equals, I can only say that the quality of her love proved that they are rightly the objects of our non-condescending treatment, that we should do all in our power to respond in that way. But if someone were now to ask me what informs my sense that they are *rightly* the objects of such treatment, I can appeal only to the purity of her love. For me, the purity of the love proved the reality of what it revealed.[8]

Here Gaita quite explicitly denies that what is disclosed in the nun's conduct can be understood, and justified, by reference to any deeper story about the nature of things. In particular, Gaita clearly takes the fittingness of her conduct to be evident independently of any account of our metaphysical context.[9] In this respect, Gaita's approach resembles Hadot's position, as described in Chapter 1: Hadot also maintains that we can simply see the goodness or appropriateness of a way of life independently of any reference to metaphysical context—and for this reason, he thinks, we can fix our fundamental evaluative commitments first, before raising the question of what picture of the world would be motivationally most productive in enabling us to enact those commitments. Somewhat similarly, Gaita seems to be saying that we can just see that certain kinds of conduct are fitting, quite independently of reference to a metaphysical, or any other, context. To the extent that his position has

---

[8] Ibid., p. 21, Gaita's emphasis.

[9] For instance, Gaita notes that the nun herself might well have offered a 'theological or metaphysical story about the people to whom she responded with a love of such purity', but adds that: 'My assent to what her love revealed did not…depend on my acceptance of an hypothesis about the grounds of that love': ibid., p 20.

this character, then Gaita's understanding of the 'impartial love of the saints', or what we might call 'neighbour love', appears to be very different from Aquinas's view, since the latter account of the goodness of neighbour love turns, I have been suggesting, on the idea that the practice is congruent with our metaphysical context.

What should we make of Gaita's stance on this point? I shall suggest that in a number of respects he and Aquinas remain of much the same mind, notwithstanding the distinction I have just noted. First of all, as Gaita presents the matter, it is clear that at the time of his encounter with the 'noble' psychiatrists, and before he had witnessed the nun's behaviour, his younger self was already fully persuaded that the patients had an 'inalienable dignity'. And as he says, before he had witnessed the example of the nun, he already 'sincerely professed' that the patients were fully 'the equals of those who wanted to help them'. Given this background, it would be natural to suppose that what the nun reveals to Gaita is not so much the general truth that these patients are his equals— he already believed that much, before her arrival on the ward—but what it takes to enact this truth in bodily terms. On this reading, Gaita's 'just seeing' that her conduct is right is a matter of his seeing that the ideal of full equality can be enacted (and perhaps only enacted) in a bodily demeanour of this kind. And since he is already committed to the ideal of fully equality, he thereby grasps the appropriateness of her conduct.

Of course, this may sound like a rather deflationary view of Gaita's insight, when laid alongside his talk of 'mystery' and 'revelation', but it seems consistent with his own description of events. What the nun 'reveals' on this account is the particular quality of embodied presence that will enable a human being to enact the idea of our common humanity in their relations with afflicted human beings such as the patients on the ward. This reading of Gaita's insight does not seem to stand in any tension with Aquinas's account of neighbour love. On this view, his insight simply specifies what it takes to live according to the ideal of neighbour love, under conditions such as those that obtain on the psychiatric ward.

Let us examine now a reason for thinking that the two accounts, in fact, converge in one important respect, despite Gaita's apparent hostility to any attempt to ground the appropriateness of the nun's example in metaphysical considerations. It is clear that Gaita's insistence on the mysteriousness of what the nun reveals is connected with his refusal to see her conduct as responsive to any feature of the world that can be specified independently of that conduct. And in turn, his stance on this second point is connected, I take it, to the fundamental moral commitment that he is exploring in his book. Gaita does not want to concede that the nun's conduct is appropriate because properly responsive to some quality x in the patients, where x can be identified independently of any reference to her practical relation to them. Why? Because, I suggest, he fears that such an account will invite a two-step approach to our moral relations with others: first of all, we are to determine whether a given individual has the relevant quality x, and then, and only then, will we be in a position to judge whether or not that individual is entitled to our moral regard and the associated practical concern. Gaita's objection to this reading of the basis of our moral relations to others is, I take it, that it risks fixing on a property that is possessed by some human beings but not others—and accordingly, it risks excluding some human beings from full membership of the moral community. And the presiding theme of his book, as indicated in its title, and the focal truth that is revealed in the example of the nun, is precisely that we all of us share 'a common humanity'.

This risk of placing some individuals who are biologically human outside the moral community can be avoided at a stroke, we might suppose, if we refuse to admit that there is any quality x that can be identified independently of the conduct of figures such as the nun, and used to justify that conduct. So Gaita's insistence on 'mystery' is, to this extent, fundamentally a moral rather than some kind of phenomenological claim: it is a way of articulating the idea that the nun's conduct cannot be justified by reference to any notional property x (where, once again, that property can be identified independently of her conduct, and can therefore stand as the ground of its appropriateness), rather than directly a report on the quality of his experience. It is because it cannot be so grounded that the nun's conduct is 'mysterious': if her conduct is not evidently a response to some independently identified quality, then it cannot be rendered intelligible, and justified, by reference to any such quality.

So we might take Gaita to be saying that the nun's regard for the patients, rather than tracking their moral worth, where that worth holds independently of her regard, in some way constitutes that worth. And how might that be possible? One answer would run: for an individual to be fully a member of the moral community just is for them to stand in an enacted relationship of equality when in the presence of a saintly figure such as the nun. In support of this account, we might note that if an individual were not to stand in such a relationship when in the presence of such a figure, then the idea of their full equality with other human beings would appear to be somewhat empty: if they are not capable of standing in an enacted relationship of equality under these most propitious of conditions, when in the presence of someone such as the nun, then the idea that they are fully members of the moral community seems merely theoretical, and not capable of being exemplified in practical terms, not even under even the most favourable of circumstances.

If on the other hand, they were to enter into an enacted relationship of equality under these conditions, then there is some basis for saying that they are rightly considered fully members of the moral community, even if there is no one in their current social context who shows them, or is even capable of showing them, such regard. Why? Because in this case there is a morally significant feature of the individual which sets them apart from, say, rocks and socks, or even plants and ants, in so far as these latter kinds of thing will never stand in an enacted relationship of equality, not even when in the presence of a figure such as the nun. So there is some reason to adopt this account of what it is to be fully a member of the moral community, and if we do, then it will follow straightforwardly that the nun's conduct towards the patients on the ward, understood as Gaita understands it, will establish, and so 'reveal', that they are fully the equals of other human beings. This is one way of reading Gaita's comment that: 'For me, the purity of the love proved the reality of what it revealed',[10] where the import of this comment is, I take

---

[10] For a fuller account of Gaita's stance on these matters, it would be helpful to consider the work of his doctoral supervisor, R. F. Holland, and in particular his chapter, 'Is Goodness a Mystery?', reproduced in Holland, *Against Empiricism: On Education, Epistemology and Value* (Oxford: Blackwell, 1980), ch. 7. Gaita's example of the nun could be read as an illustration of the position that Holland develops in this chapter. But I shall not take up these questions here.

it, that the nun's conduct of itself settles the question of the moral worth of the patients, independently of reference to any further standpoint.

Of course, it is not difficult to think of moral theories that endorse precisely the stance to which Gaita is objecting, by making the moral worth of an individual contingent upon their possession of some capacity, such as the capacity for rational choice, or the capacity to feel pleasure and pain, or to flourish in certain ways, where such properties turn out to be exemplified by some but not all human beings.[11] As we have seen, Aquinas's account of the scope of neighbour love is not vulnerable to this objection: for Thomas, the appropriateness of neighbour love is not grounded in an individual's possession of some empirically discernible quality; instead, it depends on a future truth concerning human beings' life with God or, more modestly, upon the possibility of our one day sharing in that life, granted our present circumstances. So to this extent, Aquinas is committed to 'mystery' in rather the sense that Gaita is: for both, neighbour love is universal in scope, and for both, this is partly because it is not founded upon any empirically discernible property in human beings, so that it is for each of them, in this respect, mysterious.

However, while Aquinas's account does seem to issue in the kind of moral commitment that Gaita is defending, and to resemble Gaita's in refusing to ground human worth (of the kind relevant to the practice of neighbour love) in any empirically discernible property, it seems clear that Gaita would not endorse it. He would no doubt say that on Aquinas's view, the appropriateness of the nun's regard for the patients, or in general of neighbour love, is still a function of some quality that can be specified independently of the showing of such love—albeit that this is not now an empirically discernible quality, such as the capacity to feel pleasure and pain, for example, but the property of one day sharing in the life of God in the beatific vision. From Gaita's perspective, Aquinas's position still runs the risk, then, of excluding certain human beings from the scope of neighbour love. And if we are

---

[11] See for instance Gaita's comment: 'Later, reflecting on the nun's example, I came to believe that an ethics focused on the concept of human flourishing does not have the conceptual resources to keep fully amongst us, in the way the nun had revealed to be possible, people who are severely and ineradicably afflicted': *A Common Humanity*, p. 19.

not universalists about salvation, and if we ground the appropriateness of neighbour love as shown to a particular individual in the truth that that individual will one day share in the beatific vision (rather than simply in their having the capacity to do so, relative to their present circumstances, or relative to our epistemic vantage point), then we should conclude that Gaita's idea of a common humanity will indeed be impossible to sustain.

However, we might defend Aquinas from this line of questioning by noting that Gaita's own position leaves open the possibility that some individuals who are biologically human will even so fall outside the moral community. On Gaita's account, such individuals are fully members of the moral community to the extent that they stand in an enacted relationship of equality, or would do so in relevant circumstances. On this approach, the scope of neighbour love turns out to be contingent upon the capacity of human beings, and figures such as the nun, to extend such love to their fellows. By contrast, Aquinas's position depends, in effect, upon the capacity of God to extend the love of charity or friendship to human beings—since on his account, a human being is entitled to the regard of neighbour love providing that they will share in the beatific vision, or at least, providing that they are capable of participating in the beatific vision given their present circumstances, where their sharing in that vision is directly a consequence of God's love for them.

If faced with the choice between these two ways of developing the idea of a common humanity, or the idea that every individual who is biologically human is fully a member of the moral community, one of which is grounded in a truth concerning the range of human love, and one of which is grounded in a truth concerning the range of divine love, then we might well prefer the second approach. Why? Because the divine love is after all, by definition, a perfectly inclusive love, freed from any of the constraints that can restrict and warp human love. In sum, we might say that Aquinas and Gaita share the same sort of commitment to 'mystery': for both of them, the appropriateness of our love of other human beings is ultimately grounded in the fact of their being loved, rather than in their possession of a property which can be specified entirely independently of that love, and which serves to justify the love.

It's just that for Gaita, this is a human, saintly love, while for Aquinas it is a divine love.[12]

Let us turn to one further feature of Gaita's handling of his example. While Gaita is insistent that the nun's example does not admit of a metaphysical or any other kind of grounding, he is also clear that so far as there is a vocabulary or way of talking that will allow us to articulate what she reveals, that vocabulary is religious, and specifically it is one that involves the idea of divine parental love. Hence he writes that:

> I doubt that the love expressed in the nun's demeanour would have been possible for her were it not for the place which the language of divine parental love had in her prayers.[13]

Or again, generalizing from this case, he comments:

> For us in the West, the claim that all human beings are sacred is the one that bears most directly on the question of how to characterise the nun's behaviour. Only someone who is religious can speak seriously of the sacred, but such talk informs the thoughts of most of us whether or not we are religious, for it shapes our thoughts about the way in which human beings limit our will as does nothing else in nature.

And he continues:

> If we are not religious, we will often search for one of the inadequate expressions which are available to us to say what we hope will be a secular equivalent of it. We may say that all human beings are inestimably precious, that they are ends in themselves, that they are owed unconditional respect, that they possess inalienable rights, and, of course, that they possess inalienable dignity. In my judgement, these are ways of trying to say what we feel a need to say when we are estranged from

---

[12] There is of course an extended theological debate about these matters, which in its modern form begins with Anders Nygren's text *Agape and Eros: Pt. 1, A Study of the Christian Idea of Love*, tr. A. G. Hebert (London: Society for Promoting Christian Knowledge, 1932). But we do not need to be drawn into that literature here.

[13] *A Common Humanity*, p. 22.

the conceptual resources we need to say it. Be that as it may: each of them is problematic and contentious. Not one of them has the simple power of religious ways of speaking.[14]

In these texts, Gaita's stance may seem to resemble Hadot's: like Hadot, he seems to be suggesting that a religious or philosophical 'discourse' can be introduced to support a way of life, and that the motivational efficacy of the discourse need not be tied to the conviction that it is, in all its detail, true. (Gaita's own position is after all agnostic, if not atheist.)

However, I don't detect in Gaita any counterpart for Hadot's thought that the world view articulated in the discourse is radically provisional—so that it is always open to being revised and updated, depending on shifts in the intellectual culture of the age. The connection that Gaita finds between theistic ways of talking, especially in so far as they involve the idea of divine parental love, and our capacity to acknowledge discursively the worth of human beings, and to act on that worth, seems to run much deeper than that. This is perhaps because Gaita takes the commitment to our common humanity to rest most fundamentally on the thought that all human beings are intelligibly the objects of love (whether or not they are in fact shown such love); and in turn, he may well think that the language of divine parental love is the surest buttress we have for the plausibility of the idea that all human beings are intelligibly the objects of love.[15] (Even saintly love, we might suppose, can fail, given familiar constraints on human beings' sympathies and powers of attention.) If this is the right way to read Gaita, then once again his position bears a striking resemblance to Aquinas's: for both authors, the language of divine love is of fundamental importance for our capacity to represent to ourselves, in storied terms, the deep significance of human lives.

It might be said that there remains one rather important difference, since Gaita is committed simply to the intelligibility of the thought that

---

[14] Ibid., p. 23.
[15] See Gaita's comment that: 'We would not find it even intelligible, I think, that we have obligations to those whom we do not love unless we saw them as being the intelligible beneficiaries of someone's love. Failing that, talk of rights and duties would begin to disengage from what gives it sense': ibid., p. 26.

human beings are loved by God, whereas Aquinas is committed to the truth of this thought. Let us think a little further about this point of distinction.

In the course of our discussion in this volume, we have been developing the idea that certain fundamental spiritual goods, what we have been calling hybrid goods, depend for their possibility on metaphysical context. But when considering Aquinas's treatment of neighbour love, I suggested that it would be a mistake to suppose that, on his view, we are to begin with a characterization of our metaphysical context, considered independently of any reference to human lives, and move from there to a conception of the good life, where the goodness or fittingness of that life is taken to follow from its congruence with the metaphysical context. This approach overlooks the fact that on standard accounts, and on Aquinas's own account, religious faith—understood as assent to a body of metaphysical teaching—is voluntary. On some such approaches, I have proposed, what elicits the person's assent to a particular metaphysical story is not simply the evidence that can be assembled in its support, but the fact that the truth of that story would significantly extend and deepen the range of goods that can be realized in a human life here and now. For instance, to revert to an example that we have discussed at some length, if we human beings will one day participate in the beatific vision, then in our relations to one another here and now, we can realize a profound good that we could not otherwise realize, namely, the good of a life that is congruent with this truth concerning our shared future.

If all of this is so, then the assent of faith is not in the first instance to the truth of a world view, and only then to a way of life that is seen to be appropriate relative to this metaphysical scheme; it is instead an assent to the metaphysics and way of life considered in combination. This suggests, once more, that Gaita's position and Aquinas's are not so far apart as might at first seem. On the reading I have just suggested, Gaita's account turns on the intelligibility of the thought that God loves all human beings. A position which starts not from the mere intelligibility but the evident truth of that thought, and moves from there to the idea of a common humanity, would stand in very direct contrast with Gaita's approach so understood. But Aquinas's view is not to be identified with this second position, and seems, rather, to occupy a middle ground between these two: it is not the evident truth, nor the mere intelligibility of the idea of divine parental love that matters, but the idea that the relevant hybrid goods, which will obtain if the doctrine holds true, are worth pursuing, even in the face of uncertainty about our prospects of success. In this way, Aquinas's account respects, I take it, one key emphasis in Gaita's discussion, namely, the thought that our moral commitments have a measure of autonomy relative to our metaphysical commitments, and are not to be seen, therefore, as mere byproducts of a view of the world that is formulated in value-free terms. But these are matters to which we can return in more detail in Chapter 6.

To conclude this phase of our discussion, let us note briefly one final point of convergence between Gaita's position and Aquinas's. While Gaita suggests that he did not need to invoke any metaphysical scheme to see the appropriateness of the nun's example, since the 'purity of her love' was of itself enough to establish the appropriateness of her conduct, it seems he would agree that *if* we were required to pair metaphysical schemes with ideals of life, where the first serve to ground the second, then the idea of divine parental love and the ideal of neighbour love would be a particularly apt pairing. And it also seems to follow from his account that neighbour love would not readily form part of any other such combination, because of its integral connection to theistic categories of thought, and notably the idea of divine parental love. If all of this is so, then while Gaita is no Thomist, his position on the relationship between theistic categories and the love of the saints can be inserted fairly straightforwardly within a broadly Thomistic story concerning the nature and grounds of neighbour love as an ideal of life.

Bodily Demeanour and Spiritual Traditions

We have been exploring various parallels between Gaita's account of the nun's example, and its role in sustaining the idea of our common humanity, and Aquinas's discussion of neighbour love, with particular reference to the connection between Gaita's insistence that the nun's conduct is 'revelatory' or discloses a 'mystery', and Aquinas's thought that neighbour love is answerable to a 'divine rule', rather than a 'rule of reason'. I want to think a little more closely now about the significance of Gaita's example for the question of how a person may come to be inducted into a spiritual tradition.

It is notable that on Gaita's account, the nun's revelation is communicated in her 'demeanour' towards the patients—what matters is 'the way she spoke to them, her facial expressions, the inflexions of her body'. So it is implied in Gaita's discussion that bodily demeanour can be integral to the handing on of a particular moral or spiritual ideal, and it is natural to ask how, more exactly, it is able to play this role.

It is not clear whether Gaita hears anything that the nun says to the patients; and in any case, it is not, it seems, what she says, but the 'inflexions of her body' that reveal to Gaita the full equality of the patients with other human beings. Moreover, Gaita's insight is not readily recorded in verbal terms, it seems. So far as we can tell, he is committed to the thought that the patients are fully his equals before he has seen the nun, as well as after: it is just that he now has a deepened appreciation of what is signified by those words. We know in general terms what kind of bodily demeanour Gaita has in mind. We know that the nun cannot be 'talking over' the patients, as we sometimes put it, or talking at or down to them: we know that her bodily demeanour cannot take the form that is typical of that kind of encounter. But it is significant that Gaita does not try to spell out more exactly what is involved, and we might wonder why that is. Of course, he can describe the nun's demeanour in generic terms—as, say, behaviour that connotes respect. But what strikes him as 'revelatory' in the nun's manner is presumably the way in which through this particular stretch of bodily movement, she succeeds in acknowledging the humanity of the patients, or in recognizing their status as fully her equals. It is having seen this particular, gesturally specific enactment of the ideal of the patients' equality with the rest of us that Gaita comes to the conclusion that, despite their best efforts, he and the psychiatrists have in fact treated them with condescension.

On this view, even small variations in, say, the inclination of the head, or the set of the mouth, will result in a significantly different interpersonal meaning. And given the constraints on our powers of description, it is hard to see how we human beings could convey, in verbal terms, the character of such an ensemble of gestures—understood simply as a set of movements that can be plotted according to their spatiotemporal coordinates—at the level of detail that would be required to fix their moral sense. Moreover, even if we could describe in the requisite detail the inflexions of the nun's body—the particular inclination of her head, and so on—at a particular moment, the sense of her gesture at that moment will be a function of a larger context which is itself comprised of earlier such movements, both her own and those of the patients. And given even small variations in this larger context, this inclination of the head will bear a different interpersonal meaning. So for these reasons, it is not surprising that Gaita does not attempt to set down in verbal terms the particular quality of the nun's bodily presence, considered simply as a set of spatio-temporal movements. In brief, he does not attempt to do so because it is not possible for him to do so.

When read in this way, Gaita's example points, I think, to a larger truth that is of some importance for our appreciation of spiritual traditions. In Chapter 3, we explored the idea that for a rounded understanding of the ideal of life of a given spiritual tradition, we need to have recourse to two vantage points, and the correlative vocabularies: those of metaphysics and experience. Gaita's example suggests that for a full understanding of a given moral or spiritual ideal, a further vantage point, though not perhaps a further vocabulary, is also required, namely, the vantage point of enacted example.

This further dimension of understanding cannot be simply read off from the first two. It cannot be read off from any metaphysical narrative, because even if we see that a given metaphysical narrative establishes that we ought to relate to others as our neighbours, it is another matter to see what particular bodily demeanour is required for the enactment of this ideal. And the idea that there is a deep disjunction between the sincere verbal profession of a given set of moral ideals, abstractly specified, and an appreciation of what it takes to enact those ideals is, I take it, at the core of Gaita's example of the nun. (This is, of course, the condition of the doctors, and of his pre-conversion self, in this example.) Moreover, even if we have first-personal experience of relating to others in this way, or can describe what it feels like to enact the relevant moral ideal, it is a further matter to grasp the associated bodily demeanour.

After all, the nun in Gaita's example does not, presumably, represent to herself a particular quality of demeanour in purely mental terms, and then resolve to act accordingly. Rather, her bodily relation to the patients is directly an expression of her regard for them, rather than being the product of any process of ratiocination. (Compare the case where you view a video recording of your conduct in a certain setting: it can, of course, be a surprise to see from this third personal vantage point what your bodily demeanour looks like, however familiar you may be with what it felt like to act in that way.)

Once more, one fundamental reason why we cannot understand what bodily demeanour is required to realize the ideal of our common humanity, or other such ideals, independently of witnessing the enactment of the ideal is that this insight cannot be recorded in verbal terms. Why not? Because, once again, the relevant inflexions of the body constitute a spatio-temporally extended gestural gestalt, which resists description at the level of mere bodily movement, since even small variations in these movements can make for large variations in interpersonal meaning, relative to a given interpersonal context, which itself comprises a set of such finely tuned movements of the body.[16]

In sum, understanding a spiritual tradition depends partly upon familiarity with the concepts that are required to define the world view of the tradition, partly upon relevant first-hand experience of what it is like to inhabit the tradition (which in turn enables a grasp of the phenomenal content of the concepts that are required to describe what it is like to participate in the tradition), and partly upon an encounter with individuals who live out paradigmatically the tradition's core values. We could put this point by saying that if we are to understand the way of life propounded by a spiritual tradition, we need both a first-personal

---

[16] If we follow one standard reading of Aristotle's treatment of the matter, then we will say that in general we need to defer to exemplars if we are to know what the good human life amounts to. See for instance his comment that 'Virtue, then, is a state of character concerned with choice, lying in a mean, i.e., the mean relative to us, this being determined by a rational principle, and by that principle by which the man of practical wisdom would determine it': *Nicomachean Ethics*, tr. W. D. Ross, revised J. L. Ackrill and J. O. Urmson (Oxford: Oxford University Press, 1980), Book II, 6. Here, I am suggesting that we need not only to defer to the exemplar, but to have first-hand experience of them, to the extent that their example cannot be communicated in verbal terms. I am grateful to Simon Oliver for helpful discussion of this point.

vantage point on that way of life (whereby we can apprehend what it is like, experientially, to live according to the tradition's core values), and also a third-personal vantage point (whereby we can grasp, through witnessing the enacted example of figures such as the nun, what kind of bodily demeanour is appropriate to the tradition's core values). In Gaita's example, the nun has the first kind of vantage point, and Gaita himself the second. Or we might perhaps put the point, rather differently, by saying that for a rounded appreciation of a spiritual tradition's ideal of life, we need a first-personal vantage point (such as the nun's), a third-personal vantage point (such as Aquinas offers, through his metaphysical depiction of the nature and ends of the spiritual life), and also a second-personal vantage point (here supposing that if we are to appreciate the example of figures such as the nun, then we will need to see their conduct as the embodiment of an I–Thou relationship, so that the insight will count in that sense as second-personal).

There is arguably one other thing that Gaita learns from the nun's example: not only what it takes to enact the ideal of a common humanity, but also the significance that this value can hold in a human life. Suppose we imagine another kind of rational creature, whose mode of embodiment is very different from ours; and suppose that this creature is also committed to the ideal of full equality between members of its kind. Let us assume, in addition, that this creature has a relatively limited gestural range, and that the ideal of full equality can be embodied in interactions between creatures of this nature only rarely. Their bodily encounters standardly connote, let us suppose, neither respect nor disrespect, but are simply neutral in this regard, for the reason that the inflexions of their bodies lack the expressive depth and nuance of human facial and gestural movements.

The ideal of equality would play a very different role in the life of such a creature from the role it plays in our lives. This ideal makes a pervasive claim upon human beings: given the expressive depth of the human bodily form, we are at risk of failing to treat our fellow human beings with due respect in each of our interactions with them, and equally in each of those interactions, we have the opportunity, at least in principle, to behave in ways that connote, in bodily terms, regard for the other person as fully our equal. So the ideal of equality has a particular significance in the lives of human beings that it need not have, it would seem, in the lives of rational creatures whose embodiment takes a different form. And perhaps this too is part of the insight that Gaita wins in his observation of the nun: part of what Gaita is describing is, arguably, his shocked recognition of the significance of the ideal of equality in a human life, and how easy it is to fall into forms of behaviour that connote not respect but condescension, or some other attitude that falls short of respect.

So far in this chapter, we have been exploring two ways of drawing out Gaita's example of the nun: first, by noting some points of resemblance between Gaita's handling of this example and Aquinas's account of neighbour love, and secondly by examining the implications of the example of the nun for the idea that for a rounded appreciation of the character of a given spiritual tradition, we need to supplement metaphysical and experiential accounts of its nature with an understanding of the bodily demeanour that is appropriate to the tradition's core values. To conclude this chapter, let us return to the theme of spiritual goods, and consider the relevance of bodily demeanour for the constitution of hybrid goods in particular.

Bodily Demeanour and Spiritual Goods

In Chapter 1, we examined the idea that the goodness or appropriateness of some spiritual practices consists, at least in part, in their being existentially congruent with their metaphysical context. In Chapter 3, we extended this account, by noting how it is not only bodily practices (such as habits of food consumption) that can be assessed for adequacy relative to a given metaphysical context but, in addition, our world-directed experience. It seems plausible to suppose, for example, that if a Christian is to practise abstinence, then it is not only their consumption of food that needs to take the right form, but also their experience of food, and the other objects of the bodily appetites, so that they experience food and these other objects in ways that befit their relationship to God. Having considered in recent pages various way of connecting neighbour love, as Aquinas understands it, and Gaita's example of the nun, it is natural to wonder whether we can further extend Aquinas's account of neighbour love, and the other infused moral virtues, by taking bodily demeanour to be more or less congruent with our metaphysical context. Let us turn to this matter now.

Religious communities are commonly concerned to regulate the disposition of the body in worship and other devotional contexts. There are also, of course, iconographical traditions which take a keen interest in the representation of the posture and facial expressions of figures of acknowledged sanctity, such as the Buddha and Christ. Or again, we might think of depictions of the annunciation, and the attention to the inflexions of Mary's body that is evident in a picture such as Botticelli's Cestello Annunciation.[17] It is worth distinguishing this kind of interest in the comportment of the body from the kind that we encountered in our discussion of neighbour love in earlier chapters.

If I am to treat someone as my neighbour, then in relevant circumstances, I need to show them beneficence; and in standard cases, beneficent action will require that I move my body appropriately. For instance, love of neighbour may require me to offer someone a drink, and to do that I may need to extend them a cup of water. Here, the movements of my body turn out to be appropriate, relative to theological context, in so far as they are morally efficacious. But the interest in the body that is evident in, for instance, depictions of the annunciation does not seem to be of this kind, where the focus is upon the beneficial consequences of my action. In the case where I hold out a cup of water, there is no interest in the body as such: all that matters is that its motions should secure the desired moral outcome. By contrast, in his representation of the annunciation, Botticelli's interest is evidently in the gracefulness that is displayed in the inflexions of Mary's body: it is the gracefulness of her demeanour relative to the relevant theological context that marks out her response as fitting. Here, and similarly in depictions of, say, Christ or the Buddha, attention is fixed not on the body's role in bringing about good outcomes, but on its capacity to register directly, in bodily terms, the significance of a religious context. Let us mark this

[17] A reproduction of the painting is available at: https://www.virtualuffizi.com/the-cestello-annunciation-by-sandro-botticelli.html, accessed 28 January 2019.

distinction by talking on the one side of 'behaviour' and on the other of 'bodily demeanour'.

Thomas Aquinas's account of neighbour love invites us to suppose that a person's thoughts, feelings, attitudes, and desires, and in the relevant sense behaviour, are all open to assessment as more or less adequate relative to theological context. But his discussion, and standard treatments of the idea of neighbour love, do not, so far as I can see, touch on this further way in which a person's dealings with the world may turn out to be appropriate relative to theological context. So by introducing the notion of bodily demeanour, we can, potentially, identify a further kind of hybrid good, in addition to those that are involved in Thomas's account of the infused moral virtues.

There is some discussion of related matters in the philosophical and theological tradition. For instance, C. S. Lewis remarks that the 'new' humanity of Christians is evident in their bodily demeanour, suggesting that: 'Their very voices and faces are different from ours; stronger, quieter, happier, more radiant.'[18] While he does not address the point directly, it seems clear that Lewis takes this transformation in the bodily appearance of Christians to be appropriate not as a means to effecting some change in the world, but because this is a way of registering in bodily terms the sense of the Christian theological narrative: if a person subscribes to that narrative, then it is only right that they should greet the world, in bodily terms, in this spirit of quiet radiance.

Bodily comportment seems to play a similar role in other contexts, where it is the significance of an interpersonal context, rather than, directly, some metaphysical conception of the nature of things, that is acknowledged appropriately in the person's bodily demeanour. For instance, famously, bodily comportment, in the sense that concerns us here, is integral to Aristotle's account of the rightly 'proud' or great-souled man. As he says: 'a slow step is thought proper to the proud man, a deep voice, and a level utterance.'[19] Here too, a certain bodily demeanour is taken to be appropriate not because it is apt to bring about good outcomes, but as a way of registering the significance of the relevant

---

[18] C. S. Lewis, *Mere Christianity* (Glasgow: William Collins, Sons & Co., 1944), p. 186.
[19] *Nicomachean Ethics*, Book IV, 3.

context: the 'great-souled' man is a person of superior accomplishments, and in his bearing, he enacts this truth about his capacity to manage his affairs on his own terms, and free from dependence on others. And of course, Gaita's discussion of the nun and her relationship to the patients also invites this sort of reading. As we have seen, what arrests the young Gaita's attention is 'the way she spoke to them, her facial expressions, the inflexions of her body'. Gaita comments that the nun's comportment towards the patients revealed their 'full humanity', and for him too, it seems that it is the movements of the body themselves, and their appropriateness relative to context, rather than their tendency to bring about good outcomes, that is the focus of interest.[20]

It is not too difficult to multiply examples of this kind. In Chapter 2, following Aquinas's discussion of infused temperance, we considered the ways in which a person's consumption of food and drink may be congruent with their theological context. And by extension, it seems reasonable to suppose that the bodily gestures relevant to the consumption of food can be judged as appropriate to the ideal of abstinence not only in so far as they involve ingesting food of the right kinds and the right amounts, but also in so far as the gestures themselves exhibit the requisite kind of grace. Snatching at food, for example, even if it involves no violation of the requirements of abstinence with respect to the kind or amount of food consumed, could still breach those requirements, in so far as this comportment is not properly attuned to the significance that food should hold given our theological context.[21] My references

---

[20] Raimond Gaita, *A Common Humanity*, p 18. We might be inclined to say that Gaita takes the bodily demeanour of the nun to be appropriate as an acknowledgement of the moral status of the patients. But that way of putting the matter would not be faithful to the strand of his thought which represents this sort of response as, at least in part, constituting the 'common humanity' of human beings, rather than simply recognizing it. Given his indebtedness to the work of Wittgenstein, we can be confident that when writing about the nun, Gaita was mindful of Wittgenstein's remark that 'the human body is the best picture of the human soul': *Philosophical Investigations*, tr. G. E. M. Anscombe (Oxford: Basil Blackwell, 1958), II, iv.

[21] Aquinas notes that gluttony concerns both 'the food we eat, and the eating thereof', and under the second heading, he comments that 'inordinate concupiscence is considered as to the consumption of food: either because one forestalls the proper time for eating, which is to eat "hastily", or one fails to observe the due manner of eating, by eating "greedily"' (ST 2a2ae. 148. 4, tr. Fathers of the English Dominican Province, New York: Benziger Brothers, 1947). Here we find the beginnings of an account of how a person's manner of eating can be spiritually significant, and not only the amount and kind of food that they consume.

to worship, and depictions of the saints or of a scene such as the annunciation, may have suggested that the interest of spiritual traditions in bodily demeanour extends only to certain special individuals, or to rather restricted domains of thought and action. But as the case of food consumption indicates, and as the examples I have drawn from Lewis, Aristotle, and Gaita confirm, ideals of bodily comportment can, in fact, be applied very readily in our everyday relations with the material world, and other people, where those ideals derive, once again, from the relevant relations of congruence.

In sum, we can elaborate on Aquinas's account of the goods of the infused moral virtues by supposing that a person's demeanour, as well as their behaviour, can be deemed more or less adequate relative to their theological context. In our discussion in Chapter 3 of hybrid goods involving experience, I suggested that some such goods will be aesthetic goods. And it is natural to suppose that some hybrid goods involving bodily demeanour will also have an aesthetic character. Let's take again Botticelli's depiction of the annunciation. Here, the inflexions of Mary's body constitute a fitting response to the relevant theological context, that is, the context that is presented to Mary in the angel's address. And the resulting hybrid good has, it seems, inherently an aesthetic dimension. Why? Because the appropriateness of Mary's demeanour is in part a matter of its being a graceful acknowledgement of the angel's address. Of course, from a purely secular point of view, it will also be evident that her demeanour is graceful. But in this scene, there is, in addition, a further kind of beauty, one which cannot be identified independently of reference to the relevant theological context. Why? Because this kind of beauty arises in so far as the disposition of Mary's body presents a graceful response to that context.

As we saw in Chapter 3, in his discussion of the goals of the religious way of life, Richard Swinburne notes how certain activities which will count as aesthetically valuable independently of reference to any theological context (activities such as 'beautifying the universe' and displaying 'artistic creativity') can acquire an additional dimension of goodness once we introduce a theistic context—for granted such a context, these activities will be able to realize further goods, such as the good of satisfying an obligation to God as our benefactor, which could not otherwise obtain.[22] By contrast, in the case of the annunciation scene, as in the case of the hybrid goods involving experience that we considered in Chapter 3, it seems that the additional good that arises in relation to the relevant theological context is itself aesthetic. It is not just that the gracefulness that is evident in Mary's enacted response to the angel's address will be additionally good if there is a God—say, because it will then satisfy an obligation to God, or in some way contribute to her friendship with God. Rather, we should say that if there is a God, then the inflexions of Mary's body will realize an additional aesthetic good, because they will now count as graceful not only for the reasons that are evident from a secular perspective, but also considered as an acknowledgement of the theological context that is disclosed in the angel's address.

So here is a further way in which we can extend Aquinas's discussion of the goods of the infused moral virtues, namely, by recognizing that bodily demeanour, and not only bodily 'behaviour', can stand in a relation of existential congruence to theological context. Allowing for the similarity in the character of the goods that are realized by bodily demeanour, on the one hand, and the appearance of the everyday world, on the other (to the extent that both kinds of good are inherently aesthetic hybrid goods), there remain some differences between these two cases. In the annunciation scene, the relevant beauty rests on the body's agency: it is as minded and purposeful, rather than simply as a set of movements, that the inflexions of Mary's body count as a graceful, and therefore beautiful, acknowledgement of the angel's address. By contrast, from the convert's perspective, the new-found beauty they find in the world, following conversion, does not appear to follow from anything they have done, but seems, on the contrary, to result from God's agency, at work in them. Moreover, in this case, the beauty that is encountered in the world is taken to be beautiful, at least in part, because translucent to the divine beauty. And there is no parallel for this relationship in the annunciation scene, where the beauty in the inflexions of Mary's body, although theologically grounded, can be identified independently of any

---

[22] See Swinburne, 'The Christian Scheme of Salvation', in Michael Rea (ed.), *Oxford Readings in Philosophical Theology*, vol. 1: *Trinity, Incarnation and Atonement* (Oxford: Oxford University Press, 2009), pp. 304–5.

reference to the divine beauty. So while the relevant value is aesthetic in character and has a theological structure in each of these cases, there remain some notable differences.

The Spiritual Significance of Art

Given this account of the inherently aesthetic character of some hybrid goods, it is natural to consider what might follow for an appreciation of the spiritual importance of the arts—and especially those arts that are concerned in some way with the depiction of the human body. Let us turn now to two views on these matters that have been propounded in the recent literature in theological aesthetics. Having introduced these approaches, I shall then return to the broadly Thomistic understanding of aesthetic value that we have been sketching in this chapter, and consider how this account offers a rather different understanding of the relationship between aesthetic goods and theological commitments.

In the following passage, Jeremy Begbie is discussing the figure of Christ on the cross, and considering how even such a figure can be considered beautiful:

> in and through this particular torture, crucifixion and death, God's love is displayed at its most potent. The 'form' of beauty here is the radiant, splendid form of God's self-giving love. As Cardinal Ratzinger...put it: 'in his Face that is so disfigured, there appears the genuine, extreme beauty: the beauty of love that goes to the end.'[23]

On this account, despite being twisted and distorted, the face of the crucified Christ is properly regarded as beautiful—indeed, it is to be reckoned as beautiful precisely in its twistedness, in so far as Christ's self-sacrificial love is made manifest in his disfigured appearance. Here, the notion of beauty is being moralized: even if a body is by

---

[23] Jeremy Begbie, 'Beauty, Sentimentality and the Arts', in D. Treier, M. Husbands, and R. Lundin (eds), *The Beauty of God: Theology and the Arts* (Downers Grove, IL: IVP Academic, 2006), p. 63.

conventional aesthetic standards an object of horror rather than aesthetic attraction, it can still be deemed beautiful, if it discloses the beauty of an edifying moral purpose. Ratzinger's comments suggest, indeed, that Christ's example does not simply illustrate the nature of true love, and true moral beauty, but serves as the paradigm case of such love, by providing the standard against which other examples are to be judged. Similarly, Begbie writes as follows of James MacMillan's representation of the events of Easter morning in his work *Triduum*:

> The 'resolution' enacted in *Symphony: Vigil* neither effaces the harshness of the memories of the preceding days nor accords them any kind of ultimacy... Its beauty is anything but tidy; the forms overlap, material is scattered, dropped and picked up again...[24]

On Begbie's account, when measured against a Christological aesthetic standard, MacMillan's piece is aesthetically excellent, since it mirrors the ragged, 'untidy' kind of beauty that is evident in the New Testament account of the days leading up to Easter morning. So here again, we are concerned with a moral ideal of beauty, which is realized primordially in the Jesus story—only in this case, that beauty is reproduced in musical rather than visual form.

Although he does not develop his example in these terms, it is natural to ask whether Gaita's discussion of the nun is open to being read in this same way. Gaita is evidently struck by the 'inflexions of the nun's body' and by 'her facial expressions'—and he appears to be fascinated by her comportment. We might infer, then, that he finds a kind of beauty, or aesthetic allure, in her conduct. And following Begbie's examples, we could understand this idea by supposing that a moral value, here the ideal of our common humanity, in some way shines through her gestures, so that they are perceived as morally beautiful.

So in Begbie's comments, we find one conception of beauty, and its spiritual import, to set alongside the Thomistically inspired account that we have been examining. Let's consider now a further account of these matters. In the following text, George Pattison is discussing a video

---

[24] Ibid., p. 68.

installation which was located for a time next to the baptismal font of Durham Cathedral. The video, entitled 'The Messenger', depicts a naked man sinking down through a body of shimmering water, until lost from view, before returning gradually to the surface, so that his form comes slowly into focus once again. This cycle lasts about thirty minutes, and is then repeated. The artist, Bill Viola, was commissioned to produce the installation for this site, but did not intend his work to bear any specifically Christian doctrinal meaning. Pattison comments:

> Although Viola himself is informed more by Buddhist than by Christian spirituality, the work projects itself almost effortlessly towards Christian appropriation precisely because of its use of a language before language that is the primary matrix of symbolic formation and that is shared by Christian and non-Christian art alike.[25]

Pattison's suggestion is that when seeking to apprehend the religious import of an artwork, we should first of all appreciate the work simply for itself, by attending to its sensory qualities, and bracketing out any theological or other interpretive frame. When we approach the work in this mode, we are reliant upon what he calls in this passage, following an expression he has borrowed from the sculptor Antony Gormley, the 'language before language' of the body: it is in the body's preverbal, pre-discursive responses to the work that we apprehend its primordial meaning. In this case, the bodily impact of this sequence of images, of the man sinking through the water and then returning to the surface, produces in the viewer thoughts of drowning, of death and rebirth, and perhaps also of cleansing, independently of reference to any culturally specific interpretive lens. In these ways, according to Pattison, a work of art can communicate a meaning to us, non-verbally, and in that sense, it can function as a 'language before language'. Here, as for a number of the other examples that Pattison discusses, what is communicated in the work is the universal, bodily significance of the elemental constituents of the sensory world—in this case, water.[26]

---

[25] George Pattison, *Art Modernity and Faith* (London: SCM, 1998), p. 185.
[26] For a similar approach, see Pattison's treatment of, for example, Antony Gormley's sculpture *Sound II*, located in the crypt of Winchester Cathedral: ibid, pp. 182–4.

According to Pattison, we are then to take a second interpretive step, by reading the work in terms of the categories of a particular cultural or religious tradition. To return to this same example, we can understand Viola's work by reference to specifically Christian categories, and the significance that water bears in the Christian rite of baptism, as an instrument of spiritual cleansing and rebirth. Pattison's suggestion is that the religious power of a work for a given religious tradition is apparent when we consider how this second phase of interpretation relates to the first. When apprehended in terms of the language before language of the body, The Messenger discloses the elemental significance of water for creatures such as ourselves, and the work's specifically Christian import is then evident when this same scene is understood in terms of the categories of the Christian narrative of baptism. It is the directness of the fit between these two readings of the video, the pre-discursive and the doctrinally articulated, that allows the work to speak, as Pattison says, 'almost effortlessly' into a specifically Christian cultural context. And in turn, the relative effortlessness of this communication indicates the spiritual suggestiveness or potency of Viola's work from a Christian point of view.

So on this account, works of art can contribute to the spiritual life by grounding spiritual ideals, such as cleansing and rebirth, in the life of the body, and its primordial sensitivity to the fundamental constituents of the sensory world, such as water. Or to put the point another way, Viola's work has a spiritual resonance because it sensitizes us to the elemental significance of water for human beings, and thereby prepares the way for a deepened appreciation of the symbolic meanings of water when used in, for example, the rite of baptism.

We have now sketched three conceptions of the contribution of the arts and, more broadly, aesthetic values to the spiritual life: those of Begbie and Pattison, and the Thomistically informed perspective that I have expounded with reference to Botticelli's Cestello annunciation. As we have seen, these accounts share an interest in the spiritual and aesthetic significance of the human body. Let's consider next how each understands the relationship between spiritual and aesthetic values.

Begbie's account and the account we have been exploring by reference to Aquinas are alike in supposing that there is a kind of beauty in the human body that can be discerned only from the vantage point of the relevant theological frame. On Begbie's account, that frame is provided by the story of Jesus, which generates a distinctively theological measure of aesthetic value, which in turn makes it possible to find a kind of beauty even in a twisted and distorted body, in so far as it is relevantly Christ-like. Here, the introduction of a theological frame has the effect of displacing more conventional measures of aesthetic excellence, which would yield a very different verdict in this case. The Thomistic account we have been considering differs on this point, since it retains conventional aesthetic categories such as gracefulness. On this approach, the theological frame does not challenge our established measures of aesthetic value, but instead provides a new and expanded context within which those measures may be deployed. For instance, in the Cestello annunciation scene, Mary's demeanour can be seen as graceful from a purely secular point of view, but appears as additionally graceful once we have introduced the relevant theological frame. So here the introduction of a theological perspective results in a deepening of the aesthetic judgement we would anyway be inclined to make, whereas on Begbie's approach, that perspective seems to overturn the aesthetic judgement we would otherwise make.

While Begbie's approach starts from a theological frame, Pattison's account of aesthetic value invites us, as a first step, to set aside theological and other reference points, and to consider the artwork in terms simply of its import for the body. We might see this procedure as somewhat reminiscent of Aquinas's appeal, when discussing the virtues, to a 'rule of reason': after all, Pattison is proposing that, in the first instance, we are to understand the artwork solely on the basis of our humanity, and independently of any culturally, or theologically, specific frame of reference. However, Pattison is concerned with an assessment of the work that is, at first, simply bodily in character, rather than being ordered in discursive or conceptual terms, and in this respect, his approach clearly remains distinct from that of Aquinas.

Once we have appreciated the work in these terms, Pattison suggests, we can then introduce, as a second interpretive step, a theological frame of reference. This move may sound rather like Thomas's account of the way in which the infused moral virtues build on the acquired virtues, rather than displacing them. But again, the two accounts are also significantly different. For Pattison, a work seems to count as theologically fruitful in so far as it introduces, via the first phase of interpretation, various humanly universal themes, such as death, birth, and bodily vulnerability, which can then be further specified in theological terms. Following our discussion, we might add that a work can be more or less rich theologically, depending on the closeness of fit between these universal themes and the concerns of a given theological tradition. On this view, the theological significance of the work depends most fundamentally on its capacity to lead us into a conventional theological subject matter, through a set of thoughts that are elicited in the first instance by the work's pre-theoretical, pre-discursive impact upon the senses. For example, Viola's installation discloses the primal significance of water in human life, and thereby lends itself to theological appropriation, since theological perspectives on the import of water can be grafted onto this pre-discursive apprehension of its role in a human life.

So we should say that on Pattison's view, the introduction of a theological frame does not establish a new set of aesthetic values, but simply enables the further specification of various theologically suggestive themes that are elicited in our initial encounter with the artwork. That initial encounter will have an aesthetic focus in so far as it involves an appreciation of the work in sensory terms and for itself, that is, independently of any framing narrative.[27] So to this extent, Pattison's narrative is concerned with aesthetic values, but once again, the introduction of a theological frame does not evidently deepen our appreciation of, say, water in aesthetic terms, but instead allows us simply to elaborate on the sense in which water is, for instance, a source of cleansing.

By contrast, on the broadly Thomistic view we have been exploring, the introduction of a theological frame will make a difference to our assessment of the work in aesthetic terms. To revert to our earlier example, once we have introduced the relevant theological context, we can find a new beauty in Mary's demeanour, as represented by Botticelli. So we

---

[27] For an account of why this sort of stance counts, for some traditions, as 'aesthetic', see Nicholas Wolterstorff, 'Art and the Aesthetic: The Religious Dimension', in P. Kivy (ed.), *The Blackwell Guide to Aesthetics* (Oxford: Blackwell, 2004), ch. 18.

could formulate the difference between Pattison's approach and the Thomistically informed perspective that we have been developing here by saying that on the first account, aesthetic values, of the kind that are evident from a secular vantage point, serve as a route into theological themes, whereas on the second account, theological themes serve as a route into aesthetic values which are theologically grounded and therefore not discernible from a secular vantage point.

In these ways, each of these approaches offers a set of recommendations for understanding the spiritual import of a work of art. Think, for instance, of any traditional depiction of the annunciation, say, Fra Filippo Lippi's picture that hangs in the National Gallery in London.[28] If we read this image in the style of Begbie, then we will take as our focus the resemblance between Mary's demeanour and the attitudes we might associate with the historical Jesus. For instance, perhaps we will take her downward gaze and slightly stooped figure to express a Christ-like humility, and to be beautiful for this reason. Or again, if adopting this reading, we might be struck by the way in which Mary's gestures give physical form to the sentiment expressed in her words when she remarks 'be it unto me according to thy word' (Luke 1:38 King James Version); and we might, therefore, see the disposition of her body as an anticipation of Christ's submission to the will of the Father in his passion and death. If, on the other hand, we follow Pattison, then we will bracket out any reference to theological context, and attend first of all to the play of shapes and colours on the canvas, and only then introduce theological categories, in order to elaborate on the themes that are suggested by the bodily impact of the work.[29]

By contrast with these other approaches, on the Thomistic account we have been considering, Mary's gestures are gracefully adapted to a particular theological context, and additionally graceful for that reason. Independently of that context, we could still see those gestures as beautiful by reference to the usual standards of aesthetic excellence, and

---

[28] A reproduction of the painting is available at: https://www.nationalgalleryimages.co.uk/imagedetails.aspx?q=NG666&ng=NG666&frm=1, accessed 28 January 2019.

[29] Compare Pattison's treatment of Craigie Aitchison's *Crucifixion 1994*. Despite its overtly religious subject matter, he seeks to read the picture in the first instance independently of any theological frame: *Art, Modernity and Faith*, pp. 186–8.

perhaps as morally beautiful, in so far as they connote humility. But from this Thomistic perspective, it is only when we know the theological context within which Mary is acting, and know, for instance, the content of the angel's message, that we can grasp in full the beauty of these very gestures, and see how they bear a certain gravity, and exhibit a certain grace, as responses to this particular theological context. So this approach occupies a middle ground between the others: it allows for a distinctively theological assessment of aesthetic value (here like Begbie), while at the same time affirming our conventional aesthetic standards (here like Pattison).

These three approaches to the spiritual significance of the arts need not be in competition with one another: as we have just seen, a given artwork can be read in all three ways, without falling into contradiction. And it may well be that some works will lend themselves more readily to one kind of construal, and others to another. Following on from our discussion in earlier chapters, what I hope to have shown here is that Aquinas's account of infused moral virtue is important not only for an appreciation of the spiritual significance of our world-directed thoughts, attitudes, behaviour and experience, but also for an understanding of the contribution of bodily demeanour to the spiritual life. Many spiritual traditions promise, at least implicitly, to bring their adherents not simply to a condition of right belief, and right experience, but to a state wherein their very bodies become transparent to a transcendent value. In this discussion, we have been trying to consider how that might be.

Concluding Thoughts

This chapter has had three broadly defined aims. First of all, I have tried to sketch a new vantage point on neighbour love considered as an infused virtue, to support the metaphysical and experiential perspectives on the virtue that we developed in earlier chapters. Aquinas does not consider what kind of bodily demeanour is required if the ideal of neighbour love is to be enacted by a creature with our particular kind of embodiment. And in the ways we have explored, Gaita's example of the nun allows us to provide at least a sketch of the relevant kind of demeanour, although not, of course, to represent that demeanour in all its gesturally specific detail. While some features of his example may be open to dispute, Gaita is surely right to suppose that there is a logical gap between, on the one hand, understanding the core values of a tradition, where those values are expressed in relatively generic terms, using phrases such as 'human dignity' or 'a common humanity', and on the other, understanding the particular bodily comportment that is required for the enactment of those values. And to give a rounded account of the various dimensions of a given spiritual tradition, it is necessary, therefore, to allude not only to its world view, and the generic ideals of life that can be specified by reference to that world view, but also to the particular quality of bodily demeanour that is integral to the living out of the tradition in practical terms.

Secondly, I have tried to establish how it is possible for bodily demeanour to bear this sort of significance, by employing once again Aquinas's account of the goods that are the object of the infused moral virtues—what we have been calling hybrid goods. As we have seen, while Aquinas does not consider hybrid goods of this kind, it seems that the theoretical structure that he develops can be invoked to understand not only the spiritual significance of our world-directed thoughts, desires, experience, and morally efficacious behaviour, but also the importance for the spiritual life of the disposition of the body, or what we have termed bodily 'demeanour', in distinction from mere behaviour.

Finally, I have tried to show how this appreciation of the spiritual significance of bodily comportment suggests a new perspective on the aesthetic dimension of the spiritual life, to set alongside familiar models of the kind advanced in the recent literature in theological aesthetics. Hence a further, related objective of the discussion has been to develop an understanding of the attractiveness, and in particular the aesthetic allure, of the saintly life.

5

The Epistemic Significance of Tradition

Introduction

In the course of earlier chapters, I have often used the phrase 'spiritual traditions'—and implied in this expression is of course the idea that, typically, the thoughts, practices, and experiences that constitute particular forms of the spiritual life are not simply static but develop over time. The aim of the current chapter is to consider more closely the traditioned character of the spiritual life, and the nature and source of change in the conceptions and habits of action and experience that define particular forms of spiritual commitment. Two familiar themes from earlier chapters will be particularly relevant for this discussion: first of all, the idea that, in some central cases, spiritual goods are relative to metaphysical context; and secondly, the idea that spiritual traditions can be understood from different vantage points—from what we can call, following our earlier usage, the perspectives of metaphysics, experience, and enacted example.

On one natural account, the revealed truths that are disclosed in some founding event or text are to be communicated to others, or 'handed on', and the role of tradition is, then, to preserve these foundational truths as they are passed from one person to another. (The English word 'tradition' derives, of course, from the Latin 'tradere', meaning 'to hand on'.) Given an account of this structure, it is natural to suppose that the epistemically interesting category is really revelation—since the role of tradition is simply to recapitulate what has already been established in revelation. I am going to argue that this construal of the role of tradition is unduly narrow. I shall start by noting two more expansive conceptions

Spiritual Traditions and the Virtues: Living Between Heaven and Earth. Mark R. Wynn, Oxford University Press (2020).
© Mark R. Wynn.
DOI: 10.1093/oso/9780198862949.001.0001

of the part that tradition might play in the transmission of religious or spiritual teachings, before developing a further proposal that is rooted in our earlier discussion of infused moral virtue. In later parts of the chapter, I shall broaden the discussion to include not only religious teaching, but also the experiences and demeanours that define particular forms of the spiritual life. Let us begin by considering the account of these matters that is at least implied in the intellectual practice of Anselm and Thomas Aquinas.[1]

An Anselmian Perspective on Tradition

In his Preface to the *Proslogion*, Saint Anselm notes that he had intended to give this work the title 'Faith in Quest of Understanding', and his earlier work the *Monologion* the title 'An Example of Meditation on the Meaning of Faith'—and both titles reflect the tenor of his approach to theological enquiry.[2] On this view, we are to begin from 'faith', or a particular construal of the content of revelation, and work from there to an account of other matters. So on this Anselmian model, we might think of tradition not as a matter of adapting the content of revelation so that it will fit our developing secular understanding of the world, but as an ongoing meditation on the data of revelation considered in themselves, so as to draw out their meaning and implications.

Let's take an example of this general approach. For Anselm, it was of course a datum of revelation that God is, among other things, living, wise, and powerful. And in the *Monologion*, he proposes that, by the exercise of reason, we can discover a further divine property, one that is

---

[1] Here we are concerned with the importance of tradition for an understanding of the data of revelation, and what it takes to live appropriately relative to those data. In his justly influential account of traditions of moral enquiry, Alasdair MacIntyre has been occupied with some related questions, and his approach is, I take it, broadly consonant with the perspective developed here. See for instance his remarks on how our understanding of the goods internal to practices, such as portraiture, can be extended over time, and on Aquinas's work as an integration of Aristotelian and Augustinian traditions. These themes are explored in, respectively, *After Virtue: A Study in Moral Theory* (London: Bloomsbury, 3rd edn, 2007), ch. 14, and *Three Rival Versions of Moral Enquiry: Encyclopedia, Genealogy, and Tradition* (London: Duckworth, 1990), ch. v.

[2] *Proslogion*, in *Anselm of Canterbury: The Major Works*, ed. Brian Davies and G. R. Evans (Oxford: Oxford University Press, 1998), p. 83.

not disclosed directly in revelation, but which accords with, and indeed
helps to explain, the divine properties that are presented, directly, in
revelation. This further property is the meta-property of being whatever
it is in all cases better to be than not to be. (To adapt one of Anselm's
examples, being gold is not such a property, because while it is a perfection in a coin, being gold is not a perfection in a human being.[3] By contrast, Anselm suggests, it is in all cases better to be wise.[4]) For present
purposes, we don't need to rehearse Anselm's argument for the claim
that 'the supreme essence is alive, wise, all-powerful, true, just, happy,
eternal... and whatever is likewise better without qualification than not-
whatever', that is, whatever it is in all cases better to be than not to be.[5]
What is significant is that Anselm claims hereby to have arrived at a
deepened insight into the data of revelation. We already knew from
Scripture that God is living, wise, and powerful. But now we see that
these properties are not just isolated attributes, but bound together in so
far as they are all logically entailed by a truth concerning what God is:
namely, that God is whatever it is in all cases better to be than not to be.
And of course, having identified this meta-property, of being x for every
x which is such that in all cases it is better to be x than not to be x,
Anselm is also in a position, in principle, to ascribe further first-order
properties to God, in addition to those disclosed in Scripture, on the
grounds that these properties also satisfy the condition of being such
that it is in all cases better to be in that way.[6]

So if we take Anselm's practice as our guide, we should say that
Christian theologians can elaborate on the data of revelation in two
related ways. First, they can identify the logical structure that informs, at
least implicitly, the claims of revelation. In the instance we have just

[3] *Monologion*, ibid., ch. 15, p. 27. The background thought here is that being human is a
higher form of existence than being gold.
[4] Hence Anselm writes: 'Omne quippe non sapiens simpliciter, inquantum non sapiens est,
minus est quam sapiens; quia omne non sapiens melius esset, si esset sapiens', ibid., ch. 15,
available at: http://www.logicmuseum.com/authors/anselm/monologion/anselm-monologion%
2015-17.htm, accessed 28 January 2019.
[5] Ibid., ch. 15, p. 28, ellipsis in the translation. The Latin text reads: 'Quare necesse est eam
esse viventem, sapientem, potentem et omnipotentem, veram, iustam, beatam, aeternam, et
quidquid similiter absolute melius est quam non ipsum.'
[6] One example of such a property might be necessary existence. See Anselm's discussion in
Proslogion, ch. 3.

discussed, this is a matter of seeing that the various properties ascribed to God in Scripture can be explained by God's possession of a further, meta-property, where this property is not itself ascribed to God, at least not directly, in Scripture. And secondly, theologians can elaborate on the data supplied by Scripture, by seeing how a given reading of the structure of the data of revelation gives us a reason to affirm claims that are not themselves made in Scripture. To take the same example, once we recognize that Scripture is committed, at least implicitly, to thinking of God as being whatever it is in all cases better to be, we can then conclude that further properties may be attributed to God, properties which are not mentioned in Scripture, but which we are logically required to ascribe to God, once we have supposed that God is whatever it is in all cases better to be.

So as it is enacted in Anselm's thought, tradition plays the dual role of identifying the interconnectedness of the data of revelation, and showing how we might extrapolate from those data to consider further matters that are not addressed directly in the scriptural text. On this approach, we can say that relative to an initial deposit of 'revelation', tradition has an ordering and also an extrapolative or projective function, and not simply a recapitulative function. As Anselm's example indicates, these roles are connected: it is by virtue of arriving at a new ordering of the data of revelation that we can understand more clearly their implications.

So here is one way in which tradition may involve more than the mere reiteration of the data of revelation. Let us consider now a further way in which tradition may be able to play this more expansive kind of role.

Thomas Aquinas as an Exemplar of Tradition-Informed Reflection

As embedded in Aquinas's theological practice, 'tradition' has to do not so much with the elaboration of the data of revelation considered in themselves, as in Anselm, but, rather, with the question of how Christian revelation is to be articulated in a radically new, and potentially subversive, intellectual context. With the emergence in Latin translation of various of the works of Aristotle in the twelfth and thirteenth centuries, the Christian world view found itself with a possible rival, which was capable of addressing all the central topics of Christian theology in its own terms—by reference to Aristotle's thoughts on metaphysics, physics, philosophy of mind, and ethics. In this respect, Thomas's intellectual context is rather reminiscent of our own. In our time, the apparently comprehensive world view that promises to address all the central themes of Christian theology is, of course, natural science, broadly conceived so as to include, for example, evolutionary psychology—and given this parallel, a consideration of how tradition functions in Aquinas's work is evidently of more than antiquarian interest.

I am going to take two examples of how Aquinas engages with this newly re-discovered Aristotelian world view. Perhaps the most striking feature of Aquinas's procedure in these circumstances is his willingness to articulate the fundamental claims of Christian theology in the terms provided by the conceptual framework of the Aristotelian tradition. For example, in the First of the Five Ways, in *Summa Theologiae* 1a. 2. 3, Thomas sets out a proof for the existence of God which tracks the proof that Aristotle had given in Book Lambda of the *Metaphysics*: for Aquinas as for Aristotle, God is to be understood as the unchanging source of change.[7] Given simply the text of the First Way, the reader would naturally suppose that by *potentia*, potentiality, here, Aquinas means exactly what Aristotle had meant by *dunamnis*. But the highly systematic character of the *Summa* means that, here as elsewhere, Aquinas's text has to be read in the light of what he says in later discussion. And in the immediately following question, in ST 1a. 3. 4, Aquinas considers whether God is 'composed of essence and existence'. In the second of the arguments that he develops in the body of the response, he writes that:

existence is that which makes every form or nature actual; for goodness and humanity are spoken of as actual, only because they are spoken of as existing. Therefore existence must be compared to essence, if the latter is a distinct reality, as actuality to potentiality. Therefore, since in God there is no potentiality, as shown above (Article [1]), it follows

---

[7] See Aristotle, *The Metaphysics*, tr. H. Lawson-Tancred (London: Penguin, 1998).

that in Him essence does not differ from existence. Therefore His essence is His existence.   (ST 1a. 3. 4)[8]

Aquinas appeals here to Article 1 of this same question to support the idea that there is no potentiality in God; and in turn that article directs the reader to Question 2, Article 3—that is, to the text of the Five Ways, and at least by implication to the First Way in particular, where Aquinas is concerned directly with the idea that there is no potentiality in God. But in Question 3, this idea has taken on a new significance, since it is now being taken to support not simply the thought that God is immutable, but the idea that in God there is no distinction between essence and existence. The underlying proposal is, evidently, that if a thing's existence is distinct from its essence or nature, then the thing will not exist by nature, with the consequence that it will depend for its existence upon a cause—which is to say that the thing's nature stands in need of actualization. But of course, we cannot think of God, who is the Creator, in these terms, and accordingly we should suppose that there is no distinction of existence and essence in God or, to put the matter otherwise, that God exists by nature, or simply by virtue of what God is.

Whatever we make of this line of argument, it is clear that the notion of potentiality is here being stretched, as it is employed in a new intellectual context, to articulate a distinctively Christian affirmation, one that Aristotle did not assert or even entertain: namely, the claim that the existence of all things, with the sole exception of God, involves the actualization of the relevant nature's potential to exist, so that God is the source not only of change in things, but also of their very being. Given the role that this argument gives to the idea that there is no potentiality in God, it is clear that we need to go back to the First Way, and read Aquinas's claim that there is no potentiality in God, as it is developed there, in the requisite way. In other words, when Aquinas says when developing the First Way that there is no 'potentiality' in God, we need to take that claim to be relevant not just to the possibility of change in

---

[8] Tr. Fathers of the English Dominican Province (New York: Benziger Brothers, 1947). Unless otherwise indicated, I shall follow this translation in later quotations.

God, but also to the possibility of there being any 'distinction' in God between existence and essence.

Aquinas's deploys the notion of potentiality in a further context when he considers the Trinitarian nature of God in *Summa Theologiae* 1a. 27. From his use of the notion in 1a. 3. 4, one might well have concluded that the existence of the Son, and also of the Spirit, requires the actualization of a potentiality. After all, in orthodox Christian teaching, which Aquinas of course upholds, the Son is said to 'proceed' from the Father; and it seems natural to conclude that the Son's existence must therefore involve the actualization of this potential to proceed. Aquinas, of course, denies this, and to make sense of his stance on this point, we need to introduce a further refinement into the notion of potentiality.

On Aquinas's account of the matter, to say that the second person of the Trinity proceeds from the first is to say that there is self-understanding in God.[9] And it is of course essential to God that there should be self-understanding in God. It follows, then, that the second person of the Trinity exists by nature, because it is God's nature both to exist and to understand God. So when Aquinas maintains that the existence of the second person does not involve the actualization of a potentiality, since there is no potentiality in God, he is saying not that the second person does not derive, in some sense, from the first, but that this derivation does not compromise the claim of the second person to exist by nature, since it is the Father's nature to exist, and also the Father's nature to generate the Son, so that the Son, as well as the Father, exists by virtue of what He is.[10] So here the denial of potentiality turns out to amount to the denial that the Son's existence is contingent, in the sense of not being guaranteed by His nature.

---

[9] See for instance his comment: 'For it is clear that the more a thing is understood, the more closely is the intellectual conception joined and united to the intelligent agent; since the intellect by the very act of understanding is made one with the object understood. Thus, as the divine intelligence is the very supreme perfection of God (Question [14], Article [2]), the divine Word is of necessity perfectly one with the source whence He proceeds, without any kind of diversity.' (ST 1a. 27. 1 ad 2). Here the Word proceeds from the Father, and is the divine understanding, the object of which is the Father.

[10] Again, the key text for the denial of potentiality in God is ST 1a. 2. 3, which is in turn picked up in the way we have noted in ST 1a. 3. 4. This claim is not retracted when Aquinas turns to discuss the Trinitarian nature of God.

So as he moves from Question 2 to Question 3, and then to Question 27 of the first part of the *Summa Theologiae*, Aquinas gradually elaborates on the notion of potentiality that he has inherited from Aristotle. In Question 2, considered in isolation from the remainder of his text, the notion of potentiality seems to be functioning exactly as it does in Aristotle, namely, as part of an explanation of how change in the world ultimately derives from a transcendent source that is devoid of change. But the later questions show that Aquinas wants to use this same notion to address questions that were of no concern to Aristotle—questions concerning God's role as creator, and God's Trinitarian nature. And to apply the notion of potentiality in these new domains, he needs to draw out its sense, in the ways that we have noted. What does this procedure tell us about Aquinas's understanding of the contribution of tradition in the handing on of an initial deposit of revelation?

Quite independently of his interest in the concept of potentiality, Aquinas anyway believes, of course, that God is the ultimate source of change, and that God is the creator and a Trinity. But in the *Summa*, he succeeds in articulating these familiar theological affirmations in terms of the favoured conceptual vocabulary of the best secular learning of the day. Aquinas's procedure in this respect suggests two general conclusions about tradition. First, it implies that the Christian theologian has a responsibility to make the claims of revelation intelligible to their contemporaries, so far as they can, which in turn issues in a requirement to articulate those claims using the concepts that are current in the intellectual culture of the time. There is a measure of intellectual humility and of charity in this approach: of humility in so far as others' concepts are given a certain precedence, as the theologian accommodates herself to their habits of thought, and of charity in so far as this exercise is motivated by a concern for the well-being of others, which is taken to depend on their capacity to understand the data of revelation.

Secondly, Aquinas's procedure reflects a certain confidence in the powers of secular reason, and in turn a certain conception of the relation between 'grace' and 'nature'. He is inviting us to suppose that if the best secular learning finds that the concept of potentiality is integral to a developed appreciation of the nature of things, then there is to that extent a reason to suppose that this concept will also be of use in theological enquiry. And implied in this conviction is the idea that secular reason is able to track the fundamental ordering of things, albeit that its vision is not, of course, comprehensive. Accordingly, it is also implied in Aquinas's approach that 'revealed' insights are not simply discontinuous with those that are available on the basis of 'natural' reason, but involve instead a kind of deepening or extension of those insights. Aquinas's handling of Aristotle's notion of potentiality provides a very direct illustration of how a concept drawn from secular enquiry can be elaborated by applying it to, and in turn adapting it to fit, new contexts of enquiry. And this reflects a wider truth: revelation does not overturn the findings of natural reason, or occupy some self-contained epistemic sphere that is sealed off from human understanding as it operates in other domains. Instead, revelation calls for the analogical extension of the concepts that are integral to the exercise of natural reason. Of course, not all theologians have subscribed to this view of the relation between revelation and the findings of natural reason: some have been more content with a picture of discontinuity, or even contradiction. But for those who share Aquinas's perspective, it will make sense to suppose that when trying to understand and to communicate the data of revelation, it should be possible to put to productive use the key concepts that have emerged in the course of our secular enquiries.

In sum, on this Thomistic approach, when theology encounters some newly developed secular conception of the nature of things, its response ought not to be one of simply recapitulating the data of revelation in terms of the concepts that are embedded in theological tradition. Its approach ought, rather, to be one of trying to articulate the import of the data of revelation by means of the concepts that are current in our best secular understanding of the world, where this exercise will involve, most likely, the analogical re-working of those concepts. So in this way, theological tradition draws on secular reason, without simply deferring to it: tradition borrows various concepts from secular thought, while at the same time stretching those concepts, as they are applied in the new intellectual context that is constituted by the Christian revelation. Along the way, of course, the theologian may discover a new unity in the Christian vision of the nature of things—as Aquinas arguably does when he discovers that the single notion of potentiality, when analogically extended, can be used to chart God's nature as the ultimate source of change, as creator, and as Trinity.

Although I have been talking of two Christian theologians—Anselm and Aquinas—their understanding of the role of tradition is easily generalized to other, non-Christian forms of religious life, where there is some initial 'deposit' of spiritual insight, or 'revelation', that is to be transmitted to later generations. In brief, if we follow Anselm, then we will suppose that the role of tradition is to identify the deep structure of revelation, so that its key themes can be extrapolated and projected into new contexts. And if we follow Aquinas, then we will think that tradition's role is to articulate the claims of revelation using concepts drawn from the best secular learning of the day. Anselm's approach in a way involves a movement from the perspective of revelation and into the world, as the data of revelation are newly organized, so that they can be applied to new questions—including, potentially, 'mundane' questions and not simply (as with the example I have given) questions concerning the divine nature. Aquinas's approach involves, in a way, a movement in the other direction, from an understanding of the world, and towards the perspective of revelation, as the concepts that are current in secular learning are used to order the data of revelation, so that the data become newly intelligible, through the analogical extension of the relevant concepts.

A Further Example of Tradition-Informed Reflection: Thomas Aquinas on the Moral Life

Let us consider now one further way of developing the idea that tradition's role is not simply one of reiterating insights that have already been established in some initial event of divine self-disclosure. For this account, I shall turn once more to the guiding category of this enquiry: Thomas Aquinas's conception of infused moral virtue. Since we have already examined that category at some length, I shall proceed relatively quickly, without pausing to record the nuances of Aquinas's position.

Aquinas reproduces Aristotle's understanding of the moral virtues, to the extent of allowing that virtues such as courage, justice, and temperance can be acquired by way of habituation. In this respect, his thought extends earlier theological traditions, which had been inclined to think of the virtues as what God 'works in us without us' (ST 1a2ae. 63. 2). So at this juncture, Aquinas's procedure is one of allowing secular learning to extend received theological opinion. His reasons for taking this approach are no doubt various, but his stance indicates once again a certain confidence in secular reason, and a willingness to defer to secular understanding where the subject matter is human nature and the ends of life that are relative to human nature.

But of course, at the same time, Aquinas retains the view, long inscribed in Christian tradition, that the theological virtues of faith, hope, and charity are 'infused', rather than acquired. He might have simply set this view alongside the Aristotelian view, so as to divide the virtues into two varieties—those that concern our relation to creatures, and those that are God-directed. And he could then have assigned one mode of production to the first and another to the second, by speaking of habituation and infusion respectively. And, in turn, he could have proposed one measure of success for the first and another for the second, namely, fulfilment of human nature and flourishing in relation to God. But characteristically, Aquinas wants a closer relation between the 'natural' and 'theological' narratives, and he finds a way of holding together these two kinds of virtue by supposing that in addition to the acquired moral virtues and the infused theological virtues, there is a further category of virtue, what he calls infused moral virtue. The role of virtues of this further kind is to relate us to creatures (hence they are 'moral' rather than 'theological') and at the same time to direct the person to God (hence the requirement that they should be 'infused' rather than grounded simply in our natural capacities) (ST 1a2ae. 63. 3). So the role of the infused moral virtues is to ensure that our world-directed habits of thought, feeling, and so on, are fitting not only relative to those ends of life that are proportionate to our human nature, but also relative to our ultimate goal of sharing in the life of God. So the infused moral virtues share their subject matter with the acquired moral virtues, and their teleology and mode of production with the theological virtues, and in this way serve as a kind of conceptual bridge between the Aristotelian and the theological virtues.[11]

Let us consider now the implications of this case for an account of the traditioned character of theological enquiry. While the example of potentiality may have suggested that, fundamentally, the role for innovation in the development of tradition is to find new formulations of familiar theological truths, this further example suggests that there is also a role for innovation in so far as developments in the secular sciences can lead to a significant extension in our theological understanding.

In the case we are considering, Aquinas follows Aristotle in supposing that there are acquired moral virtues. Here again, we see his commitment to the authority of secular enquiry in the domain of the simply human, that is, so far as human beings are considered independently of reference to their theological context. Granted this Aristotelian account, it is natural to ask, next, how these virtues are to be related to the theological virtues. That was not a question the tradition had put to itself, since formerly it did not have any use for the category of acquired moral virtue. But once that category has been introduced, there is a need to show how the acquired and theological virtues are to be related, assuming, once again, that we do not wish to think of God-referenced and world-referenced accounts of the good life as discontinuous. So here the unfolding of tradition involves not simply the re-articulation of the data of revelation in a new idiom, but a new insight into the relationship between the creaturely order as understood in the secular sciences and the data of revelation. In brief, on this approach, according a measure of

[11] We can see an anticipation of this teaching in Augustine's development of the *uti/frui* distinction in his *De Doctrina Christiana*. As Augustine puts the point, 'this world must be used, not enjoyed': *On Christian Doctrine* (Milton Keynes: Lightning Source, 2013), Book I, ch. 4, p. 14. On this account, God alone is to be 'enjoyed' for his own sake (ch. 22), while creatures are simply to be 'used' in the sense that our relationship to them is to be integrated into our relationship to God. Augustine's position on this point reflects his reading of Christ's commandment to love God 'with all your heart, and with all your soul, and with all your mind' (Mt 22:37 and parallels). He offers this gloss: in 'loving his neighbour as himself, a man turns the whole current of his love both for himself and his neighbour into the channel of the love of God, which suffers no stream to be drawn off from itself by whose diversion its own volume would be diminished': ibid., ch. 22, p. 25. Hence it is love of God that is properly fundamental, and all other attachments are to be folded into this love. Similarly, on Aquinas's understanding of the infused moral virtues, our relationship to creatures is to be folded into a God-directed teleology.

autonomy to the secular sciences means that tradition will need to evolve or innovate, as it encounters new questions concerning the 'hinge' between what we know by revelation and what we know of the world and of human nature from the secular sciences.[12]

In our own time, we are all familiar with the question of how to relate the understanding of the human person that is available in the secular sciences, such as evolutionary psychology, and the understanding of this same subject matter that has been purveyed in religious and spiritual traditions. We could see this modern debate as a further instance of the kind of enquiry with which Aquinas was occupied, when he was considering how to relate Aristotle's teaching on the acquired moral virtues to the conception of human possibilities that was propounded in his Christian sources. In both cases, the question is one of how to trace the relationship between revealed and secular perspectives when they share a subject matter, and how to understand the hinge that will allow one vocabulary to be brought into constructive alignment with the other.

We have now considered three examples of the role that may be played by tradition in the evolution of a given understanding of the spiritual or religious life. First, tradition has a role in setting the data of revelation, considered in themselves, in new order, so that novel questions can be addressed: here tradition has an integrative and projective function. Secondly, there is the case where concepts which have their origins in secular enquiry are brought into contact with the data of revelation, so making the data newly intelligible, through the analogical extension of these concepts. These two approaches are both concerned with the conceptual ordering of the data of revelation, but in the first case the key concepts are internal to the tradition (for example, the notion of a quality that in every case contributes to the perfection of a thing is, I take it, one that arises out of Anselm's reflections on his Christian

---

[12] Thomas's Dominican predecessor, William Peraldus, had already in effect introduced the idea of infused moral virtues. But Peraldus's account does not include the acquired moral virtues. So Aquinas's position on the infused moral virtues remains innovative in the sense that matters here—that is, in so far as it provides a way of articulating the hinge between Aristotelian and theological perspectives. For an account of Peraldus's position, see John Inglis, 'Aquinas's Replication of the Acquired Moral Virtues: Rethinking the Standard Philosophical Interpretation of Moral Virtue in Aquinas', *Journal of Religious Ethics*, 27 (1999), 3–27.

sources, rather than being imported from secular understanding), whereas in the second case the relevant concepts have been developed in secular fields of enquiry (as with Aristotle's concept of potentiality).

There is in addition, I have been suggesting, a third kind of traditioned enquiry, whose focus is the interface between secular and theological perspectives when they have a common subject matter. This case is different from the first two in so far as it is concerned in the first instance not with the ordering of the data of revelation, by reference to concepts that are internal or external to the tradition, but with the question of how to construct a bridging story that will relate the data of revelation to an emerging secular conception of the themes that are addressed in revelation. The second of these kinds of investigation (involving the analogical extension of concepts) occupies a kind of middle ground between the other two. It is concerned with how to order or articulate the claims of revelation—and in this respect, it is like the first investigation. But at the same time, it appeals to concepts that have been fashioned within secular contexts of enquiry, and for this reason it bears, at least indirectly, on the relationship between secular and theological perspectives on the world—and to this extent, it resembles the third kind of investigation. In practice, a particular episode of traditioned enquiry may exhibit features of more than one of these approaches, over time and even at a given time.

So far, we have largely been concerned with the question of how a spiritual tradition may develop with respect to its doctrinal teaching: whether we are thinking of God as exhibiting all those properties that invariably contribute to the perfection of a thing, or of the divine nature as devoid of potentiality, or of certain moral virtues as infused by God, we are in each case using a broadly metaphysical idiom. In our earlier discussion, in Chapters 3 and 4, I have been arguing that for a rounded appreciation of a religious tradition, we need to grasp not only whatever metaphysical story it may have to tell about progress in the spiritual life, but also the habits of experience and of bodily demeanour that are integral to participation in the tradition. And it is natural to ask, therefore, how we are to understand tradition—or the 'handing on' of what has been received—when our attention moves from the transmission of doctrinal teaching to the handing on of bodily practices and forms of experience. When we change our focus in this way, I am going to propose, we find that tradition assumes a rather different character.

Tradition and Experience

In Chapter 3, we considered Aquinas's account of spiritual development, which he represents as a movement from the production of the acquired moral virtues to the receipt of the infused virtues. And we noted how John of the Cross's description of the transition from the active to the passive phase of the night (that is, from a time when the person is engaged in various spiritual exercises, to a time when it seems to them that their agency has been reduced to nothing) can be related to the story that Aquinas rehearses in terms of the categories of acquired and infused virtue. In this way, a narrative of spiritual change that is formulated in experiential terms can be mapped onto a narrative that is recorded in the language of metaphysics.

While the experiential and metaphysical stories present certain structural parallels, in general, it is not possible, I have suggested, to simply deduce the experiential account of the phases of the spiritual life from the metaphysical account. To take this same example, considered in itself, Aquinas's narrative would not lead us to suppose that the later phases of the spiritual life will be registered in experience in terms of bewilderment and rupture. So while John's description of the spiritual life conforms to the general structure of Thomas's, its emotional tone is not one we could have anticipated given simply Thomas's account—on the contrary, on that account, we might well have expected progress in the spiritual life to be manifest in experience as a process of smooth, incremental change.

This disjunction between the perspectives of metaphysics and experience is of some importance when we come to consider the role of tradition in shaping our understanding of what it is like, in experiential terms, to live in fidelity with the doctrinal teachings of a given spiritual tradition. Suppose we grant the truth of Thomistic metaphysics, and the phenomenological verisimilitude and theological aptness of John's account of what it is like, in experiential terms, to develop in spiritual terms in a world so conceived. In that case, we should suppose that John's discussion represents a deepening in our understanding of the experiential dimension of spiritual progress. And this deepening could not have been achieved, I have been arguing, simply by scrutinizing the story that can be told using the categories of Thomistic metaphysics: John's story rests, rather, upon first-hand experience, and upon his own practical commitment to leading the spiritual life in a world conceived in theistic—and indeed in broadly Thomistic—terms. To generalize the point, even if a tradition succeeds in producing a gradually deepened understanding of doctrinal matters over time, this will be no guarantee of any deepening in its appreciation of the experiential dimension of progress in the spiritual life. Why? Because, once again, the nature of spiritual progress so far as that is manifest in experiential terms cannot be simply read off from an account of spiritual development that is cast in purely doctrinal or metaphysical terms.[13]

When thinking about the nature of doctrinal change, I suggested that we can identify three general patterns of development, involving: integration and projection; the analogical extension of secular concepts when they are put to work in specifically Christian contexts; and the construction of a conceptual hinge that will connect our theological understanding of a given subject matter to our emerging secular understanding of these same themes. It is an implication of what I have just been saying that whichever of these forms doctrinal change takes, that will not of itself enable a deepened understanding of the experiential dimension of the spiritual life. So our earlier typology of the ways in which doctrinal understanding may be deepened over time does not straightforwardly carry over to the question of how our understanding of the experiential dimension of the spiritual life may be deepened over time. And we might wonder, therefore, whether we can give a similarly structured account of progress in our appreciation of the kind of world-directed experience that is appropriate with respect to a given metaphysical or doctrinal story.

---

[13] Even if a record of progress that is cast in experiential terms should conform to what we might have expected given the metaphysics, this will still count as a significant discovery, granted that this record could easily have turned out otherwise, for all we could have said when presented simply with the metaphysical facts.

Such progress will involve, of course, a deepening apprehension of the relevant relations of congruence between a given conception of our metaphysical context and our world-directed experience. And in general terms, we know that what is required for such progress is: an accumulation of relevant first-hand experience, and a capacity to record that experience with the requisite phenomenological exactitude. And in turn, the accumulation of such experience will depend upon the efforts of particular individuals to live in fidelity to the relevant doctrinal scheme. Is there anything more we can say about the nature of the insights that are involved in a deepening of our understanding of the experiential dimension of the spiritual life? If a tradition is developing productively in this respect, then we might expect it to generate two kinds of insight.

First of all, it will throw new light on the range of ways in which a person's orientation to their ultimate end can, in principle, be realized in their world-directed experience. We have considered some examples of this possibility in our earlier discussion. For instance, the habits of consumption of the person of infused temperance will be directed not only to the goal of bodily health, but also to the end of relationship to God. And the experience of such a person can participate in this same God-directed teleology, in so far as they not only consume food of the kind and amount that is appropriate to their relation to God, but also desire food, savour it, and afford it prominence in the perceptual field, in ways that are proportional to its significance for their relationship to God. To the extent that this is possible, there will be a set of food-based spiritual goods—what in earlier discussion, we have termed hybrid goods—that are experiential in form.

Secondly, as a tradition's understanding of the experiential dimension of the spiritual life unfolds, so it will be able to pronounce not only upon the possibility in principle of various experientially grounded hybrid goods, but also upon the extent to which such goods are in practice realizable in a human life: allowing that it is possible for our world-directed experience to be attuned to our final end at least occasionally, in various domains, it is a further matter to determine whether it is possible for our experience to realize hybrid goods with any frequency. When John of the Cross observes that in the period of 'awakening' that follows the Dark Night, it is possible to experience all things 'in God', he is addressing this further question, and proposing that once a person has reached a condition of spiritual maturity, it is possible for their world-directed experience to be adapted to their final end pervasively. In sum, a tradition's understanding of the contribution of experience to the spiritual life may be deepened both on account of its new insights into the nature of the relevant hybrid goods and on account of its growing appreciation of the extent to which these goods may in practice be realized in a human life. The first of these kinds of insight is broadly conceptual, while the second is, we might say, more anthropological in character. If we take the example of a figure such as John of the Cross to be at all representative, then we should expect this deepening of insight into the experiential implications of a given doctrinal scheme to extend not simply over years or decades, but centuries.

This suggestion points to a significant disanalogy with the case of Mary the colour scientist. In our earlier discussion, we noted a parallel between Mary and the participant in the spiritual life: just as there is no ready way for Mary, while she remains confined to her black-and-white world, to anticipate what it might be like to see red, however much she may know about the physics of vision, so there is no ready way for the spiritual practitioner, when confined to a metaphysical vantage point on reality, to anticipate what it might be like, in experiential terms, to inhabit a world so conceived. However, once she has left the room, all that Mary has to do, in order to come to an understanding of what it is like to see red as red, is to open her eyes—assuming of course that she has normally functioning colour vision. By contrast, John of the Cross's work suggests that coming to experience the world in a properly Christian way standardly requires an extended process of moral and spiritual purification. And if we follow John's account, then we should also say that no amount of effortful spiritual practice will be enough to bring the person to a state of spiritual maturity: for that, they also need to receive a new, divinely infused centre of thought and agency. These considerations provide at least part of the explanation of why the process of coming to understand the experiential implications of a given doctrinal scheme can extend over centuries.

This difference between sensory experience and spiritual experience reflects the fact that in the latter case, we are not concerned simply with the kind of experience a person will in fact have if placed in relevant circumstances; what matters is the kind of experience they ought to have, if their experience is to be appropriate to their context. (It is also true of course that, for spiritual experience, the relevant context is metaphysical, and not simply physical.) So both in the case of Mary and in the case of the spiritual practitioner, the particular phenomenal feel of the relevant experiences cannot be anticipated in experience-independent terms; but by contrast with the case of Mary, in the spiritual case, this experience cannot be produced simply by training one's physical gaze upon a relevant object, but instead presupposes an extended period of moral and spiritual formation, not all of which is subject to the person's control.

We began this chapter by asking whether tradition may involve more than the mere recapitulation of some insight communicated in an initial event of revelation. The account we have been developing here suggests that, so far as our understanding of the contribution of experience to the spiritual life is concerned, then tradition will indeed play this more expansive kind of role. I shall return shortly to the question of the significance of this finding for our understanding of tradition, but first of all I want to say a little about the nature of tradition so far as it concerns the handing on of a particular style of bodily presence in the world.

Tradition and Enacted Example

Just as a metaphysical account of the various phases of the spiritual life is not of itself sufficient to determine what it would be like, in experiential terms, to develop spiritually in a world so conceived, so an account of spiritual progress that is cast in metaphysical and experiential terms, however comprehensive it may be considered in those terms, is not of itself sufficient to determine, in all the requisite detail, the bodily demeanours that are appropriate to each phase of the spiritual life. Again, for a knowledge of these matters, we are required to defer, it seems, to the lives of particular individuals who live in fidelity to the metaphysical and experiential narratives of the tradition.

Raimond Gaita's account of his encounter with the nun provides one illustration of this proposal. As we have seen, before he witnesses the nun's example, Gaita is already committed to the idea that the patients on the psychiatric ward are fully his equals. But on observing her enacted relationship with the patients, he comes to a new insight into what it takes to live in fidelity to that ideal of equality. And he evidently thinks, not only that he did not reach, but that he could not have reached this new insight independently of the example of the nun or another such figure: hence he speaks of her demeanour as affording a kind of 'revelation', which is to say, I take it, that the relevant insight could not have been produced simply by extrapolation from what he already knew.[14] Indeed, Gaita is emphatic that the fittingness of the nun's demeanour cannot be grounded in any property that can be identified independently of her conduct.[15] So on this account, there is no conceptual space for the idea that we might be able to anticipate the nun's comportment, so that it is no longer revelatory, by reference to some story about the world that is articulated simply in metaphysical, or experiential or, in general, demeanour-independent terms.

As in the case of experience, so here, we might suppose that a deepening of our understanding of the contribution of bodily demeanour to the spiritual life will involve two kinds of insight: first of all, an insight into the nature of the hybrid goods that involve what Gaita calls 'the inflexions of the body', and secondly, an insight into the extent to which these goods can be exhibited in a human life in practice. In our earlier discussion, I argued that when interpreted through the lens of Aquinas's understanding of neighbour love, Gaita's story of the nun provides one example of how the inflexions of a person's body can contribute to hybrid goods. When so interpreted, this account shows how it is not just a person's thoughts, desires, and experiences that can be appropriate to the truth that we will one day share with others in the beatific vision: their facial expressions and the expressive cast of their body can also be congruent with this same truth, and thereby partake in the fundamental

---

[14] See for instance his reference to her behaviour's 'power of revelation': *A Common Humanity*, p. 19.

[15] For further discussion of this point, see Chapter 4.

good of a life that is adequate relative to our theological context. It is also at least implied in Gaita's discussion that the goods that are realized in the nun's demeanour can be widely exemplified, since the same sort of enacted sensitivity, one that acknowledges the full humanity of the other person, will be appropriate in our dealings with human beings in general.

So in the case of enacted example, as in the case of experience, it turns out that we can only understand the condition of spiritual maturity by reference to the example of particular individuals, who have lived in fidelity to the tradition, so revealing what kind of demeanour is required if a human life is to be properly aligned with its metaphysical context.

The Role of Tradition on Pierre Hadot's Conception of the Spiritual Life

These reflections point to an understanding of the significance of tradition which is rather different from that implied in Pierre Hadot's conception of the spiritual life. As we saw in Chapter 1, on Hadot's account, 'ethics' is to be privileged over 'metaphysics', and 'philosophy' over 'philosophical discourse'—or to make the same point in the terms that we have been using, ways of life are to be privileged over world views. It is a consequence of this approach, I think, that traditioned reflection is of relatively little importance for the spiritual life.

On Hadot's account, it seems that I can simply see, immediately and non-inferentially, what constitutes a good life. If I am an Epicurean, for example, then I will simply see that a life free from anxiety is good, and on the basis of this insight, I will then commit myself to leading such a life, with the support of the requisite spiritual practices. This insight into the nature of the good life (here, a life free from anxiety) seems to be attainable independently of any tradition of enquiry. And it is not hard to see why, on this view, we do not need any such tradition: after all, for Hadot, the goodness of a given way of life is to be apprehended prior to any metaphysical or other commitment. There is, therefore, no need to consider whether the way of life is appropriate relative to some further context: as no such context is required, when deciding whether the way of life is good, it is enough for me to examine the way of life in itself—and simply note how it strikes me. At any rate, this is the picture to which Hadot's account seems to point, though he does not venture an opinion on precisely this question.

It may be thought that traditions can have a larger part to play on Hadot's account when we direct our attention away from the choice of a way of life and to the choice of a world view that will provide the necessary motivational support for the leading of that way of life. We can after all study the history of attempts to lead a given way of life, and consider whether some world views have been more successful in motivating that way of life than others. But here too, Hadot's own discussion has a tendency to downplay the role of tradition. He evidently thinks of world views as relatively dispensable: we can indeed be Stoics today, he affirms, but only if we substitute for the world view of the ancient Stoics one that is better suited to our own intellectual proclivities.[16] However, if ongoing commitment, across generations, to Stoicism or any other form of the spiritual life standardly requires us to ditch the world view of former exponents of that life, and to substitute a world view of our own choosing, then it would seem that there is not so much that we can learn from our spiritual forebears about the motivational connection between world views and ways of life, for the reason simply that our world view is not theirs, so that their experience of this connection cannot speak directly to our own situation.

In response it may be urged that even if we cannot retain the world view of, say, ancient Stoicism, or ancient Epicureanism, we can at least reflect upon the type of world view that has in the past successfully supported a Stoic or Epicurean way of life. But here again, Hadot's stance leaves only a very minimal role for tradition. To take one example, the fit between the ancient Epicurean world view and their way of life, as Hadot represents the matter, is very straightforward. The Epicurean world view, namely atomism, helps to dispel anxiety about post-mortem, divine judgement. How? Because atomism has the consequence that the person ceases to exist at death, so that there is no afterlife. To see that such a world view can help to support such a way of life, there is no need

---

[16] See Chapter 1 for further discussion of his position in this regard.

to appeal to tradition. And to develop a modern counterpart for the Epicurean world view that will, in our time, help to sustain an Epicurean mode of life, with respect to the fear of post-mortem judgement, there is again no need for traditioned reflection: all we need is to identify a world view which guarantees that there will be no post-mortem existence. And once again, we can see the motivational relevance of such a world view for the leading of this way of life independently of any reference to the experience of the ancient Epicureans—because this connection is self-evident.

The perspective that we have been developing points to a much larger role for traditioned enquiry than does Hadot's account. This is fundamentally because of the use we have made of the idea of hybrid goods, following Aquinas's discussion of the infused moral virtues. Granting the importance of hybrid goods, it will follow that we cannot characterize the spiritual life, and progress in the spiritual life, independently of reference to our metaphysical context. Why? Because on this view, a person's spiritual development will consist in large part in a deepening of the alignment between their world-directed activities and their metaphysical context. And if an understanding of the spiritual life depends on an understanding of our metaphysical context, that provides, I have been suggesting, two kinds of reason for supposing that religious and spiritual insight will be traditioned.

First of all, allowing for an initial datum of revelation, which sets out key features of our metaphysical context, there will remain a threefold role for tradition in drawing out and elaborating, rather than simply recapitulating, these primordial, revealed truths. As we have seen, the contribution of tradition will include the integration and projection of the data of revelation, the new appropriation of the data using analogically extended concepts, and the articulation of the changing joint between revelation and our secular understanding of the world. Secondly, our understanding of the spiritual life will evolve not only in terms of its doctrinal component, including here our representation of our metaphysical context, but also with respect to the question of what it takes for our world-directed thoughts, desires, and conduct to be properly aligned with a given doctrinal narrative. And here again, I have been arguing, there is a role for tradition that exceeds the mere reaffirmation of the data of revelation. In particular, we should expect our understanding of those hybrid goods which involve experience and bodily demeanour to have a traditioned character. For the reasons we have been considering, if we are to understand what world-directed experience is really adequate to the metaphysical teachings of a given tradition, or what kind of bodily demeanour is congruent with those teachings, we will need to proceed inductively, by appeal to the lives of exemplary individuals. And accordingly, our understanding will have a traditioned character, where the relevant tradition will extend, potentially, across centuries. In my concluding remarks, I return to the question of what the experiential and enacted dimension of the spiritual life may suggest for an assessment of the nature of tradition.

Concluding Thoughts on the Significance of Tradition for the Spiritual Life

This discussion of how we come to understand which forms of experience and which kinds of bodily demeanour are adequate to a particular world view suggests that we will need a rather different account of the evolution of a spiritual tradition depending upon whether we are concerned with its metaphysical, experiential, or what we might call its bodily commitments. In the ways we have examined, a tradition can progress in metaphysical terms simply through force of reflection: Anselm can come to understand, by thought alone, that the notion of a quality which is in every case perfection-making can helpfully unify scriptural ways of talking about God; and Aquinas can reason his way to the thought that the notion of potentiality can be analogically extended, so that it can be used to speak of the Christian God, who is not only the First Mover, but also the Creator and a Trinity; and Aquinas can also see simply by intellectual means that the notion of infused moral virtue allows the acquired moral virtues to be caught up into the God-directedness of the theological virtues. So these insights are all capable of being won from the vantage point of the study.

There remains a difference here from the position of Hadot, whose view might seem to be similar in this respect. As we have seen, on

Hadot's account, subject to certain fairly minimal epistemic constraints, it seems that we are free to introduce whatever world view, or 'philosophical discourse', will be motivationally helpful for the enactment of a given ideal of life. And as we have also seen, on this approach, the motivational connection between a given world view and the ideal of life that it is designed to support appears to be just obvious. So for Hadot, there is, it seems, no call for serious reflection on the question of which world view we are to adopt. By contrast, on the account we have been sketching, there remains a role for the serious, extended, and disciplined examination of the belief-worthiness of world views, and accordingly a role for traditioned enquiry, of the kinds we have discussed.[17]

By contrast with the story about the development of doctrine that I have just rehearsed, we can't 'just see', by reflection alone, that the pattern of human experience that John of the Cross describes is appropriate to a given conception of our metaphysical context, any more than we can just see that a certain bodily demeanour is congruent with that conception. For an understanding of these matters, we are dependent, it seems, on the first-hand experience of the spiritual life of figures such as John, and on our own experience of the enacted example of figures such as the nun in Gaita's example. So in these domains—of experience and enacted example—traditioned enquiry takes on a rather different form.

This difference reflects, once again, the nature of hybrid goods. To understand the contribution of experience and bodily demeanour to the spiritual life, we need to think about how these dimensions of a human life may be more or less congruent with a given conception of our metaphysical context. By contrast, when we consider the data of revelation from a metaphysical vantage point, we are not in the first instance concerned with the relationship of congruence, but only with how to order and then project the data, or how to understand them anew in the light of some analogically extended concept drawn from our secular enquiries, or how to conceive of the hinge between our emerging secular understanding of the world and the metaphysics bequeathed to us in revelation. So one consequence of taking hybrid goods to be important for the spiritual life seems to be a commitment to the different roles of

---

[17] These are matters we shall discuss in further detail in Chapter 6.

tradition with respect to metaphysics, on the one hand, and bodily demeanour and experience on the other.

Another, related way of framing this difference would be as follows. It can be said that in the domain of experience and enacted example, spiritual traditions are the source of various insights into human nature and associated life possibilities. Independently of the reports of figures like John of the Cross, or for that matter of an observer such as Raimond Gaita, we would, arguably, have little notion that human nature admits of these possibilities for experience and bodily interaction. So here tradition is not simply a matter of reflecting upon the data of revelation, as on the Anselmian model, but of generating new data, concerning what is possible, experientially and behaviourally, for creatures such as ourselves. Perhaps, then, there is a parallel here with the case where our doctrinal understanding evolves as we learn to represent, in new ways, the bridge between the data of revelation and our developing secular understanding of the world. Similarly, perhaps, our religious and spiritual understanding can be deepened as we learn how to relate the data of revelation to a newly extended conception of human beings' capacities for experience and enacted relationship. But in the latter case, there remains this difference: here, our newly extended conception of the world is itself grounded in spiritual tradition, to the extent that it arises out of an attempt to live in fidelity to a given metaphysical vision.

In sum, in the case of experience and bodily demeanour, spiritual traditions generate new, spiritually freighted data: they don't simply re-order the existing data of revelation, or relate them to our developing secular understanding. Instead, they are themselves the source of a new assessment of human possibilities: but for spiritual and religious traditions, and the attempts of particular individuals to lead lives that are faithful to the metaphysical and moral ideals of those traditions, we would never have known that these forms of experience and these forms of bodily life are possible for human beings. In this way, spiritual traditions offer a distinctive and also existentially profound vantage point upon human nature and its possibilities.

In earlier chapters, I have argued that when we choose between spiritual or religious traditions, we are not choosing, as Hadot supposed, between ways of life considered independently of metaphysical context.

Instead, we are choosing between ways of life and world views considered in combination. Again, we need to reckon with world views for this purpose, and not just with ways of life considered independently of any world view, because certain fundamental spiritual goods are relative to world view: these goods—what we have been calling hybrid goods—arise in so far as a person's world-directed thoughts, experience, and so on, are aligned with the relevant metaphysical context, as described in the world view. If that is so, then when we consider whether we have good reason to participate in a given spiritual tradition, it is vital that we understand the ways in which human experience and bodily demeanour, along with the other dimensions of a human life, may be congruent with the world view of that tradition; and it is vital that we understand, in addition, the degree to which these relations of congruence can in practice be realized in a human life. Why? Because it is only if we understand these matters that we will be able to judge the nature and extent of the spiritual goods that are purveyed by the tradition, granted the truth of its account of our metaphysical context. It follows that traditioned reflection concerning experience and bodily demeanour is not incidental to our appreciation of spiritual traditions, but at the core of our assessment of the contribution they can in principle make to the good of a human life. Let us consider these matters further in our next chapter.

6

The Nature of Faith

Introduction

In our discussion so far, we have been considering the nature of
distinctively spiritual goods, and the ways in which metaphysical commitments, world-directed experience, and bodily demeanour can
together define various forms of spiritual life. The view we have been
developing builds on Thomas Aquinas's conception of the infused moral
virtues, and specifically the idea that, in central cases, spiritual goods
have what I have called a hybrid character, since they arise in so far as a
person's world-directed thoughts, desires, behaviour, and so on, are
aligned with their theological context. Given this account of the nature
of the spiritual life, it is important to ask: what conditions must be satisfied by my assent to a given conception of our theological context, if that
conception is to provide a proper focus for spiritual practice? That is the
question I am proposing to address in this chapter.

These are matters we have touched on already, in Chapter 1 of this
discussion. As we saw there, Pierre Hadot has suggested that it is the
choice of a way of life that comes first; and a world view—or, in our
terms, a theological narrative—is to be introduced only to make the way
of life, once chosen, motivationally more accessible. Hadot is clear, then,
that a world view is postulated in the first instance not because of its
capacity to explain features of the world, or on account of its epistemic
merits in some other respect, but for its psychological efficacy. Nonetheless,
I have suggested, on Hadot's approach, the spiritual practitioner cannot
treat their world view as simply a matter of make-believe. On the contrary, the motivational power of the world view depends at least in part
on the thought that, in relevant respects, it has some prospect of providing at least an approximation to the truth. After all, to revert to the

Spiritual Traditions and the Virtues: Living Between Heaven and Earth. Mark R. Wynn, Oxford University Press (2020).
© Mark R. Wynn.
DOI: 10.1093/oso/9780198862949.001.0001

example we discussed in Chapter 1, if the Epicurean were to suppose that atomism fails to meet this minimal condition, then it is hard to see how the mere fact that the truth of atomism *would* rule out the possibility of a post-mortem judgement can be relevant to the question of whether we ought, in fact, to fear such a judgement. So in Hadot's discussion, we find, at least implicitly, a conception of the kind of assent to a given world view that is required if that world view is to function as a focus for spiritual practice.

The account of these matters that I am going to develop in this chapter is indebted, once again, to the work of Thomas Aquinas. This time, I shall be building on his discussion of religious faith. I am going to begin by expounding some key elements of Aquinas's understanding of faith, before proposing a further, broadly Thomistic conception of the nature of the spiritual practitioner's assent to the theological narrative that structures their practice. As we shall see, this account of faith is rather different from Hadot's reading of the kind of assent that the ancient Epicureans, Stoics, and others gave to the world views that supported their spiritual practice.

Thomas Aquinas on Religious Faith

In the very first article of the very first question of his famously voluminous work the *Summa Theologiae*, Aquinas asks about the point of theology, by putting to himself this question: 'is another teaching required apart from philosophical studies?' By 'philosophical studies', he means any rationally ordered enquiry that proceeds independently of appeal to scripture or 'revelation'. So, in brief, here Aquinas is asking whether a purely secular kind of enquiry might be sufficient for an understanding of how we are to live. Here is his reply, given in the opening lines of the *Responsio*:

> It should be urged that human well-being called for schooling in what God has revealed, in addition to the philosophical researches pursued by human reasoning. Above all because God destines us for an end beyond the grasp of reason; according to Isaiah, Eye hath not seen, O God, without thee what thou hast prepared for them that love thee.

[Isaiah 64. 4] Now we have to recognize an end before we can stretch out and exert ourselves for it. Hence the necessity for our welfare that divine truths surpassing reason should be signified to us through divine revelation.[1]

From this text, set down at the very beginning of the *Summa Theologiae*, we can see why the notion of faith is going to be fundamental to the account of the spiritual life that Aquinas goes on to develop (and, indeed, to any orthodox Christian conception of the spiritual life), even when it is not the immediate focus of his discussion. In sum, on the view presented here, the spiritual life is an enacted response to a theological narrative; and since this narrative cannot be established by 'reason', or by reference simply to 'philosophical research', it is to be affirmed in faith.

On the account presented here, the vision of reality given in revelation is 'beyond the grasp of reason', or 'surpasses reason', which is to say that while this vision cannot be established by means of reason, it equally cannot be refuted by reason. Although Aquinas does not address the point here, it may also be that secular reason can from its own resources show why any such vision is bound to elude its grasp. In that case, then while faith may affirm more than can be established by secular reason, we would still be able to give an account grounded in secular reason of why 'philosophical researches' are of no avail in this domain—and the commitment of faith would be to that extent rationally intelligible.

This text also emphasizes the practical significance of revelation: we need revealed truths not to satisfy the speculative intellect, but so that we may order our lives to the ends disclosed in revelation, and 'exert ourselves' accordingly, here and now. In earlier chapters, we have seen how these brief remarks can be located within a larger conception of the nature of the spiritual life, according to which a revealed theological narrative, such as the story of the beatific vision, can structure a person's relations to other human beings and the material order in general. How

[1] ST 1a. 1. 1, here following the Blackfriars edition of the *Summa Theologiae*, ed. T. Gilby (London: Eyre & Spottiswoode, 1964–74). Later citations will also be drawn from this translation, unless otherwise indicated.

is this possible? Because our world-directed thoughts, desires, behaviour, and so on, can be more or less closely aligned with a theological narrative, and can therefore be more or less successful in realizing a range of distinctively spiritual goods. Hence theological narratives can serve as a lure, drawing human lives into the shape that is required for the realization of what we have been calling hybrid goods. As we have seen, key elements of a particular narrative, as presented in 'revelation', can then be elaborated through the creative work of traditioned forms of enquiry.

If the spiritual life has in general terms this structure, of being ordered to a certain vision of reality as communicated in a reason-transcendent revelation, then it is of some importance to determine on what basis we are supposed to assent that vision. It is only much later in the *Summa Theologiae*, in the *Secunda Secundae*, that Aquinas turns to this issue explicitly, when developing his account of the nature of Christian faith or *fides*. Let us note briefly some of the presiding themes of this discussion.

We know, from *Summa Theologiae* 1a. 1, that the assent of faith cannot be grounded simply in our secular enquiries. In this respect, faith is different from, for instance, my assent to the thought that I am at present typing at a keyboard, or to the thought that if I step outside, then it will be cold. These everyday kinds of belief can be established by reference to secular reason (including here the deliverances of the senses), and in standard cases are established so compellingly indeed that my assent follows ineluctably from the relevant data. When he turns explicitly to the nature of faith, Aquinas expands on this picture, noting that 'the act of faith is belief, an act of mind fixed on one alternative by reason of the will's command' (2a2ae. 4. 1).[2] It is natural to ask: granted that the assent of faith is at 'the will's command', what is it that leads a Christian to make the commitment of faith? Aquinas comments:

> it is clear that faith's act is pointed as to its end towards the will's object, i.e. the good. This good, the end of faith's act, is the divine good, the

---

[2] This account holds for faith of all kinds, including demonic faith, since faith involves 'belief', not 'knowledge': ST 2a2ae. 5. 2. My thanks to Maria Rosa Antognazza for helpful discussion of these matters.

proper object of charity. This is why charity is called the form of faith, namely, because the act of faith is completed and shaped by charity.

(ST 2a2ae. 4. 3)

In this text, it becomes clear that faith is motivated by love or *caritas*: it is the person's love of what Aquinas here calls 'the divine good' that elicits their assent to the propositions of faith. Aquinas is proposing, I take it, that the believer's love of what is proposed in revelation leads them to assent to the truth of revelation. There is much more to be said about how this picture is supposed to work—and why it does not amount to mere wish fulfilment, that is, to the affirmation of some claim for the reason simply that we would like it to be true. We shall return to these matters shortly, but for now, it is important to note that for Aquinas, there is another kind of faith, one that is different from Christian faith in terms of its relationship to the evidence. This further form of faith is, he explains, the faith of the devils, which 'is, so to speak, forced from them by the evidence of signs'. Aquinas concludes: 'That they believe, then, is in no way to the credit of their wills.' (ST 2a2ae. 5. 2 ad 1; compare James 2: 19.) From this text, it is clear that the devils' faith is involuntary, because compelled by the evidence. And Aquinas is inviting us to suppose that authentically Christian faith differs in this respect. Not only is it not compelled by the evidence furnished by our secular enquiries, as indicated in ST 1a. 1, but it is not forced upon believers by any kind of evidence. Why not? Because were it to be so, then it would not be 'to the credit of their wills'. Accordingly, Christian faith, Aquinas is suggesting, is free and voluntary.

While Christian faith is not 'forced', it is not, for Aquinas, simply the product of the believer's will. On the contrary, as a theological virtue, it is infused. As he puts the point:

As to the assent to matters of faith, we can look to two types of cause. One is a cause that persuades from without, e.g. a miracle witness or a human appeal urging belief. No such cause is enough, however; one man believes and another does not, when both have seen the same miracle, heard the same preaching. Another kind of cause must therefore be present, an inner cause, one that influences a person inwardly to assent to the things of faith. The Pelagians thought this cause to be free will alone… This is a false doctrine. The reason: since in assenting to the things of faith a person is raised above his own nature, he has this assent from a supernatural source influencing him… the assent of faith… has as its cause God, moving us inwardly through grace.

(ST 2a2ae. 6. 1, my ellipses)

It is notable that Aquinas moves here from empirical considerations (citing the fact that one person assents to the articles of faith, in response to preaching or a miracle, while another, when presented with the same evidence, does not) to a conclusion about the grounds or cause of the believer's assent: those grounds must be internal. And we might speculate that in the history of Christian thought, empirical considerations are also relevant to Aquinas's further claim that these internal grounds involve, in particular, God's infusing activity. Viewed historically, this doctrine presumably derives from the believer's sense, rooted in their own experience, that while faith does not flow from the force of the evidence, neither is it produced by their unaided volitional effort. Accordingly, faith is seen to invite another, less naturalistic kind of explanation. At the same time, it is clear that Aquinas thinks of the act of faith as free: the view that he disavows here is not that the human will has a part to play in this process, but that the will 'alone' explains the assent of faith. Of course, in this passage, Aquinas makes a more ambitious claim than the one that I have just presented: it's not just that believers find that their assent has not, in fact, arisen in certain ways (from their unaided effort, for example), but also that in so far as this assent raises a person 'above their own nature', then it requires a certain kind of cause: a supernatural cause. For present purposes, we can bracket that further claim, and Aquinas's case in its support.

To conclude this exposition of some key elements in Aquinas's account of religious faith, let us note one further affirmation that is integral to his discussion. In ST 2a2ae. 2. 1, Aquinas proposes that faith occupies a kind of middle ground between 'science' or 'understanding', on the one side, and opinion, on the other. (By *scientia* here he means, of course, Aristotelian science, involving necessary first principles and what follows deductively from them.) In support of this thesis, Aquinas observes that as an act of belief, faith is confident—and in this respect, it resembles 'science' rather than opinion. As he puts the point, 'this act "to believe" cleaves firmly to one side'.[3] But, he continues, faith 'is not completed by a clear vision', but instead depends on 'the will's command'— and in this respect, it is like opinion, rather than 'knowledge'.

While Aquinas maintains that the act of faith is confident, this is not to say that it is certain. Indeed, we might suppose that, in general, authentic Christian faith must fall short of certainty, since it is, after all, supposed to be under-evidenced. However, while his position does admit as a possibility, if not require, that faith is in this sense uncertain, Aquinas is also clear that in a further sense faith is supremely certain. Hence he comments: 'There is nothing to stop a thing that is objectively more certain by its nature from being subjectively less certain to us because of the disability of our minds, which, as Aristotle notes, blink at the most evident things like bats in the sunshine. Doubt about the articles of faith which falls to the lot of some is not because the reality is at all uncertain but because the human understanding is feeble.' (ST 1a. 1. 5 ad 1). So in brief, while the content of faith is objectively certain, because grounded in God's truthfulness, it may also be, subjectively, that is, from the vantage point of the believer, uncertain.[4] But even if faith is subjectively uncertain, Aquinas seems to be suggesting, the person of faith will still hold unwaveringly to the truth of what is proposed in revelation.

In sum, on Aquinas's account of the matter, the spiritual life is grounded in the person's free, divinely enabled assent to a theological narrative that is communicated in revelation. For Aquinas, this assent is cognitive, in so far as it involves what he calls 'belief'. That is, faith, on

---

[3] Tr. Fathers of the English Dominican Province (New York: Benziger Brothers, 1947).

[4] Here Aquinas seems to endorse an externalist perspective on the epistemic status of faith: while this fact may not be evident to the believer, because of 'the disability of our minds', the truth-directedness of the assent of faith is in fact divinely guaranteed. On some accounts of knowledge, we ought therefore to speak of the beliefs affirmed in faith as knowledge. Compare Alvin Plantinga's comment: 'these beliefs will…have warrant for believers: they will be produced in them by a belief-producing process that is functioning properly in an appropriate cognitive environment (the one for which they were designed), according to a design plan successfully aimed at the production of true belief': Alvin Plantinga, *Warranted Christian Belief* (Oxford: Oxford University Press, 2000), p. 246. On Plantinga's warrant-based epistemology, this is to say that the beliefs affirmed in faith count as knowledge.

this account, is not a matter of living simply as if some picture of the nature of things were true, but of affirming the truth of that picture, and seeking to live in accordance with reality so conceived. On this view, faith is also evidently action-guiding: the assent of faith to a given theological narrative is a matter not of mere speculation, but of orienting oneself in the world in practical terms, so as to align one's life with the good that is disclosed in revelation. As Aquinas says in *Summa Theologiae* 1a. 1. 1, the point of revelation is to enable us to recognize a reason-transcendent end, so that 'we can stretch out and exert ourselves for it', here and now. Moreover, on this account, as we have seen, faith is voluntary, and flows from the person's loving attraction to what is presented in revelation, rather than simply from the force of a body of evidence. And yet faith remains different from opinion, since it cleaves to its favoured theological narrative unswervingly. And as infused, its truth-directedness is divinely guaranteed. So in brief, on Aquinas's account of the matter, faith is cognitive, action-guiding, voluntary, unwavering, and in the relevant sense certain.

Having expounded some of the rudiments of Aquinas's understanding of faith, I am now going to develop a further account of the nature of faith, one that is intended to track key features of his view. This account will draw out Aquinas's conception, by returning once again to the abiding themes of this enquiry: the infused moral virtues, and the distinctively spiritual goods to which they are ordered.

Building on Aquinas's Account

Let us begin by thinking about some situations of practical choice which resemble in some measure the commitment of faith as Aquinas understands it. Suppose that as a young person, I would like to attend a certain university. And suppose that to that end, I need to achieve certain exam grades. And suppose that, so far as I can tell, I have only a limited prospect of achieving those grades, even if I apply myself to my studies unstintingly. This is a familiar situation of practical choice and it is entirely evident, I take it, that in this case, under normal circumstances, I can commit myself to working hard for the sake of securing a place at my preferred university, without thereby falling into any kind of irrationality.

When I consider the reasonableness of embarking upon some such practical project, there will typically be a trade-off, of course, between the goodness of the goal, on the one side, and, on the other, the likelihood and cost of attaining it. For instance, if the end at which I aim involves a significant good, then I may have good reason to pursue it even if the commitment required should be costly, and my chances of success slight. In assessing the reasonableness of a given course of action, it will also be relevant to consider the likely consequences of failure: the case where failing to achieve my goal has the result that I achieve a somewhat similar (even if lower-ranked) outcome will present a very different kind of choice from the case where failing to achieve my goal is in some way ruinous. To put these points in general terms, my choice of action should be guided by the relative 'expected value' of the various possible actions open to me—where the expected value of an action is given by the sum of the values of the possible outcomes of the action, where each of those values is discounted by the probability of the associated outcome.

It is also true, of course, that people vary in their preferences in these matters. For example, some are more risk averse, and would sooner pursue a project of relatively low expected value, if there is then a diminished risk of a significantly bad outcome. Allowing for such variations across persons and circumstances, it is clear that, in general, pursuing a goal under conditions of uncertainty need not involve any failure of rationality, not even if the attainment of the goal is highly unlikely. Indeed, if such ventures were to be irrational of their nature, then we would have to regard a large swathe of the practical lives of human beings as rationally defective.

Let us take another example, structurally similar to the first, but with a rather different target good. Suppose that my great uncle was killed in the First World War. And suppose that while uncertain, there is a reasonable chance that he is buried in a common grave just outside the village of Passchendaele. And suppose I decide to make a journey from my home in England to this site, because I want to honour his memory at the very place where his body lies. (If this undertaking seems unduly demanding, do modify the example to suit your own commitments. Suppose for instance that I find myself in the near vicinity of the grave site, because I happen to be visiting the area for some other reason, and at that point decide to make the short journey to the site with this end in view.)

In this case, my action is motivated by the thought that I will be able to honour my uncle in a special way when remembering him at the place where he is buried. Of course, I can recall my uncle in other, place-independent ways, simply by thinking about him, while remaining wherever else I happen to be. But for many of us anyway, it makes a difference if we can remember a person at the very place where they are buried: in that case, we think, we can remember them, and honour them, with a kind of seriousness that would not otherwise be possible. It is not difficult to understand why we should think so: in many contexts, it matters for interpersonal relations that we are present to another person in bodily terms. And perhaps the body continues to be important in mediating our relations to other persons even after death. It is also true that we commonly take the history of a place to shape the practical claim that it makes upon us in the present.[5] The example I have given also rests on this association of ideas, but if you do not share these intuitions, do just substitute an example of your own choosing!

The case where I visit the putative grave is structurally similar to the case where I seek admission to my preferred university. Again, I aim at a certain outcome, while knowing that my efforts may well be fruitless. And once more, my actions are motivated by the goodness of the hoped-for outcome: here, the good of honouring my uncle in the special way that is possible when I am located at the very place where he is interred. And we can surely say of this case, as we did of the first, that my decision to pursue that good can be practically rational, even if I believe that my chances of success are relatively low.

---

[5] For a recent, large-scale example, see the extended debate, in the United States, about what sort of building, for what sort of purpose, it would be appropriate to construct on the site of the 9/11 attacks. For further discussion of the role of historical considerations in fixing the identities of places, and the claim they make upon us in the present, see my text *Faith and Place: An Essay in Embodied Religious Epistemology* (Oxford: Oxford University Press, 2009).

However, in this second example, the target good, and in turn what it takes to realize the good, takes a rather different form. In the case of the examination, I need to apply myself to my studies in such a way that I will be able to recall various items of information effectively under certain circumstances, and so on. And providing that these causal conditions are satisfied, then I will succeed in my goal of doing well enough, relative to others taking the same exams, to secure my place at my university of choice. In the second case, I also depend on the causal structure of the world: I need, for instance, to rely on some form of transport to reach the site where my uncle may be buried. But in this case, I realize the relevant good, most fundamentally, not because what I do brings about causally the desired state of affairs, but because what I do counts as an act of a certain kind—here one of acknowledging a story-mediated, place-relative existential significance. Specifically, if my uncle is buried at this place, then I can succeed in honouring him here, in the special way that is possible when we are in the presence of the deceased person's body, simply by virtue of adopting the relevant phys-ical and mental comportment when located at the site. By contrast, an account of how I come to pass the exam can be told simply in terms of the causal properties of various revision practices, and without reference to the existential import of particular places.

Spiritual practices, as we have understood them here, evidently resemble in certain respects my action in visiting the site where my uncle may be buried—supposing that my aim hereby is to acknowledge in practical terms a place-relative, narratively-mediated significance. Of course, the narratives that inform spiritual practices are typically of very wide import: here we are dealing with a particularly far-reaching or even global significance, one that attaches not simply to some local place, but to the material world as a whole. Hence if a person is to live congruently with, say, the story of the beatific vision, then their world-directed thoughts, attitudes, and behaviour will need to be ordered accordingly across a very wide range of contexts—with respect to their relations to other human beings, their habits of eating, and so on. By contrast, when I visit the putative grave, my aim is to acknowledge the significance of a very particular place in a very localized way. Allowing for this difference of scope, it seems that in each case, the goal of the person's practice is the sort of good that arises in so far as we succeed in acknowledging, in practical terms, the storied import of a place.[6]

So the case where I visit the putative grave site and the case where I order my world-directed thoughts and actions by reference to a theological narrative involve similarly structured target goods. The two cases are also alike in so far as the success of each of these projects is, of course, uncertain. For instance, I may seek to align my life with the beatific vision, and there may be no such vision, nor any other truth about my metaphysical or other context that will confer a comparable significance upon my efforts. Even so, it seems that in this case, as in the case where I visit the putative grave site, my commitment can still be practically reasonable—depending on, among other things, the likelihood of the beatific vision, and the value that will attach both to a life that is congruent with that vision and to a life that aims at such congruence when there in fact is no beatific vision.

Let's consider briefly the first of these two values: the good that will arise if my life is aligned with the beatific vision. In general, it seems plausible to suppose that the magnitude of the good that is realized when I live congruently with some state of affairs will be directly proportional to the value of that state of affairs. (Granted that there is some variation in the good that is realized when I live congruently with states of affairs, $S1$, $S2$, and so on, and allowing that the degree of congruence is the same in each case, what could account for that variation other than a difference in the value of these states of affairs?) And from a theistic point of view, God's reality is of course the supremely valuable state of affairs. And in the beatific vision, our lives will be aligned with that reality as perfectly as is humanly possible. Why? Because in the beatific vision, we shall 'see' the divine nature and be brought into union with it, so far as that is humanly possible. And in turn, therefore, a life that is lived, here and now, in conformity with the beatific vision will be aligned so far as is possible for us here and now with the divine nature. Why?

---

[6] There is, of course, a difference between the story concerning my uncle and the story of the beatific vision in so far as only the first concerns directly a location in the world. But allowing for this difference, the narrative of the beatific vision carries implications for the significance of particular places in the world, and how we are to relate ourselves to them, for the reasons we have discussed in earlier chapters.

Because such a life will be a rendering under the conditions of this life of the ideal of life that is realized in full in the beatific vision, where our relationship to the divine nature will be perfected. It follows then that in so far as my life is, here and now, aligned with the beatific vision, then I will realize a particularly profound good, since my life will, to that extent, be aligned with a particularly valuable state of affairs—and indeed, in so far as my life is hereby aligned with the divine reality, then I will realize the greatest of goods that it is possible for me to realize, here and now, by living congruently with some state of affairs.[7]

Here we have the beginnings of an account of the practical reasonableness of the spiritual life that is at least closely parallel to Thomas's understanding of the nature of religious faith. Let us take stock of some of these resemblances. As we have seen, Aquinas represents faith as 'cognitive', in so far as it involves assent to the truth of the relevant theological narrative. Similarly, in the example we have just discussed, I seek to bring my world-directed thoughts, feelings, actions, and so on, into alignment with the beatific vision—and in this sense, I commit myself to the truth of this doctrine. How so? Because I aim at a good that will only obtain if there is indeed a beatific vision.

Of course, there are circumstances in which it can make good practical sense to act as if a claim were true, while supposing that it is not. For instance, I may have reason to act as if Stumpy the cat is dangerous, when I know that she is not, if doing so will help to instruct an infant in the need to show caution in the presence of cats in general. It would not be difficult to construct spiritual analogues for this example, but by contrast with such cases, the spiritual practitioner, as we have understood them here, does not merely act as if some doctrine were true, but strives to realize a state of affairs which depends constitutively upon the truth of the doctrine. So we have some reason to follow Aquinas on this point, by supposing that there is a sense in which the spiritual life involves

---

[7] It is perhaps worth adding that on this account, in being aligned with the divine reality, my life will thereby be aligned with all else that is good, since that reality is the source and measure of all else that is good. (So we do not need to consider the putative case where my life is aligned not only with the divine reality, but with some further state of affairs in addition—and to consider whether a greater good may be realized when my life is aligned not just with the divine reality, but with this compound state of affairs.)

'belief'. The spiritual practitioner, we could say, commits themselves in practical terms to the truth of the relevant doctrine, because they commit themselves in practical terms to an end that can only obtain if the doctrine holds true.

In ordinary life, outside of religious contexts, to believe some proposition p is standardly to believe that p is more probable than not.[8] But Aquinas's account of the believing that is proper to religious faith cannot have quite that character, for the reason that believing that p is overall probable, relative to some body of evidence, is not normally subject to (direct) voluntary control. The account we have given indicates how we can take seriously both the idea that faith is voluntary, as Aquinas proposes, and the idea that it affirms the truth of the relevant theological narrative. In brief, I am suggesting, it is in the practice of the spiritual life that the truth of the narrative is affirmed, because the practice aims at a good that presupposes the narrative's truth; and since the practice is voluntary, so is the commitment to the narrative's truth that is established in that practice. To this extent, there is a sense, indeed, in which the spiritual practitioner is *more* committed to the truth of the narrative than the person who simply affirms that the narrative is more probable than not, without that claim making any difference to their practice. Why? Because it is only in the first case that the person actively binds their happiness or well-being to the truth of the narrative. And on the view we have been expounding here, the second kind of affirmation, one which remains practically disengaged, will not count as religiously or spiritually serious, however high a probability it may assign to the beatific vision or some other such narrative.

So the account of the spiritual life we have been developing tracks Aquinas's understanding of faith both in proposing that the spiritual practitioner affirms the truth of the relevant theological narrative, and in supposing that this affirmation is voluntary. These two features are also evident in the practical example we have taken to present an

---

[8] As Richard Swinburne comments: 'Normally, to believe that p is to believe that p is more probable or more likely than not-p': *Faith and Reason* (Oxford: Clarendon Press, 2nd edn, 2005), p. 5. As Swinburne goes on to note, sometimes belief is used in a rather different sense, when believing that p is simply a matter of committing oneself to p being more probable than relevant alternatives, even if not overall probable.

analogy with the case of spiritual commitment. It is, clearly, for me to decide whether I shall visit the putative site of my uncle's burial. And if I do so choose, that will be because my will is engaged by the attractiveness of a state of affairs that I have some prospect of realizing thereby: namely, the state which consists in my honouring my uncle in the special way that is possible when I am located at the very place where he is buried. So in this way, by choosing to visit this site, I commit myself voluntarily to the truth of a certain narrative, concerning where he buried. Similarly, on the conception of spiritual practice that we have been sketching, when I seek to live congruently with a theological narrative, I thereby commit myself voluntarily to the truth of that narrative.

This account of spiritual practice also resembles Aquinas's understanding of religious faith in taking the affirmation of a theological narrative to be action-guiding. More exactly, on the perspective we have been exploring, the affirmation of the narrative is established in the person's practice: we could say, then, that the assent to the narrative is action-guiding in the sense of being constituted by certain practical commitments. For instance, when I practise neighbour love, in order to realize the goal of living congruently with the beatific vision, I thereby assent, in practical terms, to the truth of the beatific vision. Here my assent is not speculative, but realized in a body of practice, which is directed at the relevant hybrid good.

Lastly, the account we have been developing is also comparable to Aquinas's understanding of faith in proposing that my commitment to the truth of the relevant doctrine will be confident and unwavering. Why think this is an implication of our account? Because, as we have seen, my practical assent to a given theological narrative will be a function both of the narrative's epistemic standing, and of the magnitude of the good that will ensue should my life be aligned with the narrative. Hence it is possible for the epistemic status of a given narrative to vary significantly, even to the point where I take the narrative to be of fairly low probability, without my practical commitment to its truth being compromised thereby—providing that the good at which I aim is of sufficient value. By contrast, if my assent to the narrative were to be based simply on epistemic considerations, then that assent would be more or less firm, more or less confident, according to variations in the strength of the epistemic case in its support.

Now the good at which I aim when I assent to the truth of the doctrine of the beatific vision is, as we have seen, a particularly profound good. Why? Because this good arises in so far as my world-directed thoughts, feelings, experience, behaviour, bodily demeanour, and so on, are aligned with a state of affairs that is of supreme value for a human being, namely, the condition of sharing with other human beings, and the angels, in the contemplation of God. Accordingly, my commitment to the truth of this narrative can, in principle, make sound practical sense, even in the face of significant fluctuations in the narrative's epistemic standing.

Reaching a more precise verdict on these questions will depend on a further matter, one that Aquinas does not consider directly. As we have noted, the appropriateness of a given practical commitment is a function not only of the value that will be realized should we succeed in that commitment, but also of the value (or disvalue) of the outcomes that will result should we not. Why? Because the expected value of a course of action is given by the sum of the values of *all* the possible outcomes of the action, where each of those values is discounted by the probability of the associated outcome. The question of what might eventuate should the commitment of faith prove fruitless was of no great interest for Aquinas. He is, after all, writing from the perspective of faith. And as we have seen, he thinks that when viewed from the relevant vantage point, faith is indeed, in one sense, certain, since its truth-directedness is divinely guaranteed. But by Aquinas's own estimation, faith can also be subjectively uncertain, and it seems we have good reason, therefore, to consider what outcomes may follow should the theological narrative which it upholds prove to be false. Why? Because, once more, the values of these outcomes (and not only the value of the outcome that will obtain should the narrative hold true) may have some bearing on faith's practical reasonableness.

Let us take the case of Amy, who has made a practical commitment, in faith, to align her life with the narrative of the beatific vision. Suppose that Amy comes in time to think that there is a compelling case against the existence of God, and in turn against the existence of the beatific vision, and suppose she therefore gives up her practical commitment to the doctrine. In such a case, how should Amy think of her former life? Should she now regret having ordered her life to the realization of goods that cannot obtain if there is no beatific vision? We can approach this question by considering the costs, if any, of the commitment of faith should the theological narrative to which it subscribes prove false.

Amy has surrendered not only her belief in the beatific vision but also her belief in God. And for simplicity's sake, let us suppose that she has not adopted an alternative religious creed. In that case, Amy will now consider the question of how she is to order her life solely from the vantage point of what we can call, following Aquinas, a rule of reason—whereas, in her former life, when she lived as a person of faith, Amy was committed to following, in addition, a divine rule.[9] For instance, in her former life, Amy sought to practise neighbour love, on the grounds that this is how we ought to relate to our fellow human beings—attitudinally, behaviourally, and so on—if our lives are to be aligned with the beatific vision. By contrast, when viewed from the vantage point of a rule of reason, neighbour love will count as supererogatory, and therefore praiseworthy, rather than obligatory. Given this understanding of how the moral status of neighbour love alters, when a person moves from the perspective of faith to a perspective that is informed simply by various rules of reason, what should Amy now make of her former life? Or to put the matter another way: given her current conception of the moral and spiritual life, does Amy have any reason to regret having lived according to a divine rule?

Suppose we distinguish two kinds of obligation: a subjective obligation is one a person takes themselves to have, whether or not they are so obliged in fact, while an objective obligation is one that holds in fact, whether or not the person is aware of having the obligation.[10] (For instance, suppose that euthanasia is in fact a serious wrong, but that, through no fault of my own, I do not recognize as much, say, because I have been raised in a culture that takes the practice to be morally

[9] For further discussion of this distinction, see again Chapter 2.
[10] Here, I am following a distinction drawn by Richard Swinburne in his essay 'The Christian Scheme of Salvation', in Michael Rea (ed.), *Oxford Readings in Philosophical Theology*: vol. 1, *Trinity, Incarnation and Atonement* (Oxford: Oxford University Press, 2009), p. 295.

178 SPIRITUAL TRADITIONS AND THE VIRTUES

unproblematic: here I have an objective but not a subjective obligation to refrain from bringing about euthanasia.) We can use this distinction to think about the change in Amy's moral context when she moves from a perspective of faith. Let us ask first of all: in making this move, has Amy thereby acquired any subjective obligations?

Well, Amy's former self lived by two kinds of rule: rules of reason and also divine rules. As we have seen in our earlier discussion, if we follow Aquinas's account of these matters, then we should say that in no case does a divine rule abrogate a rule of reason: instead, such a rule extends or radicalizes the corresponding rule of reason, by demanding that the person do all that is required by the rule of reason and more besides.[11] From this picture, it follows that Amy's former self was just as committed to observing rules of reason as she is now. It's just that her former self recognized, in addition, various divine rules, which extended those rules of reason. Hence in giving up the perspective of faith, and moving to a perspective in which she acknowledges only the authority of rules of reason, Amy has not acquired any subjective obligations.

However, in surrendering the perspective of faith, it is clear that Amy will have lost at least one subjective obligation, because previously she thought of neighbour love as obligatory, whereas now she thinks of it as supererogatory. She will also have lost any other subjective obligation that she formerly recognized because of her commitment to some divine rule, rather than a rule of reason. That leaves the question of Amy's objective obligations. What should we say on this point?

Granted the understanding of objective obligation that we are employing here—according to which an objective obligation is grounded in features of the world, rather than features of the person's perspective on the world—it will follow that Amy's surrendering of the vantage point of faith will not make for any change in the character of her objective obligations, since this change will not make for any change in the world. In sum, in giving up the perspective of faith, Amy will neither lose nor acquire any objective obligations, and neither will she acquire

---

[11] See once again the discussion in Chapter 2, concerning the relationship between the acquired and infused virtues: for instance, the relationship between religiously motivated dietary abstinence and the dietary practice that is appropriate to acquired temperance.

THE NATURE OF FAITH   179

any subjective obligations—but she will lose at least one subjective obligation. Granted this characterization of the change in her moral circumstances, does Amy have any reason to regret having lived according to a divine rule?

It seems clear that Amy would have some reason for regret if she had *acquired* any subjective obligations as a result of surrendering the perspective of faith. In that case, when viewing her former life, she would have reason to regret that she failed to recognize, and in turn to act on, various obligations that she now recognizes (and now takes to be objective). Of course, this failure need not be culpable: Amy's former self may have done all that she reasonably could have done to establish the nature of her obligations. Nonetheless, in this case, when reviewing her former self's commitments, Amy would have reason to regret that she failed to acknowledge, and in turn to act on, what were in fact her obligations, because to that extent, her life was not responsive to values that ought (objectively) to have guided her conduct. However, in the case we are considering, Amy has not acquired any subjective obligations. She has instead lost at least one such obligation. Might a change of this kind also be grounds for regret?

Let's return to the particular case that interests us. From her current vantage point, Amy considers neighbour love as supererogatory, whereas previously she thought it obligatory. Given this characterization of the change in her moral perspective, it seems that Amy has no reason to regret the mere fact of having practised neighbour love. Why? Because when viewed from her current perspective, that is, by reference to the relevant rule of reason, neighbour love appears to Amy as good, and indeed deserving of praise. So given her current moral position, Amy will suppose that she has, right now, good reason to practise neighbour love—and to that extent, it seems that she has no reason to regret having formerly practised neighbour love.

But perhaps Amy has reason to regret not the mere fact of having practised neighbour love, but the fact that she once took herself to have an obligation to practise neighbour love—and so took herself to have more of a reason for engaging in this practice (to view matters from her current vantage point) than she in fact had. On this view, it's not what she formerly did, but the strength of the reason she took herself to have for doing it, that Amy ought now to regret. But alongside this reading of her situation, we should allow that Amy may also have reason to regret that she no longer has a subjective obligation to practise neighbour love. Why? Well, were she to have a subjective obligation to practise neighbour love, then she would have more of a reason to engage in a practice that is, when judged by her current moral perspective, good and indeed deserving of praise. And other things being equal, shouldn't Amy want to have more of a reason to do what she (from her current vantage point) thinks to be deserving of praise?[12]

We have been considering the case of neighbour love. But as we have seen, as well as lifting certain actions that would otherwise be supererogatory into the realm of the obligatory, the introduction of a theological narrative may also constitute as obligatory an action that would otherwise have been a matter of moral indifference. In our earlier discussion, we considered as an example of this case dietary abstinence, where from the vantage point of the relevant rule of reason, this practice fails to produce more good than would be produced by observing a less demanding dietary rule.[13] Accordingly, when viewed from that vantage point, abstinence is not wrong, but under-motivated, to the extent that it involves a more rigorous practice than is required to secure the desired end. What should we say of this sort of case: might Amy have reason to regret the fact that she once took herself to have an obligation of this form?

Perhaps Amy has more of a reason in this instance to regret her former life. After all, here, and by contrast with the case of neighbour love, she no longer takes herself to have a reason to engage in the relevant practice in the present. For instance, perhaps she has reason to regret that the dietary practice she previously followed involved a greater expenditure of effort than was required for the production of the only good that she now associates with the practice (that is, the good of bodily health, rather than the good of a life that is aligned with the beatific vision). But in moral terms, this sort of regret will, presumably, not run

---

[12] We touched on this same issue in Chapter 2, where we considered whether a person might have reason to become a theist, in order to have more of a reason for doing what they take to be good and indeed praiseworthy.

[13] See Chapter 2 for a fuller account of this case.

very deep, since from Amy's current perspective, her former practice did not, after all, involve any wrong-doing.

We have been asking whether a person who has surrendered the perspective of faith has any reason to regret having lived according to a divine rule. On the basis of the considerations we have reviewed to this point, I have been suggesting that such a person has at most very limited grounds for feeling regret at having ordered their life in these terms. And they have indeed, arguably, some reason to feel regret about *giving up* a life that was governed by the vantage point of faith, to the extent that they now have less of a reason to do what they recognize (from their current moral perspective) it would be good, and indeed praiseworthy, to do. Again, these questions are of some interest for our purposes because in determining the practical rationality of the commitment of faith, it is relevant to consider not only the goods that will ensue should the theological narrative that is presupposed in faith hold true, but also those goods, and bads, that will obtain should that narrative be false. To the extent that a person in Amy's position has little or no reason to regret having lived according to the perspective of a divine rule, then that is a reason for supposing that the bads associated with the commitment of faith, in the case where the relevant theological narrative proves to be false, are rather limited.

But might there be other reasons why Amy should feel regret? What of the fact that her former life was ordered to a state of affairs, the beatific vision, that she now supposes does not obtain? From her present vantage point, should Amy not regret having taken a false representation of the world as the basis for her conception of how to live? That is, shouldn't she regret having organized her life around what she now takes to be a falsehood? Again, let us assume that in assenting to the doctrine of the beatific vision, Amy's former self was not guilty of any epistemic failure, relative to her circumstances at the time. So the question we are addressing is not of this form: should Amy regret not having done more to investigate the truth of the beatific vision, or more to weigh the evidence available to her, and so on? But simply: should Amy regret having based her life on a narrative that was, to judge matters from her current vantage point, false?

The following remarks of Robert Adams throw some light on this question. Here Adams is considering the contribution of worship to the well-lived human life:

> Something of ethical importance can be done in worship that we cannot accomplish except symbolically... Getting ourselves dressed in the morning, [going] to work, and then home again to dinner, we try on the way and in between to do some good, to love people and be kind to them, to enjoy and perhaps to create some beauty. But none of this is very perfect, even when we succeed; and all of it is very fragmentary... Symbolically, we can do better. Symbolically I can be for the Good as such, and not just for the bits and pieces of it that I can concretely promote... I can be for the good by articulating or accepting some conception of a comprehensive and perfect or transcendent Good and expressing my loyalty to it symbolically... The symbolism provides something for which there is no adequate substitute. Theists find this value of symbolism supremely in worship.[14]

Following Adams' suggestion, we can say that the life of faith, so far as it is guided by a conception of the fundamental nature of goodness, is one way of being for the Good as such, symbolically. Moreover, there is, I take it, a reason why 'theists find this value of symbolism *supremely* in worship'. Why do they think so? Because on the theistic world view, in worship, a person is able to relate themselves to the Good as such not only as an object of thought, but as actual. And how is that possible? Because on the theistic view, the Good is not a mere abstraction—on the contrary, the paradigm of goodness, the measure by which we are to assess the claim of anything to count as good, and in that sense the Good as such, is, for the theist, not simply an idea of goodness, but the divine nature, considered as actual.[15] Accordingly, on this perspective, I can

[14] Robert Adams, *Finite and Infinite Goods* (Oxford: Oxford University Press, 1999), p. 227, my ellipses. I am grateful to John Cottingham for drawing this passage to my attention.

[15] For a modern, now classic, account of how to develop this picture, see William Alston, 'Some Suggestions for Divine Command Theorists', in his collection *Divine Nature and Human Language* (Ithaca, NY: Cornell University Press, 1989), pp. 253–73. Platonic perspectives on the divine nature, which represent that nature as the Form of the Good, provide a further way of understanding how the divine nature can count as Goodness Itself. It is worth being clear

commit my life to the Good as such not only by ordering my life choices according to a set of moral principles or a conception of the Good as such—in addition, I can place myself in relationship with the Good as such considered as actual.

And why should it matter that I should be able to relate myself to the Good in this further way? There are various answers we might give to this question, but one is provided by the account of the infused moral virtues that we have been developing in this volume. On this account, the goods of these virtues arise in so far as our world-directed thoughts, behaviour, feelings, and so on, are aligned with sacred reality—which is to say, in so far as they are aligned with the Good as such, conceived in the way just proposed. Of course, my life can also secure various goods simply by virtue of being aligned with appropriate moral principles or ideals, even if there is no substantive reality that counts as Good as such. But in this case, my life will not realize hybrid goods as we have understood them here: that is, goods that obtain in so far as my life in relevant respects is congruent with an actual state of affairs—such as the beatific vision, supposing that this vision in fact obtains. Drawing on this picture, we can ask once again why, on the theistic view, our relationship to the Good as such is realized supremely in worship. And we may reply: because in worship, according to the theist, the person achieves not only the good that will arise whenever we align our lives with some truthful conception of the nature of the Good, but the further good that is made possible in so far as our lives are aligned, whether directly or indirectly, with the Good as such as actual.

Of course, this is how matters look from the theistic perspective. But what should Amy say when reviewing her former life, given that she has surrendered a theistic world view? As we have seen, from her new, secular perspective, Amy will not have acquired any additional subjective obligations, and those obligations she has surrendered will concern

---

that the points I make here about relationship to the Good as such considered as actual will also apply to non-theistic forms of Platonism. So they will also hold for a position such as that advocated by Iris Murdoch in 'The Sovereignty of Good over Other Concepts', in her text *The Sovereignty of Good* (London: Routledge & Kegan Paul, 1970), ch. 3. While Murdochian Platonism may not be a conventionally religious position, neither will it count as simply secular on the usage that I am following here.

courses of action that from her current vantage point will appear morally permissible, and in some cases praiseworthy. So for the reasons we have considered, it seems Amy does not have any deep-seated moral reason to regret her former way of life. But to return to our original question, might she not regret all the same the fact that she previously lived according to a conception of reality that she now takes to be false?

Amy could indeed regret having been guided by what she now takes to be a falsehood, but against this consideration we should weigh the fact that in giving up a theistic perspective, she has also surrendered a certain way of being related to the Good as such. For instance, to take the case of neighbour love again, it's not just that when she lived according to a divine rule, Amy had more of a reason to engage in various practices that from her present vantage point seem praiseworthy. It is also true that when she lived according to a divine rule, she could take her world-directed activities to have as their ultimate focus the Good as actual. So the mode of her pursuit of the Good as such was then different, to the extent that it was targeted at what she took to be a substantive reality, relationship to which would enable her to realize a range of hybrid goods in her day to day relations with the sensory world. And of course, on the standard monotheistic view, the ultimate object of Amy's practice, in her former life, was the Good not only as actual, but as personal. And for this reason too, in psychological terms, the form taken by her commitment to the Good as such would have been very different. Notably, that commitment would then have been one of (inter-personal) love. For these reasons, we might say that Amy's sense of connection to the Good as such was formerly more tangible and indeed more intimate, to the extent that it was directed at a reality that she took to be actual and even personal, relationship to which could be enacted in her encounter with the everyday, sensory world, through the realization of the associated hybrid goods. So in brief, while Amy does have reason to regret having oriented her life towards what she now supposes is a false representation of reality, she also has reason to regret having set aside the perspective of faith, to the extent that she cannot now relate herself to the Good, or express her allegiance to her most fundamental ideals, with the kind of embodied seriousness that is possible for the person who occupies the perspective of faith.[16]

Let us press this thought a little further by considering an illustration. Suppose I am a fourteenth-century pilgrim, journeying to the cathedral in St Andrews, in the hope of drawing close to, and perhaps even touching, the bones of Jesus's disciple, Andrew, who is reputed to be buried there. So I am seeking to realize the good, a hybrid good, of being oriented to the Good as such through my bodily relation to a portion of the material world—here the relics of St Andrew. And how is it possible for these bones to bear this significance for me? Because I take these remains to be hallowed, on the grounds that they were once physically proximate to the person of Christ, who in turn mediates in bodily terms the presence of God or the Good considered as actual. When a modern, secular person considers my life, they may well be glad that their life is not governed by (what they take to be) the metaphysical falsehoods of the Christian world view (not to mention the falsehood in the idea that the relics of St Andrew were located in medieval Scotland). But they also have some reason, I take it, to feel a measure of regret about their incapacity to inhabit my world view. Why? Because through my allegiance to this world view, I can take my sensory engagement with the everyday world, and even, as here, my touching of material objects, to matter in the special way that is possible when this engagement is not simply ordered to a symbolic representation of the Good as such, but offers a mode of encounter with the Good considered as actual. The pilgrim's enacted relationship to the Good as such has, in these respects, a depth that it is hard to replicate in a purely secular relationship to the material world, for the reason simply that that relationship is not animated by the thought that the Good as such considered as actual can be presented to us in our relations to the everyday sensory world. Or to put the point in

---

[16] There is an echo of this proposal in the familiar suggestion that talk of God is simply a way of personifying moral or spiritual principles. The underlying thought here seems to be that by personifying such principles, we make it easier, in psychological terms, to engage with them and take them as action-guiding. Compare Don Cupitt's reading of the idea of God as a personification of the 'religious requirement' in his text *Taking Leave of God* (London: SCM, 1980).

the terms of our present discussion, the secular life is not governed by the thought that through the pursuit of hybrid goods, our relations to the sensory world can be folded into our relationship to a transcendent Good.

In sum, we have been considering some of the costs that may attach to the commitment of faith, supposing that the theological narratives that sustain the practices of faith are false. I have been suggesting that while there are indeed costs, they need to be weighed against the various respects in which the life of faith can be seen as good from a secular point of view. Here as elsewhere in this discussion, our guiding thoughts have been taken from the work of Thomas Aquinas, and specifically his account of the infused moral virtues. If we follow Aquinas in these matters, then we should say that the person who has given up the perspective of faith, on the grounds that they no longer find its world view persuasive (not even in the modest degree that is required for religious faith), has reason to regret that they have lost certain of the subjective obligations by which they once ordered their life, and reason to regret that they can no longer commune with their ideal of the Good in the specially intimate and tangible way that is possible when a person takes that ideal to be accessible to them as actual in their relations to the sensory world.

Our discussion to this point has simplified the question of the practical rationality of faith by supposing that there are before us just two possibilities: a life that is ordered according to divine rules, and a secular life that is ordered solely according to rules of reason. But in practice, when determining whether to embark on, or persist in, a life of faith, a person is likely to have multiple alternatives before them, including those presented by various non-theistic religious schemes, some of which will have no use for the idea of revelation. So our discussion has to that extent abstracted from the complexity of real-world decision making. However, I hope to have traced some of the more important considerations that are relevant for an assessment of the respective goods that are accessible, in principle, in a life of faith and in a life that is ordered in secular terms or according to rules of reason.

So far in this chapter, we have been sketching how the account of spiritual practice that we have been defending in this volume tracks on various points Aquinas's understanding of faith. In particular, this account agrees with Aquinas in supposing that the assent to the relevant theological narrative is, in the sense we have explored, cognitive, voluntary, action-guiding, unwavering, and, in principle, practically reasonable. That last claim, about the practical reasonableness of faith, can be sustained, I have been suggesting, once we take stock of the full range of the outcomes that may follow from the commitment of faith—including those outcomes that will obtain if the relevant theological narrative should prove to be false. In the case where the narrative turns out to be false, the commitment of faith will fail to secure, of course, the hybrid goods at which it is targeted. But even if a person of faith should come to discover that this is how things stand, they need not feel, I have argued, any deep-seated regret about having ordered their life to that narrative—and they may indeed have reason to believe that in surrendering the perspective that is afforded by a divine rule, their life has been, if anything, impoverished.[17]

Having propounded an account of religious faith that is, at least, broadly convergent with Aquinas's understanding of these matters, I want to consider next how this reading of the nature of spiritual commitment compares with three others which are well-known from the literature. In this way, I hope to bring into clearer focus the distinctiveness of the conception of the spiritual life that we have been developing here.

Pierre Hadot on the Nature of 'Faith'

Let us begin by considering Pierre Hadot's account of the kind of assent to a world view (or what we have been calling a theological narrative) that is required for the purpose of sustaining a spiritual practice. While Hadot does not address this matter directly, nonetheless he is committed, as we have seen, to the idea that the spiritual adept should think of the world view that supports their practice as having some prospect of being, at least, an approximation to the truth.[18] To return to the example

---

[17] I have been proposing that the person of faith has reason to consider the goods that will be realized in their practice should the narratives of faith be false. This suggests that fictionalist readings of theological narratives are to that extent of some interest for the commitment of faith.

[18] These are matters we discussed in Chapter 1.

of Epicureanism, if we take atomism or some doctrine relevantly like it to be a contender for truth, then we will have some reason not to fear post-mortem judgement—because in that case, we will have some reason to suppose that there is no post-mortem life. By contrast, if we suppose that atomism and kindred views are not serious candidates for truth, then it is hard to see how engaging in the spiritual practice of simply entertaining these views (rather than thinking of them with the kind of assent that is implied in taking them to have some prospect of being true) can subvert the fear of post-mortem judgement. Why? Because in this case, these views give me no reason to doubt that there will be a post-mortem existence—and to that extent, they give me no reason to doubt that there will be a post-mortem judgement.

So Hadot's account suggests that a world view needs to meet an epistemic constraint of this kind if it is to play a role in motivating a spiritual practice. The approach we have been developing proceeds differently on this point, and this difference reflects a divergence of view about the nature of the goods to which the spiritual life is ordered. For Hadot, these goods can be understood independently of reference to world view. For example, the good at which the Epicurean aims is a life of tranquillity and freedom from anxiety, and on Hadot's account, such a life can be recognized as good before we consider the nature of our metaphysical context. On this reading of their practice, the role of the Epicurean world view is to enable the person to lead such a life—and it does this, at least in part, by specifying a state of affairs relative to which this ideal of life will be rationally appropriate. And once again, if it is to play this role, then the world view must be taken to have some reasonable prospect of being at least an approximation to the truth, as a condition of giving the adept some reason to believe that her fears are in fact baseless: it is not enough that the adept should suppose simply that these fears *would be* baseless if the world view were to be an approximation to the truth.

By contrast, on the perspective we have been exploring, the ends of the spiritual life cannot be specified, with respect to their fundamental nature, independently of reference to metaphysical context. Why not? Because the goods with which we have been concerned—what we have been calling hybrid goods—obtain to the extent that a person's world-directed thoughts, feelings, behaviour, and so on, are congruent with the relevant theological narrative. So on this account, and by contrast with Hadot's procedure, it makes no sense, conceptually, to start by identifying an ideal of life, and then to search for a world view that can help to sustain the way of life (and that meets the relevant probability threshold therefore): rather, when considering how to order our lives in spiritual terms, we should take ways of life and world views in combination, and ask which combination is apt to produce the greatest spiritual good. Accordingly, on this approach, the probability of a given world view can be very low, without thereby calling into question the practical reasonableness of the associated way of life. Why? Because here the reasonableness of a given way of life depends on its tendency to realize spiritual goods, which is to say that it depends not only on the probability of the associated world view, but also on the extent of the good that will ensue should the world view be true, and should it be false. Moreover, in the case of a world view or narrative such as the beatific vision, we have seen, there is some reason to think that the correlative hybrid good is as great as any hybrid good could be—since it will arise in so far as a person's life is aligned with the divine nature, or the Good as such considered as actual. And there is also some reason to suppose that the bads that will obtain should this narrative be false will not render the life of faith ruinous, or even an object of significant regret. So in this case in particular, it seems that the probability of a world view that supports the commitment of faith can be low, and indeed lower than that of some of its rivals, without thereby jeopardizing the reasonableness of that commitment.

It may be that on these points, our approach differs from Aquinas's. Perhaps on his account, we need to treat the articles of faith as at least fairly likely[19]—although it is clear that on his view, they cannot be

---

[19] It is not clear to me that Aquinas is committed to the thought that a proposition can only be affirmed in faith if its epistemic (rather than intrinsic) probability passes a certain threshold value. Let's note one objection to this reading. As we have seen in our earlier discussion, when distinguishing faith from opinion, Aquinas appeals not (directly) to epistemic considerations, but to the relative confidence of the will's movement in faith. But perhaps that confidence would not be possible if the probability of the relevant propositions were to fall below a certain value? I am grateful to Brian Leftow for raising this question in conversation. It may be worth recalling here that in the assent of faith, as Aquinas understands it, the movement of the will is

deemed too likely, without putting at risk the voluntariness of faith.[20] If we do read Aquinas in this way, then the perspective we have been developing can still be reconciled with his. We can simply say that this perspective becomes relevant to Christian faith, in the sense delineated by Aquinas, once the relevant doctrines reach an appropriate threshold of probability—while being relevant to a different but related commitment, one that is also practically rational, when those doctrines fall short of that threshold. There is no substantive philosophical disagreement here.

In sum, the account we have been propounding differs from Hadot's in two respects. It involves a different conception of the nature of spiritual goods, and in turn it also offers, therefore, a different understanding of the epistemic preconditions for spiritually meaningful assent to a world view, or theological narrative. For Hadot, I have suggested, to assent in the requisite way is to suppose that the relevant world view is a serious candidate for truth. By contrast, on the view we have been considering, assent is not, to the same extent, tied to a particular assessment of the epistemic standing of the narrative. Why? Because in this case, assent is governed not only by epistemic considerations, but also by a judgement concerning the magnitude of the goods that will obtain should the narrative be true, and of the bads that will obtain should it be

---

supported by grace—and perhaps for that reason, a person's will can move confidently in this case even if they take the relevant probability to be very low. Once again, on the account developed in this volume, the commitment of faith is embedded in a practical project, and relatively immune to epistemic considerations for that reason.

[20] Suppose I take a given article of faith to be significantly more likely than not (so that I am bound to hold it to be true) and yet less than certain. In that case, the will can still play a role in so far as I commit myself to the truth of the article with greater assurance than would be warranted simply by reference to my estimation of its probability. I am grateful to Brian Leftow for this point. Aquinas does not, of course, cite this consideration, but it is perhaps one way of drawing out his position. It may be relevant here to recall Aquinas's treatment of the faith of the devils. Their faith turns out to be involuntary because of the evidence of signs—and so far as I can see, there is no reason to suppose that this evidence is so powerful, from their perspective, that they ought to assign the relevant propositions a probability of 1, so that there is no conceptual space for a commitment of will that runs beyond what is indicated by the evidence. If so, then it seems that Christian faith is in principle an option for the devils, or others who are swayed by signs, which is perhaps contrary to the drift of Aquinas's text. However, we might also note that because of the corruption of their wills, the devils cannot in fact affirm the propositions of faith with greater assurance than is suggested by the evidence. We do not need to settle these exegetical questions for present purposes, so I shall not consider them further here.

false. Hence if we suppose that for Hadot, in a given dialectical context, a world view needs a probability of at least p, if it is to support a way of life, then it seems that on Aquinas's account, a theological narrative could have a probability rather lower than p, while still providing the basis for a commitment of faith, providing that the corresponding way of life is apt to realize significant goods. However, even here, assent will be subject to certain epistemic constraints. For instance, the likelihood of the narrative cannot be set at zero: in that case, seeking to secure a good that presupposes the truth of the narrative will not count as a spiritually serious project, on the conception of the spiritual life provided here.

So when compared with Hadot's perspective, the account of religious faith that we have been considering generates, in these ways, a distinctive conception of the goods that are the object of the spiritual life—and in turn, a distinctive understanding of the kind of assent that is required if a narrative is to support a way of life. Let's look briefly next at two further views of the nature of spiritual commitment, and their treatment of these same issues.

Two Further Accounts of Faith: Ludwig Wittgenstein and Blaise Pascal

Wittgenstein's work, and that of his followers, is commonly taken to associate religious faith with practical, rather than metaphysical, commitment. And it is of some interest, therefore, to see how this account compares with the approach that we have been developing here.

In his 'Lectures on Religious Belief', Wittgenstein remarks:

> Suppose someone were a believer and said: 'I believe in a Last Judgment', and I said: 'Well, I'm not so sure. Possibly.' You would say that there is an enormous gulf between us. If he said 'There is a German aeroplane overhead', and I said 'Possibly I'm not so sure', you'd say we were fairly near.[21]

---

[21] Ludwig Wittgenstein, *Lectures and Conversations on Aesthetics, Psychology and Religious Belief*, ed. C. Barrett (Oxford: Blackwell, 1966), p. 53.

These comments suggest that religious beliefs are different from beliefs concerning the everyday sensory world in so far as they are not held tentatively, or do not admit of doubt. (It is for this reason that the comment 'possibly, there is a last judgement' is inadmissible, if the person is speaking in a religious mode.) The view that we have been expounding provides one way of understanding this distinction: on this view, while sensory beliefs, such as the one that Wittgenstein cites here, are typically held with more or less assurance, where variations in the degree of assurance track variations in the epistemic standing of the belief, religious 'beliefs' are not in the same way vulnerable to changes in the evidence, because they are embedded in practical commitments. For example, I can be said to believe that there is a beatific vision, or believe in the beatific vision, when my life is ordered to the realization of a hybrid good that depends constitutively on the reality of the beatific vision; and for the reasons we have been considering, it is to be expected that this commitment, and the associated belief, will be relatively immune to shifts in the evidence. So to this extent, the view that we have been developing seems to fit with Wittgenstein's proposal that religious belief is distinct from sensory belief, in so far as only the second is subject to evidence-driven variations in assurance. Again, on the account we have been considering, this difference can be explained by the fact that religious faith is held fast by the relevant practical commitment.[22]

Wittgenstein goes on to note this further respect in which religious faith is distinctive:

Suppose someone is ill and he says: 'This is punishment', and I say: 'If I'm ill, I don't think of punishment at all.' If you say: 'Do you believe the opposite?' – you can call it believing the opposite, but it is entirely different from what we would normally call believing the opposite. I think differently, in a different way. I say different things to myself. I have different pictures.[23]

---

[22] In the same way, this account is also relevant to Peter Winch's Wittgenstein-inspired comment that ceasing to pray is best conceived as an 'aspect' rather than as a 'consequence' of ceasing to believe in God. See his chapter, 'Meaning and Religious Language', in Stuart Brown (ed.), *Reason and Religion* (Ithaca, NY: Cornell University Press, 1977), pp. 207–8. Here, Winch takes religious belief to be at least in part constituted by a practical commitment, rather than as simply the logical ground of that commitment.

[23] Wittgenstein, *Lectures and Conversations*, p. 55.

Here, it is, of course, the religious person who thinks 'This is punishment'. And Wittgenstein's suggestion seems to be that what distinguishes this person from their secular counterpart is not that one asserts that we are subject, even in this life, to punishment, while the other does not, but simply that one uses a certain picture to regulate their lives, while the other does not. We could connect these remarks to the earlier passage: it is perhaps because religious belief does not involve any kind of assertion, but simply the entertaining of a picture, that it cannot be subject to doubt. After all, if religious belief does not involve any assertion, and is not concerned, therefore, with advancing any view of the nature of things, then it is not clear how it could be the object of doubt, or at least of the kind of doubt that we have when we wonder whether there is an aeroplane overhead. On this reading, we might take Wittgenstein to be defending a position that I earlier declined to attribute to Hadot: perhaps a world view, or what Wittgenstein calls a 'picture' of things, can simply be entertained, independently of any commitment to its epistemic standing, and can regulate a person's life on that basis.

The view we have been considering allows us to make some sense of the idea that there is a connection between religious belief and commitment to a picture. To revert to our well-worn example, following Aquinas, we can think of neighbour love as a spiritual practice that is aimed at various hybrid goods that will obtain should there be a beatific vision. In this case, the idea of the beatific vision functions as a kind of picture, by reference to which the person of faith can assess the significance of their relations to others. And as we have seen, in holding to this picture, the person need not assert its content, by taking this representation of the world to be overall probable. So on this view, we could say that what distinguishes the person of faith from the secular person is, indeed, the fact that the secular person does not have recourse to the same pictures. Why think that the secular person is different in this respect? Because they are not aiming at goods that require for their realization the truth of the beatific vision, or another such theological narrative or picture. Instead, the secular person assesses their life by reference to different pictures, representing other states of affairs—states whose obtaining is required if their, rather different, goals are to be realized.

It is implied in Wittgenstein's remarks that the difference between the believer and the secular person need not be fundamentally epistemic in character. It is because this difference is not epistemic, we might suppose, that one does not 'believe the opposite' of the other, as Wittgenstein puts the point in the passage I have just cited. On the approach we have been developing, we can also endorse this judgement to this extent. On this account, what distinguishes the believer from the secular person is, we can say, their practical project: the believer aims at a spiritual good whose realization involves the truth of a given theological narrative, say that of the beatific vision, while the secular person does not aim at goods that are spiritual in this sense. And this difference need not rest on any epistemic difference: it may be that the believer and the secular person assign the same probability to the beatific vision. (Most likely, neither of them will assign a very precise probability to the narrative—instead, they are likely to have some rough and ready sense of whether the doctrine has some prospect, however limited, of being true.) If they do assign the same probability to the beatific vision, then the difference in their practice, in so far as one aims at spiritual goods and the other does not, will reflect a difference in value judgement: the believer considers a life that is congruent with the beatific vision as supremely worthwhile, whereas the secular person does not consider this state of affairs so profound a good—or at any rate, even if they should subscribe to that judgement in theoretical terms, their attention is, in practice, occupied with other prospective states of affairs, which they treat as a more deserving object of pursuit.

Moreover, even if, in a given case, the difference between a religious and a secular person is in part a matter of the first assigning a higher probability to the beatific vision, for the reasons we have considered, it is likely to be the believer's commitment to the goodness of the beatific vision that holds their belief in the doctrine secure, regardless of fluctuations in, or uncertainties about, its evidential status. In sum, on this view, it is axiological, rather than epistemic or abstractly metaphysical, commitments that form the bedrock of the spiritual life, and to that extent we can agree with Wittgenstein that the difference between the believer, or spiritual practitioner, and the non-believer is not best represented in terms of 'believing the opposite'.

It is sometimes supposed that Wittgenstein's account of religion is fundamentally non-realist in intent: the believer makes no assertions, but simply entertains pictures that play some sort of action-guiding role in their life. Here, I shall simply bracket the exegetical question of how Wittgenstein is to be read on this point.[24] However, the account of the spiritual life that we have been examining here shows, I think, that central features of his approach that might seem to support a non-realist view (for instance, his ideas on the invulnerability of religious belief to fluctuations in evidence, and on the role of 'pictures' in the spiritual life) can be subsumed within a metaphysically realist conception of the religious and spiritual life. After all, the view of the spiritual life that we have been exploring takes the doctrine of the beatific vision, and like doctrines, to advance metaphysical claims, and takes the truth of those claims to matter for the spiritual life. How so? Because the hybrid goods to which that life is ordered depend constitutively upon the truth of the relevant theological narrative. Even so, on this view, we can still allow that the practice of the spiritual life, for creatures such as ourselves, of limited epistemic capabilities, may well rest, most fundamentally, on our value commitments or, to put the matter in Aquinas's terms, on what we love, rather than upon the judgement that certain metaphysical proposals are overall probable.

We could read D.Z. Phillips's remarks in the following passage in a similar spirit:

If there is an analogy between the existence of God and the existence of unicorns, then coming to see that there is a God would be like coming to see that an additional being exists. 'I know what people are doing when they worship', a philosopher might say. 'They praise, they confess, they thank, and they ask for things. The only difference between myself and religious believers is that I do not believe that there is a being who receives their worship.' The assumption, here, is that the meaning of worship is contingently related to the question

---

[24] Genia Schoenbaumsfeld notes the charge in her helpful chapter, 'Ludwig Wittgenstein', in G. Oppy and N. N. Trakakis (eds), *Twentieth-Century Philosophy of Religion* (Durham: Acumen, 2009), p. 164.

whether there is a God or not. The assumption might be justified by saying that there need be no consequences of existential beliefs. Just as one can say, 'There is a planet Mars, but I couldn't care less', so one can say, 'There is a God, but I couldn't care less'. ... But all this is foreign to the question whether there is a God. That is not something anyone could *find out*. It has been far too readily assumed that the dispute between the believer and the unbeliever is over a *matter of fact*.[25]

On the view we have been expounding here, we should say that Phillips is right to suppose that where religious beliefs are concerned, it would make no sense to assent to a belief and then to add 'but I couldn't care less'. Why not? Because on this view, in religious contexts, believing is held fast within a practical project, which is directed at a state of affairs that the believer takes to be profoundly good, and about which they care. For instance, if I believe in the beatific vision, that will not be fundamentally for speculative reasons (that is, for reasons that I would be able to recognize even if I 'couldn't care less' about the truth or otherwise of this theological narrative), but because I take the state of affairs that consists in the alignment of my life with the beatific vision to be of profound significance, and indeed of such importance that it is worth ordering my life to that goal, even while recognizing that my prospects of success may well be relatively low, or at any rate relatively indeterminate.

However, while agreeing with Phillips that religious belief cannot be isolated from attitudes of 'caring', we can still take seriously the metaphysical import of theological narratives, such as the narrative of the beatific vision, and suppose that religious beliefs are, to that extent, concerned with 'matters of fact'. On the view we have been exploring here, a metaphysical construal of the narrative will, indeed, be required if we are to make sense of the believer's practice, which aims to bring their thoughts, feelings, behaviour, and so on, into alignment with the fundamental nature of things. So in these various ways, the account we have been considering intersects quite fruitfully with some central themes in

---

[25] D. Z. Phillips, *Faith and Philosophical Enquiry* (London: Routledge & Kegan Paul, 1970), pp. 16–17, his emphasis.

the work of Wittgenstein, and writers of a similar persuasion, on the question of how we are to understand the distinctive character of religious belief. And once again, this convergence of perspective on questions such as whether religious belief is relatively immune from doubt, and whether it involves 'pictures' and 'caring', is consistent with a metaphysical reading of the fundamental goals of the spiritual life.

Finally, let us look very briefly at how the account that we have been unfolding compares with Pascal's Wager.[26] The Wager is of some interest in this context because, like the account we have been presenting, it involves the idea of an afterlife, and the idea that the practice of religious faith will afford the believer some prospect of securing a significant good. In the Wager, of course, religious belief is taken to be rational because of the possibility that faith will be rewarded with the infinite good of heaven, and because this 'bet' will result in at most a finite loss should there be no God and therefore no afterlife. The perspective on the spiritual life that we have been expounding differs from the Wager in two key respects.

First of all, the goods with which we have been concerned obtain in the present, if they obtain at all. Why? Because these goods arise, here and now, in so far as the person's world-directed thoughts, attitudes, behaviour and experience are aligned, here and now, with the state of affairs recorded in the relevant theological narrative. By contrast, on Pascal's account, the spiritual life appears to be directed at a good that is reserved for the future: namely, the good of a post-mortem life in heaven. In the Wager, this is the good that is assigned an infinite value, and that is supposed to motivate the life of faith in the present.

Secondly, on the view we have been expounding, the religious practitioner who comes to discover that there is no God, and in turn no afterlife, and who therefore gives up the practice of faith, need not conclude that their former life failed to realize any significant good. Why not? Because, as we have seen, the person who has surrendered the perspective of faith has no deep-seated moral reason to regret their former life,

---

[26] Blaise Pascal, *Pensées*, tr. W. F. Trotter (London: Dent, 1910). The relevant section is widely anthologized. See for example Pascal, 'Faith Beyond Reason', in Paul Helm (ed.), *Faith & Reason* (Oxford: Oxford University Press, 1999), pp. 182–5.

and has some reason, indeed, to regret the fact that they no longer have as robust a reason for acting in ways that, from their present vantage point, seem good and even praiseworthy. Moreover, by taking their ideal of the Good as such to exist in actuality, the practitioner of the spiritual life is able, as we have seen, to address themselves to that ideal in a particularly direct and intimate fashion. To this extent, the person who has given up the practice of faith, on the grounds that its world view is false, has good reason to think of their former life as involving, from the first-person point of view, a deeper form of engagement with moral and spiritual reality than any that is available to them now. By contrast, on one natural reading of the Wager, if a religious practitioner comes to suppose that there is, definitively, no God, and no afterlife, then they should conclude that the religious practices by which their life was formerly ordered were simply futile. They may not have incurred any great cost in engaging in those practices (they may perhaps have suffered the loss of some sensory fulfilments, which were set aside in order to conform to what they then took to be a divine rule), but neither will their former life, from their present vantage point, have realized any significant good. It will simply have missed its target, of securing the infinite good of an afterlife.

These two points of difference between the Wager and the perspective on the spiritual life that we have been developing suggest two further points of difference. In the ways we have been exploring, much of that life is built around the pursuit of hybrid goods, which arise in so far as our world-directed thoughts and feelings, and so on, are aligned with our theological context. It is the prospect of realizing these goods that provides the motivational lure for a broad swathe of spiritual and religious practice, and that generates the distinctive practical orientation and phenomenology of the spiritual life. By contrast, the Wager seems to understand the relationship between religious practice in the present and the ends of the spiritual life in something like cause-effect terms: on this view, by leading a certain life in the present, I can make a certain future outcome, namely, a heavenly afterlife, more likely. This is quite a different reading of the nature of spiritual goods, and the relationship between spiritual practice and the realization of those goods.

Moreover, according to one familiar view, the Wager appeals to self-interest: its addressee is invited to engage in various practices for the sake of a future benefit that is self-interested in character, namely, the good of an infinitely extended afterlife in heaven. It may well be that Pascal has a satisfactory reply to this objection. Notably, it is clear that he takes the practice of faith to be morally and emotionally transformative, here and now, which suggests that even if a religious practitioner's commitment to the life of faith were to be made, in the first instance, in a spirit of self-interest, we should expect them to come to participate in that life, increasingly, for moral and spiritual reasons.[27] On this reading of Pascal's text, the goal of the religious life, if not at first then in time, is not simply some future, self-interested good but also, at least in part, a present good that consists in the person's moral reformation. However, the account that we have been sketching is still more clearly not vulnerable to an objection of this kind, because on this view, the person's commitment to the spiritual life is grounded, at all times, in their attraction to the goodness of a life that is aligned with our theological context. To put the point in Adams' terms, such a person is moved by the prospect of being related, in bodily and sensory terms, to the Good as such, considered as actual.

In practical terms, the conception of the spiritual life that we have been presenting here is consistent with the Wager: a person could in principle be moved to participate in that life both for the reasons that we have been examining and for the reasons cited in the Wager. (It is possible to act both for spiritual and for self-regarding reasons, and to act for the sake of some present good as well as for a future good.) But these considerations suggest that the perspective that we have been defending has some claim to be more faithful to the animating concerns of the religious life, to the extent that that life is ordered to distinctively spiritual goods, which can be realized in a person's relationship to the everyday sensory world, in the present.

---

[27] See his comment about taking holy water and having masses said, where these practices are said to curb 'the passions': ibid., p. 185.

The Mode of Religious Understanding

We have been reviewing various features of religious faith, including its status as cognitive, action-guiding, practically reasonable, unwavering, and in the relevant sense certain. In the course of this discussion, we have been especially interested in the intellectual structure of the life of faith, so far as it is ordered to the realization of various hybrid goods. In concluding this examination of the nature of faith, I want to change our focus somewhat, by considering not so much what the person of faith needs to understand in order to participate in the spiritual life, but how that understanding is realized in their day to day practical orientation in the world. So here our attention will move from the object to the mode of religious understanding. I shall consider in turn the case of bodily demeanour and perception.

Earlier in this chapter, I suggested that the goods of the spiritual life can be compared with the good that we realize when we acknowledge in bodily terms the storied meaning of a place—such as the place where someone is buried. Similarly, in Chapter 4, we considered some of the ways in which a person's bodily demeanour may help to constitute a hybrid good. I want now to expand on this account of the role of the body in the spiritual life, by exploring the character of the understanding that guides the body's sensitivity to place-relative meanings.

When I am at a football ground or graveyard, or in a classroom, or wherever it may be, the movements of my body need to be properly adapted not only to the physical contours of the space, so that I don't bump my head or trip over, but also to its social or existential significance. In this way, we coordinate our activities with those of other people and give due recognition to the existential, rather than simply physical, import of the world. The social significance of a place can sometimes be, as with a graveyard, a function of its history. And our sensitivity to such storied meanings is not typically a matter of rehearsing various thoughts about the place and its past in a purely mental way, before reading off the implications of those thoughts for the proper orientation of the body in the place, before then enacting the relevant bodily disposition. Rather, when in a graveyard, for example, or equally when in a football ground or shopping centre, if I am attuned to the place in the normal way, then I apprehend directly, in the responses of my body, how I am to comport myself in this space, if I am to give due acknowledgement to its storied significance. And it seems reasonable to suppose that, in standard cases, other kinds of place-relative social or existential significance are also apprehended primordially in the responses of the body.[28]

In our discussion of spiritual goods, we have been concerned, once again, with the story-sensitive disposition of the body. In this context, we have been interested in particular, of course, in theological stories, for instance the story of the beatific vision, where such stories are taken to condition the significance of the objects and spaces that we encounter in the sensory world—including our fellow human beings, food and drink, and so on. Allowing for this difference in subject matter, our sensitivity to the theologically mediated significance of objects and spaces seems to be of the same general character as the sensitivity we display in the more familiar, everyday cases I have just mentioned, where we orient ourselves in graveyards and so on, by taking stock of the storied identity of a material context in bodily terms. And it seems reasonable to conclude that the same kind of understanding is at work in the theological as in the everyday case. In each of these cases, our experience is not, standardly, one of consciously rehearsing a story, and then thinking through its implications for the existential import of the relevant place, and then deciding on how that import might be acknowledged in our bodily demeanour when located at the place, and then, finally, adopting the requisite demeanour. Rather, the body's own responses guide our sense of what it takes to be attuned to the space.

Accordingly, we should say that, in standard cases, if a person is to attain those hybrid goods that are conditional upon the body's orientation in space, then their understanding of the relevant relations of congruence, between the body's movements and a given theological narrative, will need to be realized, primordially, in the body. That is, whether we are concerned with the person's bodily comportment, or

---

[28] Compare Bourdieu's account of the *habitus*, and its role in ordering the body's practical orientation in the world. See Pierre Bourdieu, *The Logic of Practice*, tr. R. Nice (Cambridge: Polity Press, 1990; first published in French, 1980), p. 53. For a broader discussion of these matters, drawing on Bourdieu and others, see my text, *Faith and Place*.

facial expression, or indeed (if we follow Aristotle's discussion of the great-souled man) with the rhythms and timbre of their speech, in each case alignment with theological context will require, in the normal case, that the person's body be capable of tracking the relevant place-relative meanings directly—rather as, when in a graveyard, I do not give my body instructions about how to move in ways that will afford proper recognition to the storied identity of this place, but instead simply reckon with its significance directly in bodily terms. It is worth noting that these considerations seem to be relevant not only to what we have been calling in the course of our earlier discussion the 'demeanour' of a person, but also to their behaviour more broadly defined. When I extend a person a cup of water, for example, so fulfilling the requirement of neighbour love, my responsiveness to the person, and to the relevant theological narrative, will in the normal case be realized directly in bodily terms.

The same kind of account seems to hold when we move from bodily comportment to perception of the everyday world. In the ways we discussed in Chapter 3, in normal circumstances, I register the significance of objects in the perceptual field directly, by virtue of their salience and hue. Of course, I can also arrive at an assessment of their import by way of some—explicit—inference, but standardly, as I navigate my way through some practical context, my understanding of the relative significance of the items in my environment is realized, in the first instance, not in some relatively discursive or theoretical mode, but directly in perceptual terms. And it seems plausible that the same kind of competence is displayed when my assessment of the relative importance of objects in the perceptual field tracks their theological significance: here too, my understanding will be realized primordially in perceptual terms. For instance, the salience of objects in the perceptual field will be proportional to their significance relative to the relevant theological narrative, where this ordering is achieved directly in perceptual terms, rather than via some process of ratiocination.

In sum, our understanding of the ways in which the body's comportment may be properly aligned with a theological narrative is not presented, standardly, in some relatively abstract, discursive mode, but realized directly in the body's dispositions to move in the relevant space.

And similarly, our understanding of the ways in which the appearance of the world may be appropriate relative to a theological narrative is, in the normal case, realized directly in the ordering and colouring of the perceptual field. So in brief, allowing that hybrid goods of these kinds, involving our bodily comportment and world-directed experience, are indeed of some spiritual importance, then in central cases, religious faith will take as its object relations of existential congruence between the body, both as moving and as perceiving, and our theological context. And that faith will be realized, primordially, in the body's tendencies to orient itself in space, and in its habits of perception. Such is the understanding that is displayed, we may surmise, in the lives of the saints, in their relations with the created world.

So in these ways, the account of spiritual practices that we have been developing is relevant not only to the content of faith, but also to the form that is taken by the understanding that is typical of faith. That is, this account bears on each of these questions: 'What is it that the person of faith understands?', and also 'How is this understanding realized, in the midst of life?'

Some Concluding Thoughts

In these closing remarks, I want to return, just briefly, to a question that we posed in Chapter 2. It is a consequence of the perspective that we have been developing in the present chapter that the question at issue between believers and non-believers may in some cases concern the attractiveness of various states of affairs, rather than their probability. This perspective therefore bears on a question that we addressed in Chapter 2, namely, the question of whether a secular person can find the religious life attractive while continuing to occupy their secular vantage point, so giving them a reason for participating in that life that is intelligible from a secular point of view.

On the account we have been exploring in the current chapter, a secular person can acquire a reason for engaging in a given religious practice without having to revise their assessment of the probability of the corresponding world view. (In this sense, the person can acquire such a reason while continuing to occupy their secular vantage point.) How is this possible? Because for a person to acquire a reason for participating in a spiritual tradition, it is enough that they should come to a new appreciation of the goods that will arise should the relations of congruence postulated by that tradition obtain—or equally a new appreciation of the goods (and bads) that will attach to the relevant spiritual practice should those relations fail to obtain. (In some cases, this may be a matter of the person forming a judgement on these questions for the first time, rather than revising some already defined view.) In particular, if the secular person supposes that the potential goods of the relevant practice are significant, then they may well have a powerful reason to commit themselves to the practice, while recognizing that their prospects of success may be limited or uncertain. And for the reasons we have discussed, we can say of the person who does engage in a spiritual practice on this basis that they 'believe', or 'believe in', the world view that is presupposed in the practice. To put this point in the terms we considered in Chapter 2, it is, therefore, not only extended goods of reason that are relevant to the secular person when they consider whether they have reason to adopt a given spiritual practice, but also the theological goods that are postulated in the practice, that is, those goods whose realization depends on the truth of the relevant world view.

It is worth adding that this case, where the religious and secular person differ not fundamentally on questions of probability, but on the attractiveness of various states of affairs, is likely to be somewhat common on the conception of the spiritual life that we have been exploring here. On this conception, the commitment of faith is rooted in the pursuit of hybrid goods, and those goods, as Aquinas represents them, depend for their realization not simply on the truth of some generic claim, such as 'there is a God', but on the truth of a relatively fine-grained account of the nature of things—for instance, on the truth of the narrative according to which we will one day share with other human beings in the vision of God. To the extent that the hybrid goods that structure a particular form of the spiritual life can only be identified relative to a world view that has been specified at this level of detail, then believers, and not only secular people, are likely to suppose that the world view implied in that form of life cannot be established with a high degree of probability. Some such perspective seems to be presupposed in Aquinas's work. As the Five Ways indicate, he thinks that it is possible to demonstrate the mere existence of God, granted simply various uncontroversial empirical claims—such as the claim that there is change. But the goods of the infused moral virtues will only come into view once we supplement the findings of natural theology with the data of revelation. And as we have seen, for Aquinas, the data of revelation are to be affirmed, most fundamentally, not on epistemic grounds, but on account of the attractiveness of the vision of human possibilities that is implied in the relevant theological narrative.

It is, then, an implication of the view that we have been examining that when considering whether I should commit myself to one or another form of the spiritual life, I should not start by trying to establish the likely truth of a world view, and only then consider what way of life I am to adopt, granted that truth. Nor should I begin with a judgement about the relative attractiveness of ways of life, and only then consider what world view I might affirm, in the manner proposed by Hadot—as though I could adequately represent the goodness of a given way of life without considering whether it is aligned to my theological context. Rather, I should examine world views and ways of life in combination, and on that basis arrive at an assessment of what form of the spiritual life I am to lead, if any.

7

Spiritual Goods and the Content of Religious Belief

Introduction

The discussion of this book has had two presiding themes. First of all, we have been examining the idea that at least some of the goods that are the object of spiritual traditions depend for their realization on the truth of the relevant world view—not for the reasons given in Pascal's Wager, but because these goods consist in the congruence between a given pattern of world-directed thought, practice, and experience, and the nature of things as represented in the world view. It follows from this perspective that if we want to identify the goods that are made possible by a given spiritual tradition, then we will need to consider the diverse ways in which the various dimensions of a human life can be aligned with the tradition's world view. And as we have seen, establishing the nature and extent of these potential relations of congruence can be the work of centuries.

It is clear that relations of existential congruence can be more or less deep, and more or less broad. Following Aquinas, suppose we take neighbour love to be congruent with the truth that we will one day share in a deep-seated relationship of fellowship with other human beings in the beatific vision. If there is such a relation of congruence, it will be, I take it, a relatively broad as well as deep kind of congruence: it will be broad because relevant to the significance of our inter-personal relations in general; and it will be deep because it concerns the alignment of our lives with the supreme good for human beings, namely, the

Spiritual Traditions and the Virtues: Living Between Heaven and Earth. Mark R. Wynn, Oxford University Press (2020).
© Mark R. Wynn.
DOI: 10.1093/oso/9780198862949.001.0001

condition of sharing with our fellow creatures in the contemplation of the divine nature.[1]

So here is a first theme that we have been exploring: in central cases, the goods that are the target of spiritual traditions are, in the sense just indicated, relative to world view. And from this it follows that, to determine the breadth and depth of the goods that are made possible by a given spiritual tradition, we will need to study the potential relations of congruence between its narratives and our world-directed thought, practice, and experience. A second, related theme is this: in deciding whether it makes sound practical sense to participate in a spiritual tradition, we need to establish the expected spiritual good of this commitment.[2] As we have noted, for some religious traditions, it is spiritually important that their world view should not be evidently true, or even evidently more probable than not. (See again Aquinas's insistence on the voluntariness of Christian faith, and his contrasting treatment of the faith of the devils.) And there is, moreover, some reason to suppose that if a world view has been specified at the level of detail necessary to sustain a richly textured spiritual practice, then it is unlikely to be evidently true.[3] In these circumstances, if I am considering whether or not to

---

[1] See Chapters 2 and 6 for further discussion of the new significance that will attach to our relationship to other human beings, once that relationship is understood with reference to the beatific vision.

[2] The expected good of a given commitment is the weighted sum of the various goods and bads that may be produced by the commitment, where each good and bad is weighted according to its probability. This is not to say that a religious or spiritual person will typically have rehearsed a calculation set out in these terms, but they will nonetheless be sensitive to such considerations, to the extent that their decision making is properly informed. As we noted in Chapter 6, once a person has been inducted into a spiritual tradition, then their apprehension of the relevant relations of congruence is likely to be realized directly in bodily and perceptual terms—so in this respect too, their understanding is unlikely to be in a theoretical mode.

[3] For further discussion, see Chapter 6. A complex world view will be expressible in a long conjunctive proposition. And the probability of this proposition being true will be the product of the probabilities of each of its conjuncts, and since the probability of each of these conjuncts will typically be less than one, the probability of the entire conjunctive proposition, so far as it can be determined with any precision, will not be high. This is a reason for supposing that believers are standardly not committed to the claim that their world view is more probable than not. For further discussion of the point, see Richard Swinburne, *Faith and Reason* (Oxford: Clarendon Press, 2nd edn, 2005), p. 152.

participate in a given spiritual tradition, and sensitive to the expected spiritual good of that commitment, then my decision will be shaped at least as much by axiological questions, concerning the magnitude of the good and bads that may flow from participation in the tradition, as by epistemic questions, concerning the probability of the tradition's world view proving to be true.

These reflections suggest a general principle that we can apply when assessing the spiritual adequacy of a theological narrative or world view: other things being equal, a world view will make more of a practical claim upon us in so far as its truth would enable relations of congruence that run relatively broad and deep—and in so far as its falsehood would not result in significant bads for the person whose life has been ordered to that narrative.[4] In this chapter, I want to consider the usefulness of such a principle for mapping the structure of religious thought. I shall argue that a principle of this form can help us to understand significant transitions in theistic traditions, and to unify a number of otherwise apparently disparate questions in philosophical theology.

I am going to begin by examining William James's treatment of some related questions in his essay 'The Will to Believe'. I shall then explore the fruitfulness of this general approach with reference to three case studies, drawn from the work of Thomas Aquinas, Martha Nussbaum, and Anthony O'Hear.

William James on Spiritual Goods and the Content of Religious Thought

In his essay 'The Will to Believe', William James remarks that:

> religion says essentially two things. First, she says that the best things are the more eternal things, the overlapping things, the things in the universe that throw the last stone, so to speak, and say the final

---

[4] Hereafter, for simplicity's sake, I shall omit the question of what goods and bads will ensue if the world view should be false.

word.... The second affirmation of religion is that we are better off even now if we believe her first affirmation to be true.[5]

The first of James's affirmations in this passage is reminiscent of the familiar claim of 'perfect being theology' that any attribute assigned to God should be 'great-making', since God is, in Anselm's formula, 'that than which nothing greater can be conceived'.[6] James's text points towards a modest version of this Anselmian principle: to say that 'the best things are the more eternal things' is presumably to say that whatever is in fact religiously and ontologically fundamental (or 'more eternal') is also whatever is in fact best. And this is not yet to say, with Anselm, that the excellence of what is religiously and ontologically fundamental is not only unsurpassed in fact, but logically unsurpassable. Relatedly, James's formula also lacks the precision of reference of Anselm's, in so far as James is concerned with 'eternal things', whereas Anselm is discussing the divine nature. Nonetheless, James is surely right to suggest that, from the vantage point of many religious traditions, a thought about whatever is religiously fundamental cannot represent that reality as other than great, or indeed the 'best'. The Anselmian tradition further specifies this proposal by suggesting that a thought about God cannot represent God as other than unsurpassably great.

Let us bundle together the various considerations that are in play here under the label the 'great-making principle', recognizing that this principle will be somewhat differently exemplified in different religious traditions. In that case, we can offer this generalization about the content of religious thought: a thought about fundamental religious reality should respect the great-making principle, which is to say that it should not represent that reality as other than great, or the best, allowing that this proposal may be differently developed in different traditions.

---

[5] William James, 'The Will to Believe', in his *Essays in Pragmatism* (New York: Hafner Press, 1948), Section X.

[6] See *Proslogion*, in *Anselm of Canterbury: The Major Works*, ed. Brian Davies and G. R. Evans (Oxford: Oxford University Press, 1998), ch. 2. The principle may need to be refined in practice. It may be, for example, that two attributes each of which would be great-making considered in itself cannot be jointly exemplified. See Yujin Nagasawa, *Maximal God: A New Defence of Perfect Theism* (Oxford: Oxford University Press, 2017), pp. 90–4, for instance.

This formulation holds at the level of individual thoughts, and leaves open the possibility that the totality of religious thought may be neutral on the question of whether fundamental religious reality is great. So to capture the position of James and Anselm, we should build this further condition into the great-making principle: taken collectively, religious thoughts should represent fundamental religious reality as great, or the best.

The first of James's two affirmations is focused on 'eternal' or divine things, and lays down a rule for our thinking about such things. His second principle appears to be, in the first instance, more human-referenced rather God- or 'eternal things'-referenced. Here his proposal is that, according to the religions, 'we [human beings] are better off even now if we believe' that 'the best things are the more eternal things'.[7] Accordingly, we might take this second principle to present a further foundational constraint on the content of thought about fundamental religious reality, of this general form: holding to the truth of a given thought about fundamental religious reality cannot be such as to detract from human well-being, and in at least some cases, such believing must be such as to benefit human beings. James's principle does not force precisely this reading upon us, but this rendering seems to be in the spirit of his approach. Philosophers of religion in the tradition of perfect being theology have, of course, applied the great-making principle to thought about God across a wide range of contexts. And it is of some interest to consider whether there might not be another principle governing thought about fundamental religious reality, similarly wide ranging in scope, but with a human-referenced focus. That there is such a principle is, I take it, what James is seeking to affirm in the passage I have just cited.

The drift of our discussion to this point suggests that there is indeed a human-referenced principle, of broadly this kind, that governs the

---

[7] James's stance on this point is of course connected to his interest in the pragmatic case for religious belief. In 'The Will to Believe', he maintains that if the relation between religious belief and non-belief is one of necessary epistemic parity, then we have good reason to rely upon the practical consequences of religious belief when deciding whether or not to believe, especially when those consequences are 'momentous'. And by introducing the thought that religious believing confers various benefits, James opens up the possibility that the consequences of such believing can indeed be 'momentous'. The case I developed in Chapter 6 shares this general structure, in so far as it takes the 'expected spiritual good' of religious commitment to be relevant to an assessment of the claim it makes upon us. As I go on to note, while James affirms in 'The Will to Believe' that religious believing extends various benefits to the believer, he does not say much there about the nature of those benefits.

content of religious thought. As I noted in my introduction to this chapter, the account of the spiritual life that we have been developing naturally issues in the thought that we can assess the adequacy of a set of religious beliefs, or what we have been calling a world view or theological narrative, by reference to its spiritual productiveness for human beings—that is, by reference to the capacity of the narrative to sustain relations of congruence that run broad and deep. Moreover, the spiritual enrichment or 'benefit' that is in view here is like the benefit of which James speaks in so far as it is relevant to the person's well-being not simply at some future time, but here and now.

This is not yet evidently to say, with James, that *believing* the relevant narrative will result in a spiritual benefit, rather than simply that the truth of the narrative will result in a benefit for the person who leads the relevant form of life. But on the position we have taken here, a person's belief in a theological narrative, such as the narrative of the beatific vision, will be constituted, at least in part, by their leading a life that aims at congruence with that narrative.[8] So on this reading of the spiritual life, we have some reason to endorse James's second affirmation: according to the religions, religious believing makes us 'better off even now'. Why? Because such believing is, at least in part, constituted by spiritual practices, and from the religious point of view, or from the vantage point of the relevant divine rule, those practices are the source of hybrid goods here and now.

However, James's position and the view we have been sketching remain different on one key point: the second of James's affirmations implies, I suggest, that we will benefit from religious believing, here and now, even if religious belief, in its various forms, should be false. And that can't be so on the approach we have presented, since hybrid goods depend constitutively upon the truth of the relevant theological narrative. Let us reflect on this difference by examining a little more closely James's account of the benefits of religious believing.

In the passage I have just cited, and in the remainder of 'The Will to Believe', James does not specify the nature of the benefits that attach to

---

[8] Why? Because when a person seeks to bring their life into alignment with the narrative of the beatific vision, for the sake of realizing the associated hybrid goods, thereby they commit themselves, in practical terms, to the truth of that narrative.

religious believing—although he does note various parallels drawn from an assortment of non-religious domains; and in these non-religious cases, it is clear enough what he takes the benefit of believing to be. However, in his later work *The Varieties of Religious Experience*, James does identify various goods that can be associated with religious belief. Take for instance the following passage. Here, he is not considering directly the benefits of religious belief, but as we shall see, he is touching on what he takes to be a closely related matter.

> In the practical life of the individual, we know how his whole gloom or glee about any present fact depends on the remoter schemes and hopes with which it stands related. Its significance and framing give it the chief part of its value. Let it be known to lead nowhere, and however agreeable it may be in its immediacy, its glow and gilding vanish. The old man, sick with an insidious internal disease, may laugh and quaff his wine at first as well as ever, but he knows his fate now, for the doctors have revealed it; and the knowledge knocks the satisfaction out of all these functions. They are partners of death and the worm is their brother, and they turn to a mere flatness. The lustre of the present hour is always borrowed from the background of possibilities it goes with.[9]

On the view presented here, there is a deep-seated connection between the subjective quality of a person's experience of the everyday world and their 'framing' assumptions concerning the future course of events. More exactly, the idea seems to be that our capacity to find sensory objects of interest or significance is tied to our ability to locate them within a future-referenced narrative, one within which we ourselves will be active participants. Why? Because these objects can only have any practical meaning for us as part of our own ongoing story. If that is so, then when I learn that my death is imminent, so that there is no future for me, my environment will become drained of significance. And what James is describing here is the perceptual counterpart of that condition:

---

[9] William James, *The Varieties of Religious Experience: A Study in Human Nature* (London: Longmans, Green and Co., 1911), p. 141.

as things surrender their practical significance for me, because they are no longer folded into my future projects, so their appearance changes, and as a consequence the perceptual world loses its 'lustre'.[10]

To put this point in the terms we used in Chapter 3, we may say that in the experience of this old man, who has just received his diagnosis, the everyday world now appears less vivid or bright, or lustrous, so that its 'hue' has changed—where this change in the appearance of things embodies his judgement that the sensory world no longer has any practical significance for him, since it 'leads nowhere'. Similarly, James notes that 'these functions [of laughing and quaffing wine] turn to a mere flatness'. And we might read this comment as an allusion to the flattening out of the contours that had previously structured the man's perceptual field. Following our usage in Chapter 3, we could say that the patterns of salience that formerly ordered his experience of the world have now been eroded. Here again, the character of the perceptual field reflects, and perhaps in part constitutes, the man's judgement about the significance of his environment: here, the flattening out of the world as it appears is the perceptual counterpart of the truth that, for this man, everyday objects have ceased to carry any differentiated import. Why? Because from his perspective, these objects are now, one and all, devoid of any deep practical significance.

James notes the description of a related condition in Tolstoy's autobiographical work *A Confession*. In the following passage, Tolstoy is not confronting the prospect of imminent death, but he is reckoning with

<hr>

[10] It might be wondered whether this reading moves too quickly from James's observations about 'gloom or glee' concerning 'present facts' to a claim about the world's appearance. In this connection, it is worth recalling that James takes emotional and perceptual states to be closely connected. We have discussed one example of this association already, when noting his treatment of conversion experience (see Chapter 3). See too his remarks on the implications of being 'stripped of all the emotions with which your world now inspires you'. James comments of the person in this condition that: 'No one portion of the universe would then have importance beyond another; and the whole collection of its things and series of its events would be without significance, character, expression, or perspective. Whatever of value, interest, or meaning our respective worlds may appear endued with are thus pure gifts of the spectator's mind': *Varieties*, p. 150. As I go on to note, there are in any case good conceptual reasons to associate a judgement about the relative practical significance of objects with the ordering of the perceptual field.

his mortality—and to this extent he too is occupied with the thought that his present circumstances 'lead nowhere'. Tolstoy asks himself:

> What will be the outcome of what I do to-day? Of what I shall do to-morrow? What will be the outcome of all my life? Why should I live? Why should I do anything? Is there any purpose which the inevitable death which awaits me does not undo and destroy?[11]

Like the man who has learnt of his terminal diagnosis, Tolstoy is struck by the thought that his projects lack any enduring significance. And again like the man with the diagnosis, Tolstoy's sense of the practical futility of his life is rooted in a lived, rather than merely theoretical, appreciation of his own mortality. James offers this gloss on Tolstoy's predicament:

> At about the age of fifty, Tolstoy relates that he began to have moments of perplexity, of what he calls arrest, as if he knew not 'how to live', or what to do. It is obvious that these were moments in which the excitement and interest which our functions naturally bring had ceased. Life had been enchanting, it was now flat sober, more than sober, dead.[12]

Here again we find the idea that a diminished sense of the practical significance of things can be written into the perceptual field. The experience is once again one of 'flatness' or 'disenchantment'—and in turn, at least by implication, one of loss of vividness or brightness in the perceptual field.

In Chapter 3, we considered James's suggestion that in conversion experience, the everyday world can appear rejuvenated, so that sensory objects seem newly 'glorified'. Tolstoy's report is to be contrasted with this case: he is describing how the sensory world may be drained of practical significance, so that it appears flatter and less vivid, whereas the person who enjoys an experience of nature as 'transfigured', as James puts the point, discovers a new significance in their sensory environment,

---

[11] Ibid., p. 155.   [12] Ibid., p. 152.

which accordingly appears brighter and in a way more fully real than before.

In these various contexts—when discussing experiences of religious renewal, or equally of life as having no enduring practical significance—James touches, at least indirectly, on the potential benefits of religious belief. From this perspective, these benefits concern the convert's capacity to find a deepened significance in their everyday environment, and in turn, therefore, to inhabit a perceptual world that is lively and structured. And conversely, the benefits of religious believing include avoiding the state of practical disorientation that afflicts Tolstoy and the man with a terminal diagnosis. And at least by implication, religious believing is able to secure these outcomes because of the distinctive way in which it 'frames' our everyday experience—by postulating an afterlife or some other theological context that will underwrite the enduring significance of our lives.[13]

The Varieties has as its subtitle: 'a study in human nature'. And the ideas that James is rehearsing in these passages are naturally read as a contribution to philosophical anthropology: it is, James seems to be saying, a fundamental truth of human nature that the prospect of imminent death, or equally a lively awareness of our mortality, can throw human beings into a state of practical arrest, where this diminished sense of the import of the everyway world is manifest in the draining away of colour and structure from the perceptual field. Let us think a little further about the relevance of James's comments for a philosophically informed anthropology.

The connection between, on the one hand, losing a sense of the practical significance of things in general and, on the other, experiencing the world as 'flat' seems to be broadly conceptual in character. After all, if the perceptual field were not to be flattened in this way, then in the subject's experience, some objects would stand out relative to others, and therefore appear as more significant than others—contrary to the supposition that the loss of practical significance extends to the person's

---

[13] As James notes in a later lecture, it's clear that Tolstoy's own malaise was resolved by religious conversion: ibid., p. 185.

relationship to the world in general. And we could tell a similar, conceptual story for changes in 'hue'.

By contrast, the connection between the judgement that one's death is imminent and the loss of a sense of the world's practical significance is not evidently conceptual in character. To the extent that it holds in any general way, this connection seems to be a function of human nature. In fact, even in the human case, it is not difficult to imagine a very different response to the discovery that one's death is imminent. On coming to believe that I do not have long to live, I might find that my everyday environment has acquired, if anything, a deepened practical significance. Why? Because I will now suppose that the set of projects that I can bring to completion, in the time that remains to me, is more tightly circumscribed than I had previously supposed. And accordingly, from my perspective, the opportunity cost of any given project will have risen, so giving the choice to pursue that project a deepened practical significance. Or to put the point otherwise, from my new vantage point, there is more at stake in my choice of a given project, because that choice will now close off a larger range of alternative projects and associated goods.[14]

Let us pause to take stock of some of the key features of this Jamesian account of the goods of religious believing. In the texts we have considered, James understands these goods in terms of a transformation of the person's practical and experiential relation to the world, in the present. And in this respect, his account fits squarely with his suggestion that religious commitment confers benefits that we can enjoy 'even now'. Here as so often, James's interest is fundamentally psychological: he is in effect exploring the ways in which religious belief can be good for mental health, where mental health is understood in terms of the capacity to

---

[14] Conversely, it might be suggested that far from securing the meaning of a human life, an endless future would actually undermine it. See for instance Bernard Williams' proposal that if a person is given an everlasting, heavenly existence, then, necessarily, there will come a time when all their desires have been fulfilled, whereupon they will be reduced to a state of boredom—or else they will need to acquire some radically new desires, in which case it may be doubted whether it is the same person who persists thereafter. See Bernard Williams, 'The Makropoulos Case: Reflections on the Tedium of Immortality', in Williams (ed.), *Problems of the Self* (Cambridge: Cambridge University Press, 1973), ch. 6. The question of how we might live in the light of an awareness of our mortality is of course a central theme of Martin Heidegger's *Being and Time*, first published in 1927, and a fuller engagement with these questions would naturally look to his work.

orient oneself in the world practically, and to enjoy a perceptual environment that is structured rather than flat, and coloured rather than 'grey'.

Comparing Approaches to the Nature of Spiritual Goods

As we have seen, our account of the goods of religious believing shares certain features with James's, but the goods with which we have been concerned have a rather different character: notably, these goods can only be specified, in terms of their fundamental nature, by reference to the relevant world view. Why? Because they consist in a relation of congruence between the person's world-directed activity in some respect and reality so conceived. The benefits James describes may perhaps be induced by adopting the relevant world view: for instance, by coming to believe in an afterlife, a person may acquire the belief that their projects have an enduring practical significance, not simply for others but for themselves, and this conviction may help to restore structure and colour to their perceptual field. But in so far as they consist in a new practical attunement to the everyday world, or in a newly vivid perceptual field, these goods can be identified independently of reference to any world view. In this sense, the benefits which provide the focus for James's discussion are broadly speaking empirical, while those with which we have been concerned are, we could say, spiritual.

We can make the same sort of point by noting the different role that is played by beliefs about the future in these two approaches. According to James, my belief that I have an enduring future may afford me access to a lively perceptual world, here and now. And on the account we have been sketching, my belief in the beatific vision, understood as a state belonging to our eschatological future, may enable me to find new significance in the everyday sensory world, here and now. But for James, this connection between a conception of the future and the character of our present experience seems to be broadly causal in character: the person who thinks of themselves as having an ongoing future thereby satisfies a psychological precondition for achieving a certain kind of experiential good in the present. By contrast, the connection with which we have been concerned is conceptual: my belief in the beatific vision, where this belief is constituted by a body of spiritual practice, will confer a deepened significance on my present experience, here and now, only if my life is in fact aligned with the beatific vision. Why? Because here the relevant experiential good is not induced by a belief about the future, but is constituted by the relationship between my belief—and the associated body of spiritual practice—and a truth about the future. The two approaches differ, therefore, both on the question of whether the contribution of belief to the spiritual life is to be understood in terms of causal efficacy and also, more fundamentally, on the question of what it is to hold a religious belief: on the account we have been sketching, a belief such as the belief in the beatific vision is, at least in part, comprised of a body of spiritual practice, which is targeted at the relevant hybrid good.[15]

One consequence of adopting a Jamesian account of the goods of religious believing is that we thereby admit the possibility of these goods being produced by other means, that is, independently of religious believing or any associated spiritual practice. For instance, to the extent that they take the form of a transformation in the appearance of the world, then it seems reasonable to suppose that the benefits James describes can be brought about by pharmacological means. Even so, there is no reason why an account of the attractiveness of a given religious world view should not appeal both to Jamesian, 'psychological' benefits and to the distinctively spiritual goods with which we have been occupied. These Jamesian benefits are real enough, and if commitment to a given world view will give us access to them, then other things being equal, that is a reason for holding the view. Nonetheless, it may be urged, Jamesian benefits do not touch the heart of the spiritual life. Why? Because the spiritual person wants, it seems plausible to suppose, not just, nor most fundamentally, psychological well-being, but to stand in

---

[15] As a pragmatist, James would no doubt be open to a practice-based reading of religious belief. And in the case of Tolstoy, as he presents it, there is clearly a close association between religious believing and practice, to the extent that Tolstoy's conversion is, in some fashion, tightly connected to his overcoming of a state of practical arrest. Nonetheless, as we have seen, in his treatment of examples such as that of the old man who has learned his diagnosis, James seems to treat belief as a psychological state that can be fully described independently of practice.

the right relation to the fundamental nature of things. And the notion of a hybrid good, which has been at the core of our account of the spiritual life, is concerned precisely, of course, with what it is for a person to stand in that relation.

It is worth adding that these two stories about the goods of the religious life are not only consistent with one another, but can also be integrated, since the psychological goods that James documents can themselves contribute to hybrid goods. How so? Because, to take just one example, a more boldly contoured perceptual field is not only a psychological good, but also, potentially, a constituent of a spiritual good, to the extent that experience of this form is congruent with a relevant theological narrative. And as we have seen, there is some reason to suppose that a person's world-directed experience should have precisely this subjective character if it is to be aligned with, say, the narrative of the beatific vision.[16]

So far in this chapter, we have been concerned with the idea that religious thought should conform not only to one or another version of what I have called the 'great-making principle', but also to a human-referenced constraint on the content of such thought, which takes as its starting point the idea that religious believing is, in some way, the source of various goods. As James puts the matter in the second of his affirmations, according to the religions, 'we are better off even now if we believe'. Drawing on James's text *The Varieties of Religious Experience*, we have been exploring one way of developing this idea: on this approach, religious believing serves as a causal precondition for various benefits that are psychological in character, and consist fundamentally in the believer's enjoyment of a perceptual world that is structured rather than flat, and vivid rather that grey. So following this Jamesian account, we could say that the relevant human-referenced principle has something like this form: in general, a proposal with religious content should be such that believing it will confer various psychological benefits upon the person, where these benefits can be enjoyed 'even now'.

---

[16] See Chapter 3 for a discussion of how Aquinas's understanding of spiritual goods can be harmonized with James's account of the phenomenology of conversion experience.

The account of the spiritual life that we have been developing takes a different stance on the nature of the goods of religious life: even when they involve experience, these goods are not simply psychological in character, but concern the alignment between the person's world-directed experience and their theological context. Nonetheless, on this view too, we have good reason to postulate a human-referenced principle which can serve as a guide to the content of religious thought. As we have seen, on this approach, the principle will have this general form: a theological narrative, or world view, makes a serious claim upon us, in spiritual terms, to the extent that its truth would enable relations of congruence that run broad and deep. Or to put the point in terms of believing, following the structure of the principle that we have attributed to James, and here assuming that the relevant narrative is true, and that religious believing is constituted by spiritual practice: a theological narrative should be such that believing it will confer significant spiritual benefits upon the person, where these benefits can be enjoyed 'even now'. Here again, we have a measure for the adequacy of religious thought that is tied to human well-being, but the relevant goods are not now simply psychological in character, or caused by religious believing, but instead depend constitutively on the person's spiritual practice and theological context.

In sum, we have taken stock of two related ways of introducing a human-referenced measure for religious thought. For ease of reference, let us term the measure that is implied in the approach that we have been following in this volume: the principle of spiritual good. Again, that principle runs: a theological narrative, or world view, makes a serious claim upon us, in spiritual terms, to the extent that its truth would enable relations of congruence that run broad and deep.

The great-making principle and the principle of spiritual good, so understood, offer independent routes into the content of religious thought, but it is possible of course that they will converge upon similar conclusions. For instance, applying the great-making principle, in the way proposed by the ontological argument, a person may conclude that there is a God, who is perfectly good; and they might then infer that there is a beatific vision, on the grounds that such a vison would be a fitting expression of the divine goodness. (I do not say that this is a persuasive line of argument: I am just offering an illustration of how the great-making principle might be deployed in principle.) Here, we begin with a characterization of fundamental religious reality, one that is grounded in an Anselmian reading of the great-making principle, and by this means, we arrive at the conclusion that there is a beatific vision.

By contrast, when applying the principle of spiritual good, we are to consider, in the first instance, human beings—and the ways in which the truth of a theological narrative may contribute to a person's spiritual well-being. Following this approach, assent to the beatific vision can be grounded in a judgement about the breadth and depth of the hybrid goods that will be possible should the doctrine be true, where this assent is realized in the practical pursuit of those goods. In this case, my affirmation of the idea that there is a beatific vision is grounded in the first instance in a judgement that concerns not the divine nature, but spiritual well-being. So here is one example of how the great-making and spiritual good principles may converge on the same belief, albeit that they take quite different routes to that belief.

Having introduced the principle of spiritual good, and recalled some of the considerations that can be cited in its support, let us examine next the fruitfulness of the principle for an account of religious thought. At the core of our enquiry to this point has been the idea of infused moral virtue. So it is natural to start by asking: might the validity of this idea be understood, at least in part, by reference to the principle of spiritual good?

Thomas Aquinas on Spiritual Goods and the Structure of Religious Thought

As we have seen, Aquinas inherited from his theological forebears, and notably from Augustine, the idea that virtue is what God 'works in us without us'.[17] He also inherited from his philosophical sources, and

---

[17] ST 1a2ae. 63. 2, in the Blackfriars translation (London: Eyre & Spottiswoode, 1968). In the following discussion, further quotations will be from this same translation, unless otherwise indicated. This is Aquinas's gloss on Augustine, rather than a direct quotation, although Aquinas treats the text as though it were a direct quotation. Aquinas applies the text to those

notably from Aristotle, the idea that virtue derives from a process of habituation.[18] In these circumstances, Aquinas might have simply partitioned the life of virtue: he could have followed Aristotle in supposing that there are acquired moral virtues relevant to the person's flourishing as human, and followed Augustine in allowing that there are, in addition, theological virtues, namely, faith, hope, and charity, which direct the person to God, and which require for their formation, therefore, God's enabling activity—or the infusion of grace—rather than simply some process of habituation of the kind that is relevant to the production of the acquired moral virtues. Why does Aquinas not take this approach? To put the question otherwise: why does he introduce the concept of infused moral virtue, to sit alongside the notions of acquired moral virtue and infused theological virtue? So far as I can see, he doesn't give his reasons—certainly, he provides no explicit account of the matter. However, we can offer a speculation, rooted in Thomistic principles, about what his reasons might have been.

In this connection, it is worth recalling that Aquinas's Dominican forebear, Peraldus, had, in effect, already introduced something like the notion of infused moral virtue—as distinct from infused *theological* virtue—when proposing that human 'effort', rather than 'cooperation', is relevant to the formation of the moral but not the theological virtues. 'Effort' here is to be understood in terms of removing an obstacle to the formation of a virtue, and not in terms of some process of habituation, involving 'cooperation', whereby human agency positively enables the development of the virtue. (Peraldus draws the analogy of opening the shutter over a window, to admit the sunlight: here, our effort enables the sun to shine into the room, but we do not cooperate with the sun in producing the light.)[19] On this reading, it seems we should attribute to Peraldus a non-Aristotelian account of the formation of the moral virtues, one that gives a role to something like infusion. Granted

---

virtues governed by a divine rule; but the Augustinian tradition tended to see all virtues in these terms. See again John Inglis, 'Aquinas's Replication of the Acquired Moral Virtues', *The Journal of Religious Ethics*, 27 (1999), 9.

[18] Aristotle, *Nicomachean Ethics*, tr. W. D. Ross, revised J. L. Ackrill and J. O. Urmson (Oxford: Oxford University Press, 1980), Book 2.
[19] The text is noted in Inglis, 'Aquinas's Replication', 9.

Peraldus's stance on these matters, and granted his own, more Aristotelian sympathies, perhaps it was to be expected that Aquinas would allow for the existence of the Aristotelian, or acquired, virtues, while at the same time retaining his Dominican confrere's suggestion that there are in addition moral virtues that are not acquired, but infused. This would be one account of Thomas's stance on these questions.

Alternatively, perhaps he was simply swayed by the thought that there are evidently Christian practices, such as fasting, which concern our relation to the created order and which are at the same time God-directed. (As we have seen, he discusses this case when introducing the notion of infused moral virtue.)[20] In so far as they bear on our relations to the created order, we might say, the virtues that support practices such as fasting should be considered as 'moral'. And in so far as they are concerned with our relationship to God in eternity, these virtues cannot be grounded in the exercise of powers that belong to us on account of our human nature, but must instead be infused. (The idea that God-directed virtues require infusion is a standard argumentative move in Aquinas.)[21] For these reasons, we may wish to say that in speaking of the infused moral virtues, Aquinas was simply offering a gloss on familiar Christian spiritual practices, in so far as those practices subordinate food and drink, and other material things, to a divinely ordered teleology. And as we have seen, we might also say that in speaking of infused moral virtues, as well as of acquired moral virtues, Aquinas was moved by a determination to adhere to the teaching of his Dominican forebear, Peraldus, while at the same time trying, characteristically, to accommodate the thought of Aristotle. Allowing for the possibility of these accounts, I want to suggest now a further reading of the drift of Aquinas's thought on these questions.

As we have seen, Aquinas introduces the idea that there are infused moral virtues in these terms:

> the theological virtues are enough to shape us to our supernatural end as a start . . . Yet the soul needs also to be equipped by infused virtues in regard to created things, though as subordinate to God.
>
> (ST 1a2ae. 63. 3 ad 2)

---

[20] See ST 1a2ae. 63. 4, a text we examined in Chapter 2.
[21] See for instance ST 1a2ae. 63. 2.

Here it is clear enough what is at stake, for Aquinas, in the idea of infused moral virtue: by introducing this notion, we create conceptual space for the thought that a person's relationship to created things can be folded into their relationship to God. In turn, therefore, the idea of infused moral virtue allows us to identify a new kind of good that can be realized in a human life: namely, the good that arises in so far as a person's world-directed thoughts, feelings, behaviour, and so on, are ordered to their theological end. So in this way, the notion of infused moral virtue is, for Aquinas, tightly connected to the notion of spiritual good. In our discussion in this volume, we have been advancing one reading of the nature of the goods that are enabled by the infused moral virtues, by proposing that there are hybrid goods, that is, goods that arise in so far as there is a relationship of existential congruence between a person's world directed activities, thoughts, and so on, and their theological context. (Alternatively, we could read this relationship in causal rather than existential terms, and take a person's world-directed thoughts, activities, and so on, to be ordered to their divine *telos* for that reason.)

Accordingly, one simple, and I think plausible, account of Aquinas's use of the idea of infused moral virtue would run as follows: allowing for the fact that the idea of infused moral virtue was already to some extent current in his intellectual context, Aquinas endorsed this idea because hereby we can assign a deepened significance to human beings' relations to the everyday world. To put the matter in these terms is to say that he was guided, at least implicitly, by the principle of spiritual good. On the version that we have proposed, that principle reads: a theological narrative, or world view, makes a serious claim upon us, in spiritual terms, to the extent that its truth would enable relations of congruence that run broad and deep. And the idea that there are infused moral virtues, if understood as itself a theological narrative, or as part of such a narrative, seems to satisfy this principle. Why? Because if there are such virtues, then it will be possible, at least in principle, for human lives to realize relations of congruence that run broad and deep. Whether or not Aquinas was in fact moved by these considerations, it is of some interest to see that the notion of infused moral virtue can be supported in these terms.

Of course, the idea that there are infused moral virtues bears a special connection to the question of whether relations of congruence are possible at all. Why? Because a given theological narrative, such as the narrative of the beatific vision, can enable relations of congruence only if it is possible for human beings' world-directed thoughts, feelings, behaviour and experience, and so on, to be aligned with the narrative. And if we follow Aquinas on this point, we should say, in turn, that it is possible for our world-directed thoughts, and so on, to be aligned with a given theological narrative only if there are infused moral virtues. Why? Because these virtues are the dispositions by means of which we can integrate our relations to the material order into our relationship to God. To put the point in Aquinas's terms, if our world-directed thoughts and actions are to be aligned with our divine *telos*, then 'the soul needs to be equipped by infused virtues in regard to created things, though as subordinate to God'—which is to say that for this purpose, we need the infused moral virtues.[22]

Hence the idea that there are infused moral virtues satisfies the principle of spiritual good in a distinctive way. In general, a theological narrative will satisfy this principle to the extent that its truth would enable relations of congruence that run broad and deep. And the capacity of a narrative, such as the narrative of the beatific vision, to meet this condition depends on there being infused moral virtues. Accordingly, the idea that there are infused moral virtues fulfils the principle of spiritual good in the special sense that it is a condition of the possibility of other theological narratives satisfying this principle.

While admittedly this remains a speculation, we have some reason, therefore, to say that Aquinas's commitment to the notion of infused moral virtue was not simply for the sake of accommodating a pre-established Dominican conception of the moral life, nor just a matter of recognizing that some Christian practices, such as fasting, are both world-directed and God-directed, but was, perhaps in addition, born of his understanding that the idea of infused moral virtue is presupposed in our concept of one important class of spiritual goods, namely, what we have been calling hybrid goods. If that is so, then we can say that the core notion of

[22] Again, this quotation is taken from ST 1a2ae. 63. 3 ad 2.

our enquiry—namely, infused moral virtue—is validated by the principle of spiritual good. This is not a coincidence: as we have seen, the idea of infused moral virtue is embedded in the conception of spiritual goods that we have been presenting here; and it follows that if we are to use the conceptual resources of this discussion to develop an account of the goods that attach to religious believing, then that account will involve the idea of infused moral virtue.

We have been considering how the principle of spiritual good lends support to the idea that there are infused moral virtues, understood as dispositions that govern our relations to the material order, where the standard of success in those relations is provided by reference to a divinely ordered teleology. Next, let us think briefly about a matter that we have not examined directly to this point: namely, the mode of production of the virtues. As we have seen, Aquinas distances himself from the view that in general, the virtues are what God 'works in us without us'; and specifically, he distinguishes the acquired moral virtues from those virtues that God brings about without us.[23] Moreover, even in his account of the infused virtues, he retains a role for human agency: so here too, it would be misleading to say that, on his view, the virtues are simply 'what God works in us without us'.[24]

Aquinas associates this conception of the virtues—as what God works in us without us—with Augustine; and for present purposes, let us follow him on this point, setting aside the question of the exegetical warrant for

---

[23]   In ST 1a2ae. 63. 2, Aquinas associates the idea that virtue is what God 'works in us without us' with God-directed virtues in particular. And he is clear that it is possible to produce the acquired virtues by means of human effort. Hence he comments: 'it is possible by means of human works to acquire moral virtues, in so far as they produce good works that are directed to an end not surpassing the natural power of man: and when they are acquired thus, they can be without charity, even as they were in many of the Gentiles': ST 1a2ae. 64. 2. At the same time, Aquinas maintains that all true virtue is directed to God, and therefore presupposes the virtue of charity, which is of course infused. See for instance his comment in ST 2a2ae. 23. 7 that 'no strictly true virtue is possible without charity'. (Here I have followed the Benziger Brothers translation.)

[24]   I am not going to consider the detail of Aquinas's position on the relationship between human agency and the infusion of grace. But see for instance ST 1a2ae. 111. 2, where he comments: 'if grace is taken for God's gratuitous motion whereby He moves us to meritorious good, it is fittingly divided into operating and cooperating grace.' And in the same place, he explains the notion of cooperating grace thus: 'in that effect in which our mind both moves and is moved, the operation is not only attributed to God, but also to the soul; and it is with reference to this that we speak of "cooperating grace".' So cooperating grace evidently supports, rather than displaces, human agency.

this attribution.[25] Interestingly, we can, perhaps, find a motivation for this Augustinian standpoint in what we have dubbed the 'great-making principle': after all, we might think that by representing virtue as 'what God works in us without us', so assigning human moral goodness entirely to the agency of God, and not at all to the agency of human beings, we succeed in magnifying the divine nature. Why might someone think so? Well, perhaps on the grounds that, by thinking of God as uniquely the source of all that is morally good in a human life, we thereby attribute more good to the divine agency than we otherwise would.[26] (I bracket here the question of whether this line of thought is persuasive.)

However, this stance seems less attractive from the point of view of a human-referenced understanding of religious thought. Why? Because it appears to diminish the significance of a human life, by making human choices and commitments, in the moral domain and perhaps more generally, merely epiphenomenal.[27] (Again, on the view under consideration, the divine agency seems to simply bypass human agency, since virtue is what God works in us 'without us'.) I have just argued that the notion of infused moral virtue is presupposed in the idea that human beings can align their lives with a theological narrative, and for this reason supported by the principle of spiritual good. And we might add that the notion that human beings are other than mere ciphers for divine agency is also supported by the principle of spiritual good—for the reason that this notion is a still more basic presupposition of the idea that human beings can align their lives with a theological narrative. Why think so? Because it is only if human agency is other than epiphenomenal that human beings can be agents at all—and therefore intelligibly the bearers of the virtues, and the subjects of a moral and spiritual life.

---

[25] See again footnote 17.

[26] Compare Augustine's remark: 'Where is he who, reflecting upon his own infirmity, dares to ascribe his chastity and innocency to his own strength, so that he should love You the less, as if he had been in less need of Your mercy, whereby You forgive the transgressions of those that turn to You?': Augustine, *Confessions*, tr. J. G. Pilkington (1887), Book II, ch. 7.

[27] We could take the more radical option here by following the example of the occasionalists, and supposing that not only the moral agency of human beings, but all creaturely activity is really the work of God.

These considerations suggest that while the great-making principle and the principle of spiritual good may tend to support convergent conclusions on certain issues, there may be other matters where their apparent findings will be harder to reconcile. And we might speculate that it is at least in part for this reason that the relationship between divine and human agency has proved to be so vexed a question in Christian as well as other religious traditions.

In sum, we have been suggesting that the principle of spiritual good can help to explain some key elements in Aquinas's thought: notably, the idea that there are infused moral virtues, and the idea that virtue is not, in every case, 'what God works in us without us'. And if we allow that the notion of infused moral virtue represents an innovation in medieval theology, a departure from earlier Aristotelian and Augustinian traditions alike, then we can also explain in this way a significant transition in theistic thought.[28] Lastly, we have also seen how the principle of spiritual good may help to account for a case of entrenched theological disagreement, if we suppose that this principle and the great-making principle have a tendency to pull in contrary directions on the question of how we are to conceive of the relationship between divine and human agency.

Atheism, Divine Ineffability, and the Principle of Spiritual Good

We have been considering how the principle of spiritual good may serve as a measure for the content of religious thought. Again, that principle runs: a theological narrative, or world view, makes a serious claim upon us, in spiritual terms, to the extent that its truth would enable relations of congruence that run broad and deep. It is notable that some atheistic critiques of religion present, in effect, a challenge to the idea that theological narratives are spiritually productive: from this perspective, these narratives cheapen, rather than deepen, human lives as they are lived

---

[28] This will be so even if we suppose that it was Peraldus, or some other figure, rather than Aquinas, who first introduced the notion.

here and now. I am not going to consider this kind of objection at any length, but it is worth pausing to note how some forms of atheism can in this way trade on something like the principle of spiritual good.

At the beginning of the *Confessions*, Augustine famously addresses God in these terms:

> You have formed us for Yourself, and our hearts are restless till they find rest in You.[29]

Some might see in this passage a tendency to diminish the significance of this-worldly experiences and concerns. Why? Because on the view presented here, it might be said, the proper focus of a human life is exclusively relationship to God: all world-directed ties are in the end unsatisfying, and indeed dispensable. Arguing that this is indeed the drift of Augustine's thought, Martha Nussbaum comments:

> we have reason to be alarmed at the insistent otherworldly direction of this longing [that is found in Augustine's theology]. Death is irrelevant, real suffering in this world is irrelevant, all that is relevant is coming into God's presence.[30]

Here something like the principle of spiritual good has been placed in the service of a critique of the narratives of Christian theology: on Nussbaum's account, far from deepening the significance of a human life, here and now, those narratives have a tendency to evacuate our world-directed thoughts and actions of any real importance. Why? Because they take the basic human project to be one of escaping from this world, to another realm, wherein lies our true home.[31] It is not

---

[29] Augustine, *Confessions*, tr. J. G. Pilkington (1887), Book I, ch. 1.

[30] Martha Nussbaum, *Upheavals of Thought: The Intelligence of Emotions* (Cambridge: Cambridge University Press, 2001), p. 552.

[31] In support of this reading of the import of Augustine's thought, see for instance this passage in his *On Christian Doctrine*: 'Suppose, then, we were wanderers in a strange country, and could not live happily away from our fatherland, and that we felt wretched in our wandering, and wishing to put an end to our misery, determined to return home. We find, however, that we must make use of some mode of conveyance, either by land or water, in order to reach that fatherland where our enjoyment is to commence. But the beauty of the country through which we pass, and the very pleasure of the motion, charm our hearts, and turning these things which

difficult to find other objections to Christian theology of this general form. Friedrich Nietzsche is perhaps the best known such critic;[32] but here is an example of the same kind of case being presented by a contemporary commentator, André Comte-Sponville:

> I have grown wary, not only of loftiness, which crushes everything, but also of interiority, introspection, the 'I myself'. I find it easier to believe in spiritualities that open out on to the world, on to other people, on to everything.[33]

According to Comte-Sponville, Christian theology invites us either to look upwards, to a transcendent, divine realm, or to look inwards, into what traditionally would have been styled the sphere of the soul. In whichever way they direct our gaze, he implies, the problem with theologies in this mode is that they disparage the world, because they imply that our attention is properly directed not 'outwards' to the world, but instead to some other domain—and thereby they encourage an attitude of carelessness towards the world and what happens in the world.

The notion of infused moral virtue, as we have understood it here, stands in clear contrast to the perspective of Nussbaum and Comte-Sponville. Why? Because the goods of the infused moral virtues—what we have been calling hybrid goods—arise in so far as human beings'

---

we ought to use into objects of enjoyment, we become unwilling to hasten the end of our journey; and becoming engrossed in a factitious delight, our thoughts are diverted from that home whose delights would make us truly happy. Such is a picture of our condition in this life of mortality. We have wandered far from God; and if we wish to return to our Father's home, this world must be used, not enjoyed, that so the invisible things of God may be clearly seen, being understood by the things that are made, Romans 1:20—that is, that by means of what is material and temporary we may lay hold upon that which is spiritual and eternal': Augustine, *On Christian Doctrine* (Milton Keynes: Lightning Source, 2013), Book I, ch. 4, available at: http://www.newadvent.org/fathers/12021.htm, accessed 28 January 2019. The implication of this text seems to be that we must not find satisfaction in creatures, in themselves, lest that satisfaction divert us from the one needful thing, which is to hasten to our true home, in another world.

[32] See for instance Nietzsche's comment that God is 'the enemy of life': *Twilight of the Idols or How to Philosophize with a Hammer*, in Friedrich Nietzsche, *The Anti-Christ, Ecce Homo, Twilight of the Idols*, ed. A. Ridley and J. Norman, tr. J. Norman (Cambridge: Cambridge University Press, 2005), p. 174.

[33] André Comte-Sponville, *The Book of Atheist Spirituality: An Elegant Argument for Spirituality Without God*, tr. N. Huston (London: Bantam Books, 2008), p. 197.

world-directed activities are aligned with a (truthful) theological narrative. So on this account, the introduction of a theological frame for our world-directed thought, experience, and behaviour, far from displacing the meaning that our lives would otherwise bear, has instead the consequence of preserving that meaning, while ensuring that our this-worldly commitments come to acquire, in addition, a further kind of significance.

Following Aquinas, we could take the consumption of food as a simple example of this general approach. In the practice of religiously motivated dietary abstinence, food retains its significance as a source of bodily health, while at the same time acquiring an additional significance, in so far as it is now ordered to the person's relationship to God. Similarly, to take another of Aquinas's examples, in the practice of neighbour love, we are to think of other human beings under the category of 'friendship', but this does not derogate from the significance they would otherwise carry, since the perspective afforded by a 'divine rule' subsumes, and does not abrogate, that afforded by a 'rule of reason'. In the same spirit, in response to Comte-Sponville, it may be said that the notion of infused moral virtue, and the associated notion of hybrid goods, invite us to see that we do not need to choose between looking 'upwards' to the truths recorded in a theological narrative and 'outwards' towards the world. Why not? Because what we find when we look outwards towards the world can be deepened once we locate our world-directed thought and activity within a theological frame.

Perhaps Nussbaum would object that this account still demeans this-worldly commitments in so far as it implies that the significance that worldly things have in themselves, in their own right, is less than their God-directed significance. The role of the beatific vision in the case that we have been developing arguably provides the beginnings of a response to this complaint. On this account, what grounds the appropriateness of neighbour love, for example, is a truth about our relations with other human beings: namely, the fact that, in the eschatological future, we will share with one another in a deep-seated relationship of friendship. It is this inter-human truth, rather than directly any truth about God, that supplies the basis for the idea that my present relations to other human beings can realize an additional good, once situated within a theological frame. At the same time, of course, a monotheist will no doubt be inclined to agree with Nussbaum's representation of their position: if we are required to make such a comparison, then we should indeed say that the God-directed significance of creatures is greater than their intrinsic significance. But the theist will add: this is not in any way to diminish the intrinsic significance of creatures, because, once again, the vantage point of a divine rule does not displace the vantage point of a rule of reason, but subsumes it. In brief, on this account, there is no reason to be exercised by the relative weight of these two kinds of significance, since they are not in competition with each other.

I am not going to comment further on this atheistic critique of theological narratives, but from this brief discussion, we can draw these two conclusions. First, the remarks of Nussbaum, Comte-Sponville, and others give us further reason to suppose that the dispute between the advocates and critics of a given religious or spiritual perspective is not necessarily—and I would add: not standardly—about the probability of the relevant world view or narrative, but instead concerns the spiritual fruitfulness of that narrative, or as we might put it, its propensity to sat isfy the principle of spiritual good. To express the point otherwise, if we are to settle such disputes, so far as we can do so, we need to ask: is a life that is lived in relation to a given theological, or secular, narrative apt to deepen, or diminish, the present significance of our this-worldly endeavours? And secondly, I hope to have shown that the account of the spiritual life that we have been defending here offers one ready response to a Nussbaumian critique of religious commitment. Why? Because this account is committed to affirming the significance of our world-directed thoughts, actions, experience, and so on—not in spite of but *on the basis of* an 'other-worldly' conception of their import. Indeed, on this view, we should say that the introduction of a theological narrative has the effect simply of extending whatever significance might otherwise attach to those thoughts and actions.

In concluding this chapter, I want to touch briefly on one further case where the principle of spiritual good may be of some help in mapping the content of religious thought. This time we shall be concerned with a general claim about the constraints on such thought: namely, the idea that ultimate religious reality, as it is in itself, lies beyond the reach of human concepts. Let us begin by considering Anthony O'Hear's treatment of this question in his essay 'The real or the Real? Chardin or Rothko?'

In the course of this discussion, we have been considering the nature of spiritual goods. O'Hear's essay also bears on these questions, and on his view, as on the view we have been presenting, such goods are relative to metaphysical context. For O'Hear, it is, in particular, the distinctiveness of human beings, relative to their metaphysical context, that reveals the deep significance of a human life. Here is how he develops the point:

> I see the contemplation of what arises in human practice as the singular contribution we as humans can make to the cosmos. Because of our status as sensory and intellectual, we alone are in a position to enjoy particular perceptions of the world, and to evaluate the fruits of those perceptions. A merely sensory consciousness could not reflect on what it perceives, while a purely intellectual being (an angel) would perceive or experience nothing.[34]

So according to O'Hear, human lives have a special significance when located within their cosmological context, because our mode of perception is unique in being at once sensory and intellectual. Accordingly, human beings can make a distinctive contribution to the wider economy of reality, and we have therefore, O'Hear is suggesting, a special kind of calling or function, namely, to engage in the distinctively human form of perception well.[35] O'Hear speaks here of our capacity to 'evaluate' perceptions, in conceptual terms, but equally we might say that because they are conceptually structured, our perceptions have themselves a distinctive character. In this, we differ from non-human animals, whose

---

[34] Anthony O'Hear, 'The real or the Real? Chardin or Rothko?', in Michael McGhee (ed.), *Philosophy, Religion and the Spiritual Life* (Cambridge: Cambridge University Press, 1992), p. 53.

[35] On this point, O'Hear's case resembles Aristotle's account of the nature of the well-lived life. Aristotle notes that the good lyre player is one who excels with respect to the distinctive capacity of lyre players, that is, by playing the lyre well; and similarly the good human being is one who excels with respect to the distinctively human capacity, which is 'an activity or actions of the soul implying a rational principle': *Nicomachean Ethics*, Book I, ch. 7. O'Hear is offering an argument of the same form, only on his account, the distinguishing human trait is a capacity for reflection upon sensory experience.

experience, even if conceptually structured in some degree, cannot be ordered according to the fine-grained conceptual distinctions that are typical of human thought. We also differ from the angels, and indeed from God, O'Hear is proposing, because, as non-embodied, they cannot register the character of colours, smells, sounds, and so on, in phenomenal terms. To cast the point in the form of an example, the beauty of a sunset is only revealed in (and to some extent it is constituted by) the distinctively human form of experience, since only we can appreciate the colours of a sunset in phenomenal terms, while at the same time perceiving the focal object of our experience as, say, a moving, celestial object. (Clearly, non-human animals do not gaze at sunsets, and presumably this is at least in part because the repertoire of concepts which they can bring to bear on this object is relatively limited.) To this extent, the beauty of the universe, along with its goodness in other respects, depends upon the distinctively human form of perception—and in turn this truth gives human lives a special importance.

In this passage, O'Hear talks of 'the singular contribution we as humans can make to the cosmos'. And it might be thought that this contribution can hardly be construed, as I have just suggested, as a calling. After all, our mode of perception is surely bound to be at once sensory and concept-infused—and it therefore makes no sense to suppose that there might be anything like a body of spiritual practice that will enable us to live accordingly. While it may perhaps be true that we have little choice but to experience the world in this way, O'Hear thinks that some of our commitments can betray, while others can honour, the distinctively human form of life. The two cases he explores concern works of art and our understanding of ultimate reality. Let's look briefly at each in turn. As we shall see, O'Hear's development of these ideas nicely intersects with some of the themes from our earlier discussion.

It is at least implied in O'Hear's account that artists have a special role to play in human life, because their work can be more or less successful in acknowledging the special worth of the distinctively human mode of perception. And at the core of his paper is a comparison between the paintings of Jean-Baptiste-Siméon Chardin and Mark Rothko. Measured by the standard of showing due regard for the human mode of perception, he suggests, Chardin's paintings succeed, while Rothko's fail:

In Rothko's work, there is no trace of the concrete, nothing appears; we are overwhelmed by hazy, empty sublimity. And before long, I find them deeply unsatisfying, longing to turn to the modesty and concreteness of a Chardin. Is engulfment, the wiping away of all determinations and horizons, what life – and art – is all about? If it is, then human effort and perception and perspective are, in the final analysis, mocked.[36]

On this account, the problem with Rothko's paintings is that they are not adapted to the distinctively human form of experience. Why think so? Because Rothko's works give us simply planes of colour, rather than objects that are bounded by 'determinations and horizons', and that can be tracked, therefore, by our conceptually structured form of perception. (We might put the point by saying: a Rothko canvas would tend appear to an animal as it does to a human being, for the reason that a plane of undifferentiated colour does not lend itself to conceptual ordering.) This is one reason, O'Hear is suggesting, why we find (or ought to find) Rothko's paintings 'unsatisfying' as objects of aesthetic contemplation. It is implied in O'Hear's comments that there is a further deficiency in Rothko's work, one that is perhaps more existential than simply aesthetic—namely, a tendency to disparage the distinctively human function, by drawing us into a different kind of experience from the one that confers deep significance on a human life. Here, O'Hear's thought seems to be that by presenting us with a perceptual object of this form, and suggesting that it is deserving of the kind of sustained attention that we afford works of art, Rothko is, at least implicitly, ranking a concept-independent sort of experience above the specifically human form of experience.

By contrast, Chardin's canvasses seek to elicit precisely the kind of perceptual response that is characteristic of the distinctively human form of life: here we are invited to discriminate between everyday objects such as pepper pots, cups, and so on, by apprehending them precisely as pepper pots and cups. Indeed, O'Hear maintains that by allowing these objects to 'emerge shyly, from a soft and often indeterminate

---

[36] O'Hear, 'The real or the Real?', pp. 50–1.

background, against which they quiver in the light almost on the edge of visibility', Chardin is able to show how our seeing them is 'a human achievement', that is, dependent upon the appropriate exercise of a particular perceptual endowment.[37] So on O'Hear's account of the matter, Chardin's work affirms the specifically human form of perception, and its capacity to summon particular kinds of sensory appearance into being, through its active, conceptually ordered appreciation of the material world. By contrast, Rothko's work disparages the human form of perception, by 'wiping away all determinations', of the kind that would sustain conceptually infused experience, and simply 'engulfing' or overwhelming rather than addressing and engaging the viewer.

It is worth pausing to record some comparisons between O'Hear's proposal and the account of the spiritual life that we have been expounding here. It is a matter of dispute whether background metaphysical assumptions can be relevant to an assessment of the aesthetic merit of a work of art. (It might be said: what matters for the appreciation of anything in aesthetic terms is precisely the bracketing out of background assumptions of all kinds.)[38] So it is notable that these approaches share an interest in the relationship between metaphysical and aesthetic commitments. In Chapter 4, we considered how a world view, or theological narrative, may inform our assessment of the beauty or grace that is displayed in the movements of the human body. And for his part, O'Hear is proposing that our appreciation of the sensory qualities of a work of art can be shaped, quite properly, by a truth that only becomes apparent once we have set the human mode of perception within its metaphysical context. These approaches are also alike in placing experience of the everyday sensory world at the heart of an account of the human good. But where O'Hear is interested in concept-infused sensory experience

---

[37] Ibid., p. 48. It is implied here that in our experience of the everyday world, we can aspire to a kind of focused attentiveness, which is to be preferred, in spiritual terms, to less effortful forms of perception, to the extent that it involves the fuller exercise of our distinctively human perceptual powers. And, certainly, there are spiritual practices that would support this sort of achievement.
[38] See again George Pattison's account of aesthetic experience, as discussed in Chapter 3. For wider discussion of the relevant intellectual tradition, see Nicholas Wolterstorff's instructive chapter, 'Art and the Aesthetic: The Religious Dimension', in P. Kivy (ed.), *The Blackwell Guide to Aesthetics* (Oxford: Blackwell, 2004), ch. 18.

in general, our concern has been specifically with the case where sensory experience acquires a deepened significance because of its congruence with a theological narrative.

As well as examining the implications of his account of spiritual well-being for our understanding of works of art, O'Hear also considers how this same account can guide our assessment of issues in philosophical theology, and specifically the question of how to represent the relationship between human thought and religious reality as it is in itself. His particular target is John Hick's approach to religious experience, as formulated in his classic text An Interpretation of Religion, but if applicable here, then O'Hear's case will have wider currency, and will count against any suggestion that the divine nature—or religious reality otherwise conceived—is ineffable, that is, in some fundamental respect, beyond the reach of all substantive human concepts.[39] O'Hear's case on this point parallels his critique of Rothko: his objection to Hick's philosophy of religion, as to Rothko's painting, is that it has a tendency to debase the distinctively human form of life.

Before turning to O'Hear's critique of his position, we should note the basic structure of Hick's case. To put the point over-simply, Hick's perspective is bound up with his pluralism about religious traditions. How so? Because if substantive human concepts were to apply to ultimate reality as it is in itself, and not simply to that reality as it appears to human beings in religious experience, and if we were to know which of these concepts so apply, then we would be committed to favouring certain religious traditions over others. For instance, if concepts such as person and good are privileged, then we will have ranked monotheistic traditions over others, contrary to the pluralist claim that all traditions are equally successful, cognitively as well as salvifically. Accordingly, on this Hickian view, fundamental religious reality, or what Hick terms, in a vocabulary that aspires to be neutral between religious traditions, the Real in itself, cannot be said to be 'one or many, person or thing, substance or process, good or evil, purposive or non-purposive'.[40]

---

[39] See John Hick, An Interpretation of Religion: Human Responses to the Transcendent (New Haven, CT: Yale University Press, 2nd edn, 2004).

[40] Hick, cited in O'Hear, 'The real or the Real?', p. 56.

Drawing out the parallel between this conception of the Sacred and Rothko's art, O'Hear remarks:

> Instead of anything specific we are, in both cases, being offered a void, an emptiness, which is said to be pregnant with noumenal meaning and to underlie the merely phenomenal.[41]

So according to O'Hear, Hick represents ultimate reality as it is in itself, that is, considered as a noumenon rather than as a phenomenon, as utterly inaccessible to human thought and experience. And why is this problematic? O'Hear's answer can't be simply, as it was for Rothko's canvasses: because Hick is inviting us to attend to a reality that is not adapted to the distinctively human mode of experience—that is, experience that is both sensory and concept-infused. After all, on any standard account, sacred reality is not going to be, directly, accessible to sensory experience. (And O'Hear's intention is not to dismiss the very idea of the Sacred.)

I take it that O'Hear's underlying objection is, rather, that Hick's representation of ultimate religious reality demeans the human form of life, because it treats that reality as utterly discontinuous in character from the objects that we apprehend in everyday sensory experience. And if that is so, then while human perception may be unique in being at once sensory and intellectual, that truth will no longer secure the importance of a human life. Why not? Because on this Hickian perspective, human experience of the sensory world will fail to offer even the most fragmentary intimation of what is, by hypothesis, of ultimate value, namely, fundamental religious reality as it is in itself. Moreover, given Hick's conception of the Real in itself, the same sort of case can presumably be made for any of our experience that is non-sensory in form. Hence, on Hick's account of the matter, human experience in general will be concerned with the mere surface appearance of things, where that appearance stands in sharp contrast with the nature of what is truly of importance. Accordingly, such an account deprives human experience

---

[41] Ibid.

of the possibility of holding any deep significance, even if the form of that experience should be unique to human beings.

So in brief, on O'Hear's account, Hick's understanding of fundamental reality is to be rejected because of its implications for the kind of significance that a human life can bear. Put otherwise, O'Hear is objecting to Hick's ineffability thesis on the grounds that its truth would be spiritually impoverishing. And in this way, he is invoking considerations at least very much like those that are embedded in what we earlier called the principle of spiritual good. Here, then, is a further point of comparison between O'Hear's discussion and the case that we have been developing in this volume.

As we have seen, when set alongside the great-making principle, the principle of spiritual good can perhaps explain why certain disagreements in philosophical theology have proved to be so deeply entrenched. And it may be that we can understand in these same terms the persistence of the dispute about whether the divine nature, or fundamental religious reality otherwise conceived, transcends all substantive human concepts. After all, if we begin with the idea that the basic task of religious thought is to magnify the divine nature (to take the theistic case in particular), then might we not suppose that we think of God most adequately when we represent the divine nature as 'radically other' in ontological terms, and therefore as altogether beyond the reach of human concepts, which are, after all, fitted for the description of finite things? On this perspective, the notion of divine ineffability serves as a buttress for the distinction between God's reality and the limited, imperfect mode of being of creatures. But if we follow O'Hear, then we should suppose that this attempt to magnify the divine nature offends against another basic principle of religious thought, namely, the principle that religious narratives should not, to put the point minimally, diminish human life. So on this question, as on the question of the relationship between divine and human agency, there is some reason to suppose that a deep-seated fissure in religious thought can be understood, in part, by reference to the principle of spiritual good.

Our earlier discussion does not quite support O'Hear's claim that the ineffability thesis is inadmissible because spiritually impoverishing, but it does appear to favour a related claim. On the approach we have been taking, theological narratives, such as the narrative of the beatific vision, are required for the identification of hybrid goods. And to that extent, the position we have been exploring suggests, with O'Hear, that the spiritual life depends upon the availability of religious concepts that afford a measure of substantive insight into the character of transcendent reality. Why? Because only so can we make reliable judgements about what it would take for a human life to be aligned with that reality, in such a way as to realize hybrid goods. However, in reaching this view, we are not thereby committed to the thought that certain of our concepts apply literally, affirmatively and informatively to the divine nature as it is in itself. (That is, we are not therefore required to deny the ineffability thesis in this or some related form.) Why not? Because it may be enough that the relevant narratives pick out some aspect of transcendent reality other than the divine nature considered in itself. For instance, it may be enough for a narrative to allude to the special character of the human relationships that will obtain when the saints share in the contemplation of the divine nature in the beatific vision. In this case, it is the idea of a certain kind of human solidarity that grounds the conceivability of various hybrid goods, rather than, directly, any description of the divine nature as it is in itself.

Concluding Thoughts

In this chapter, we have been exploring the idea that what we have been calling the principle of spiritual good, or some variant of that principle, can structure theological discussion across a range of fields. Specifically, we have seen how this principle may prove relevant to questions such as these: 'Is there an afterlife?' (if we follow James on this point). 'Are there infused moral virtues?' And: 'How are we to think of the respective roles of divine and human agency in the formation of the virtues?' Or again, the principle may be applicable when we consider whether human experience and concepts supply any substantive insight into the character of a transcendent realm. There is some reason, therefore, to suppose that the principle of spiritual good offers, potentially, a way of mapping what we might think of as the deep structure of religious thought, even when its role is not explicitly acknowledged by religious practitioners. And to the extent that it can play such a role, then the principle will help to unify a range of apparently quite disparate kinds of enquiry.

Moreover, when allied with the great-making principle, the principle of spiritual good can also serve to explain our tendency to oscillate between rival conceptions of the divine nature and activity—as for instance, when we are attracted both to the idea that the divine nature radically eludes our concepts, and to the idea that it is accessible to human thought and experience; or again, when we are drawn both to the thought that human goodness is exclusively attributable to a divine source, and to the suggestion that our own agency is implicated in some forms of human goodness. In such cases, the tensions in our thinking appear to reflect the competing pull of these two principles.

In earlier chapters, we have taken as our starting point a world view, or theological narrative, and considered what follows for our understanding of the nature of a well-lived human life. On this approach, different narratives will produce different visions of what it takes to live congruently with our theological context, and therefore different visions of the nature of spiritual goods. In this chapter, we have been examining how we can also move in the other direction: here, we begin with a conception of the spiritual good that is implied in a given narrative, and ask what follows for our assessment of that narrative. In brief, on the account we have been developing, the spiritual claim that is made upon us by a given narrative will vary with the breadth and depth of the relations of congruence that it enables. Hence, theological narratives are to be assessed not only in terms of their evidential standing, or their tendency to magnify the divine nature, but also by reference to their spiritual fruitfulness. So here we find a further reason for endorsing an overarching thesis of this discussion: serious theological enquiry needs to be grounded not only in religious teachings considered abstractly, but also in the spiritual life.

Concluding Remarks

Spiritual Traditions and Human Possibilities

In the course of this enquiry, we have been concerned with the relevance of the notion of infused moral virtue for an understanding of what it is to participate in a spiritual tradition, and an appreciation of the nature of spiritual well-being. A summary of the main phases of the discussion can be found in the Introduction, so I shan't provide a further overview here. Instead, I shall conclude by simply alluding, very briefly, to one further dialectical context within which these reflections may be located.

Secular critiques of religion commonly suppose that God-centred, or otherwise religious, world views present various challenges for human freedom. In the twentieth century, two of the best-known philosophical advocates of secularism took up this case by proposing that theistic accounts of the world, if true, would undermine human freedom in a particularly radical way, by establishing a distinction between humanly endorsed values and the values that are in some way embedded in the nature of things, by divine fiat or on account of some truth about the divine nature. Famously, Jean-Paul Sartre maintained that from a theistic perspective, human beings are like artefacts, that is, they are made for a purpose that is not of their own devising, and subject therefore to standards of success that are not of their own choosing—rather as a paper cutter, to take Sartre's now rather dated illustration, has to cut paper well if it is to count as a good paper cutter. And of course, this is in fact a view with deep roots in theistic traditions. By contrast with this picture, Sartre maintains, atheistic existentialism offers an emancipation: on the secular view, to use Sartre's slogan, 'existence precedes essence', which is to say that we are not defined, and confined, by some pre-established nature and associated purposes—or essence—but

Spiritual Traditions and the Virtues: Living Between Heaven and Earth. Mark R. Wynn, Oxford University Press (2020).
© Mark R. Wynn.
DOI: 10.1093/oso/9780198862949.001.0001

instead can, and must, choose for ourselves the values by which we are to live.[1]

Speaking from a rather different cultural and intellectual context, Bertrand Russell also placed evaluative freedom at the core of his objection to theistic religion, arguing in his essay 'A Free Man's Worship' that a secular outlook liberates us from any dependence upon alien ideals of life:

In this lies Man's true freedom: in determination to worship only the God created by our own love of the good, to respect only the heaven which inspires the insight of our best moments. In action, in desire, we must submit perpetually to the tyranny of outside forces; but in thought, in aspiration, we are free, free from our fellow-men, free from the petty planet on which our bodies impotently crawl, free even, while we live, from the tyranny of death. Let us learn, then, that energy of faith which enables us to live constantly in the vision of the good; and let us descend, in action, into the world of fact, with that vision always before us.[2]

Russell contrasts, then, 'the world of fact', that is, the world described by the natural sciences and above all by physics, with an ideal world, which he takes to be of human origin, in so far as our ultimate values, or whatever plays in our lives the role that has been played by God in traditional religion, are 'created by our own love of the good'.[3] And it is in the contemplation of this ideal realm that true, liberative religion is to be found, because here the values that we reverence are of our own making and choosing.[4]

---

[1] Jean-Paul Sartre, 'Existentialism Is a Humanism', tr. P. Mairet, in W. Kaufman (ed.), *Existentialism from Dostoyevsky to Sartre* (London: Meridian Publishing Co., 1989; first published in French in 1946), available at: https://www.marxists.org/reference/archive/sartre/works/exist/sartre.htm, accessed 28 January 2019.

[2] 'A Free Man's Worship', in Bertrand Russell, *Mysticism and Logic and Other Essays* (London: George Allen & Unwin, 2nd edn, 1917), p. 50. The essay was first published in 1903.

[3] The expression 'the world of fact' occurs again on p. 52, where Russell develops the idea that the arts present a kind of ideal world, which can provide a proper focus for our devotion. On p. 49, he speaks of 'the world of ideals'.

[4] The concluding lines of this passage echo, clearly, Plato's parable of the cave, and his proposal that the enlightened person, who has set eyes on the world of the Forms, should then return to the cave. See the *Republic*, Book VII. And there is some reason, therefore, to adopt a

In our earlier discussion, I noted an understanding of religious commitment according to which we are to begin by establishing the likely truth of a world view or theological narrative, and only then consider what way of life we are to adopt granted that truth.[5] It seems to me that in their critique of religious traditions, Russell and Sartre both have in view some such picture of what it takes to participate in a religious tradition. On Sartre's conception of how religious understanding proceeds, there is, for the religious person, a fact of the matter about what a human being's function is, which is to be identified, presumably, by reference to a sacred text, or perhaps via some empirical enquiry; and this fact then fixes the nature of the values that are to guide a human life. Accordingly, on Sartre's account, we can intelligibly suppose that religious values will be experienced as a constraint, for the reason that they cut across the values that we would choose for ourselves. Similarly, for Russell too, it seems clear that the values that are commended in theistic religion may conflict with those that are given in 'our own love of the good'. It is for this reason, of course, that acting according to the latter values can be represented as a liberation from the requirements of traditional religion. Indeed, on Russell's view, it seems that the conventionally religious person is, in fact, committed to an alien set of values, because of their conviction that whatever happens in the world happens for the best.[6] So on this view too, it seems, theistic values can be identified independently of reference to our own ideals of good.

However, on the view we have been developing here, religious commitment does not have this structure. The theological narratives that provide the background for the religious person's pursuit of various

Platonic reading of Russell's essay, by supposing that the values to which we are to orient ourselves are pre-existent, and simply mirrored so far as possible in our artistic and other ideal-informed creations. But this reading is, I take it, hard to reconcile with the theme that in true religion, 'God' or the ultimate object of our devotion is 'created by our own love of the good', rather than existing independently of human thought and activity.

[5] I note this position at various points, for instance, in the closing lines of Chapter 6.

[6] Compare Russell's remark that on 'the position which we have become accustomed to regard as specially religious', we should say that 'in some hidden manner, the world of fact is really harmonious with the world of ideals': 'A Free Man's Worship', p. 49. Of course, Russell takes the world of fact, as disclosed in physics, to be just obviously indifferent to human well-being.

hybrid goods, and thereby the basis for their values, are not simply foisted upon them, but taken to be worthy of assent because of the way in which they appeal to 'our own love of the good'. Hence whatever we may wish to say about the role of human nature in fixing the goods of the acquired moral virtues (here, I simply bracket this question), the goods of the infused moral virtues are not so defined: instead, they are relative to theological narratives to which the believer assents freely, that is, on account of their attraction to a form of life whose possibility depends on the truth of the narrative. Of course, the position we have been expounding is not to be identified with those of Sartre and Russell: I have not suggested that fundamental values, or God, are simply 'created by our love of the good', as Russell proposes, or that our choices constitute values, as Sartre maintains.[7] Nonetheless, as represented here, religious and spiritual commitment does not threaten our freedom in the way that seems to be at least implied in their accounts. Why not? Because religious ideals of life cannot, ultimately, stand opposed to our deepest values.[8] Why not? Because our assent to the relevant theological narrative is grounded in those values. To put the matter in Russell's terms, in this realm, there is no access to the world of facts that does not lead through the world of ideals.[9]

This way of understanding the nature of the difference between secular world views, such as those of Russell and Sartre, and religious world views suggests that in certain important respects, they are engaged in a common enterprise—of trying to understand how our 'love of the good' may properly guide our fundamental life choices. If we are to make

[7] See Sartre's comment on the actions of military leaders, where this remark is clearly intended to reveal the character of human action in general, properly understood: 'the action presupposes that there is a plurality of possibilities, and in choosing one of these, they realize that it has value only because it is chosen': 'Existentialism Is a Humanism'.

[8] Of course, this is not to deny that our understanding of value can be deepened and even fundamentally transformed through an encounter with religious ideals. The thought is just that a religious scheme which consistently cuts across our values, so that it can at no point be recognized as proposing a way of life that is good, can make no claim upon us.

[9] A Sartrean or Russellian might object that on the view given here, religion still entails a kind of restriction upon our freedom, for the reason that, on this view, our choices do not constitute values, and can therefore be judged from the vantage point of those values. These are matters for another occasion, but from the (conventional) religious point of view, it is clear that the phenomenology is of the values shaping us, rather than vice versa, so that for this rather different reason there is no possibility of religious values chafing against our fundamental identity.

progress in these matters, what we need above all is a multiplicity of perspectives, concerning the ways in which a human life may count as good and even as beautiful. And for this purpose, spiritual traditions are indispensable: for here we find thought out and lived out, across times and cultures, and in dialogue with the constraints that are given with our human nature, a myriad of stories concerning the sort of significance that a human life can bear. So here is a reason for thinking that far from imposing alien values, and constricting human possibilities, as some have supposed, spiritual traditions offer, in fact, our surest way of expanding and enriching the stock of those possibilities—and our clearest vision of what it would be for a human life to be lived well.

References

Adams, Robert, *Finite and Infinite Goods* (Oxford: Oxford University Press, 1999).

Alston, William, 'Some Suggestions for Divine Command Theorists', in William Alston, *Divine Nature and Human Language* (Ithaca, NY: Cornell University Press, 1989), pp. 253–73.

Anselm, *Anselm of Canterbury: The Major Works*, ed. Brian Davies and G. R. Evans (Oxford: Oxford University Press, 1998).

Aquinas, Thomas, *Summa Theologiae*, tr. Fathers of the English Dominican Province (New York: Benziger Brothers, 1947).

Aquinas, Thomas, *De Veritate*, tr. R. W. Mulligan (Chicago: Henry Regnery Company, 1952).

Aquinas, Thomas, *Summa Theologiae*, ed. T. Gilby (London: Eyre & Spottiswoode, 1964–74).

Aristotle, *Nicomachean Ethics*, tr. W. D. Ross, revised J. L. Ackrill and J. O. Urmson (Oxford: Oxford University Press, 1980).

Aristotle, *The Metaphysics*, tr. H. Lawson-Tancred (London: Penguin, 1998).

Arthur, John, 'Famine Relief and the Ideal Moral Code', in H. LaFollette (ed.), *Ethics in Practice: An Anthology* (Oxford: Blackwell, 2nd edn, 2002), ch. 57.

Augustine, *On Christian Doctrine* (Milton Keynes: Lightning Source, 2013).

Augustine, *The Confessions*, tr. J. G. Pilkington, in P. Schaff (ed.), *Nicene and Post-Nicene Fathers*, First Series, vol. 1 (Buffalo, NY: Christian Literature Publishing Co., 1887), available at http://www.newadvent.org/fathers/1101.htm (accessed 28 January 2019).

Austin, Nicholas, 'Spirituality and Virtue in Christian Formation: A Conversation between Thomistic and Ignatian Traditions', *New Blackfriars*, 97 (2016), 202–17.

Begbie, Jeremy, 'Beauty, Sentimentality and the Arts', in D. Treier, M. Husbands, and R. Lundin (eds), *The Beauty of God: Theology and the Arts* (Downers Grove, IL: IVP Academic, 2006), pp. 45–69.

Bourdieu, Pierre, *The Logic of Practice*, tr. R. Nice (Cambridge: Polity Press, 1990; first published in French in 1980).

Comte-Sponville, André, *The Book of Atheist Spirituality: An Elegant Argument for Spirituality Without God*, tr. N. Huston (London: Bantam Books, 2008).

Cottingham, John, *Why Believe?* (London: Continuum, 2009).

Cupitt, Don, *Taking Leave of God* (London: SCM, 1980).

DeYoung, Rebecca Konyndyk, McCluskey, Colleen, and Van Dyke, Christina, *Aquinas's Ethics: Metaphysical Foundations, Moral Theory, and Theological Context* (Notre Dame, IN: University of Notre Dame Press, 2009).

Gaita, Raimond, *A Common Humanity: Thinking About Love & Truth & Justice* (Melbourne: Text Publishing, 1999).

Gaita, Raimond, *Good and Evil: An Absolute Conception* (London: Routledge, 2nd edn, 2004).

Hadot, Pierre, *Exercices Spirituels et Philosophie Antique* (Paris: Etudes Augustiniennes, 2nd edn, 1987).

Hadot, Pierre, *Philosophy as a Way of Life: Spiritual Exercises from Socrates to Foucault*, tr. M. Chase (Oxford: Blackwell, 1995).

Heidegger, Martin, *Being and Time*, tr. J. Macquarrie and E. Robinson (Oxford: Basil Blackwell, 1962; first published in 1927).

Heyd, David, *Supererogation* (Cambridge: Cambridge University Press, 1982).

Hick, John, *An Interpretation of Religion: Human Responses to the Transcendent* (New Haven, CT: Yale University Press, 2nd edn, 2004).

Holland, R. F., 'Is Goodness a Mystery?', reproduced in R. F. Holland (ed.), *Against Empiricism: On Education, Epistemology and Value* (Oxford: Blackwell, 1980), ch. 7.

Inglis, John, 'Aquinas's Replication of the Acquired Moral Virtues', *The Journal of Religious Ethics*, 27 (1999), 3–27.

Jackson, Frank, 'Epiphenomenal Qualia', *The Philosophical Quarterly*, 32 (1982), 127–36.

James, William, *The Varieties of Religious Experience: A Study in Human Nature* (London: Longmans, Green and Co., 1911).

James, William, 'The Will to Believe', in William James, *Essays in Pragmatism* (New York: Hafner Press, 1948), pp. 88–109.

John of the Cross, *The Living Flame of Love by Saint John of the Cross with his Letters, Poems, and Minor Writings*, tr. D. Lewis (London: Thomas Baker, 1919).

John of the Cross, *The Essential St John of the Cross: Ascent of Mount Carmel; Dark Night of the Soul; A Spiritual Canticle of the Soul and the Bridegroom Christ; Twenty Poems by St John of the Cross*, tr. E. Allison Peers (Radford, VA: Wilder Publications, 2008).

Lewis, C. S., *Mere Christianity* (Glasgow: William Collins, Sons & Co., 1944).

MacIntyre, Alasdair, *After Virtue: A Study in Moral Theory* (London: Bloomsbury, 3rd edn, 2007, 1st edn, 1981).

MacIntyre, Alasdair, *Three Rival Versions of Moral Enquiry: Encyclopedia, Genealogy, and Tradition* (London: Duckworth, 1990).

Murdoch, Iris, 'The Sovereignty of Good over other Concepts', in Iris Murdoch, *The Sovereignty of Good* (London: Routledge & Kegan Paul, 1970), ch. 3.

Nagasawa, Yujin, *Maximal God: A New Defence of Perfect Theism* (Oxford: Oxford University Press, 2017).

Nicolson, Paula, *Post-Natal Depression: Psychology, Science and the Transition to Motherhood* (London: Routledge, 1998).

Nietzsche, Friedrich, *Twilight of the Idols or How to Philosophize with a Hammer*, in Friedrich Nietzsche, *The Anti-Christ, Ecce Homo, Twilight of the Idols*, ed. A. Ridley and J. Norman, tr. J. Norman (Cambridge: Cambridge University Press, 2005).

Nussbaum, Martha, *Upheavals of Thought: The Intelligence of Emotions* (Cambridge: Cambridge University Press, 2001).

Nygren, Anders, *Agape and Eros: Pt. 1, A Study of the Christian Idea of Love*, tr. A. G. Hebert (London: Society for Promoting Christian Knowledge, 1932).

O'Hear, Anthony, 'The real or the Real? Chardin or Rothko?', in Michael McGhee (ed.), *Philosophy, Religion and the Spiritual Life* (Cambridge: Cambridge University Press, 1992), pp. 47–58.

Pascal, Blaise, *Pensées*, tr. W. F. Trotter (London: Dent, 1910).

Pascal, Blaise, 'Faith beyond Reason', from *Pensées*, in Paul Helm (ed.), *Faith & Reason* (Oxford: Oxford University Press, 1999), pp. 182–5.

Pattison, George, *Art Modernity and Faith* (London: SCM, 1998).

Phillips, D. Z., *Faith and Philosophical Enquiry* (London: Routledge & Kegan Paul, 1970).

Plantinga, Alvin, *Warranted Christian Belief* (Oxford: Oxford University Press, 2000).

Plato, *Republic*, tr. C. J. Emlyn-Jones and W. Preddy (Cambridge, MA: Harvard University Press, 2014).

Russell, Bertrand, 'A Free Man's Worship', in Bertrand Russell, *Mysticism and Logic and Other Essays* (London: George Allen & Unwin, 2nd edn, 1917; first published in 1903), ch. 3.

Sartre, Jean-Paul, *L'Existentialisme Est un Humanisme* (Paris: Nagel, 1967; first published in 1946).

Sartre, Jean-Paul, 'Existentialism Is a Humanism', tr. P. Mairet, in W. Kaufman (ed.), *Existentialism from Dostoyevsky to Sartre* (London: Meridian Publishing Co., 1989; first published in French in 1946), available at https://www.marxists.org/reference/archive/sartre/works/exist/sartre.htm (accessed 28 January 2019).

Schoenbaumsfeld, Genia, 'Ludwig Wittgenstein', in G. Oppy and N. N. Trakakis (eds), *Twentieth-Century Philosophy of Religion* (Durham: Acumen, 2009), pp. 161–74.

Singer, Peter, 'Famine, Affluence, and Morality', *Philosophy and Public Affairs*, 1:3 (1972), 229–43.

Swinburne, Richard, *The Existence of God* (Oxford: Oxford University Press, 2nd edn, 2004).

Swinburne, Richard, *Faith and Reason* (Oxford: Oxford University Press, 2nd edn, 2005).

Swinburne, Richard, 'The Christian Scheme of Salvation', in Michael Rea (ed.), *Oxford Readings in Philosophical Theology*: vol. 1, *Trinity, Incarnation and Atonement* (Oxford: Oxford University Press, 2009), ch. 14.

Turner, Denys, *The Darkness of God: Negativity in Christian Mysticism* (Cambridge: Cambridge University Press, 1995).

Weil, Simone, *Waiting on God*, tr. E. Crauford (London: Routledge & Kegan Paul, 1951).

Williams, Bernard, 'The Makropoulos Case: Reflections on the Tedium of Immortality', in Bernard Williams, *Problems of the Self* (Cambridge: Cambridge University Press, 1973), ch. 6.

Williams, Rowan, *The Wound of Knowledge: Christian Spirituality from the New Testament to Saint John of the Cross* (Cambridge, MA: Cowley Publications, 1991).

Winch, Peter, 'Meaning and Religious Language', in Stuart Brown (ed.), *Reason and Religion* (Ithaca, NY: Cornell University Press, 1977), pp. 193–221.

Wittgenstein, Ludwig, *Philosophical Investigations*, tr. G. E. M. Anscombe (Oxford: Basil Blackwell, 1958).

Wittgenstein, Ludwig, *Lectures and Conversations on Aesthetics, Psychology and Religious Belief*, ed. C. Barrett (Oxford: Blackwell, 1966).

Wolterstorff, Nicholas, 'Art and the Aesthetic: The Religious Dimension', in P. Kivy (ed.), *The Blackwell Guide to Aesthetics* (Oxford: Blackwell, 2004), ch. 18.

Wordsworth, William, 'Ode: Intimations of Immortality From Recollections of Early Childhood', in William Wordsworth, *Poetry & Prose with Essays by Coleridge, Hazlitt and De* Quincey (Oxford: Clarendon Press, 1969; first published in 1807), pp. 111–18.

Wynn, Mark, *Faith and Place: An Essay in Embodied Religious Epistemology* (Oxford: Oxford University Press, 2009).

Wynn, Mark, 'Between Heaven and Earth: Sensory Experience and the Goods of the Spiritual Life', in D. McPherson (ed.), *Spirituality and the Good Life* (Cambridge: Cambridge University Press, 2017), ch. 6.

Wynn, Mark, 'Renewing Our Understanding of Religion: Philosophy of Religion and the Goals of the Spiritual Life', in P. Draper and J. L. Schellenberg (eds), *Renewing Philosophy of Religion: Exploratory Essays* (Oxford: Oxford University Press, 2017), ch. 5.

Wynn, Mark, 'Metaphysics and Emotional Experience: Some Themes Drawn from John of the Cross', in J. Corrigan (ed.), *Feeling Religion* (Durham, NC: Duke University Press, 2018), ch. 2.

Index of Biblical References

Index

For the benefit of digital users, indexed terms that span two pages (e.g., 52–53) may, on occasion, appear on only one of those pages.